UNDERSTANDING THE
NEW RELIGIONS

UNDERSTANDING THE NEW RELIGIONS

Edited by
Jacob Needleman
and
George Baker

A Crossroad Book
THE SEABURY PRESS • NEW YORK

Second printing

1978
The Seabury Press
815 Second Avenue
New York, N.Y. 10017

Printed in the United States of America

Library of Congress Cataloging in Publication Data
Main entry under title:
Understanding the new religions.
"A Crossroad book."
1. United States—Religion—1945—Addresses, essays,
lectures. 2. Cults—United States—Addresses,
essays, lectures.
I. Needleman, Jacob. II. Baker, George, 1941–
BL2530.U6U5   200'.973   78-14997
ISBN 0-8164-0403-8
ISBN 0-8164-2188-9 pbk.

CONTENTS

FOREWORD

THE GRADUATE Theological Union is itself a product of new forces and changing sensibilities in American religious life. Formed in 1962 as a graduate school and consortium of seminaries, the Graduate Theological Union has come to include six Protestant and three Roman Catholic theological schools, plus Centers for Judaic Studies, Urban-Black Studies, Asian-American Theologies, and Women and Religion. Its existence is thus itself a response to new impulses of ecumenism and new perceptions of religious pluralism, interdependence, and dialogue, as well as to new forms of religious consciousness.

The kind of "ecumenical pluralism" to which the Graduate Theological Union is committed leads inevitably to special interest in the variety of other newly emerging religious aspirations. They are a natural focus for our study, as movements powerfully represented in our immediate geographical context, and as of vital importance for theological education in the schools that comprise the Graduate Theological Union. We have, therefore, undertaken the serious development of a program of research into such movements and their social consequences, of organizing a major collection of resource materials, and of educational service, especially to the surrounding community. In this project we have been assisted by the Ford Foundation, the Rockefeller Foundation, the San Francisco Foundation, the Henry Luce Foundation, Inc., and the National Endowment for the Humanities.

It is a pleasure, therefore, to send forth this volume as an early fruit of the enterprise. The book itself grows largely out of the National Conference on the Study of New Religious Movements in America, which was held in Berkeley in June, 1977, with support from the Ford Foundation. It is not intended directly as a full conference report, though it includes most of the essays, thoroughly revised, that were presented at the conference, along with other important contributions subsequently solicited.

We are particularly indebted to the Ford Foundation for its help in the initiation of the project, as well as to other sponsors of the program for their generous support of the entire project. Our special thanks also go to Dr. Joel Colton of the Rockefeller Foundation, who attended the conference and himself contributed trenchant observations in his role as participant observer. His solid and sensitive support of the program is deeply appreciated. We regret that the format of this volume did not allow us to include his comments, nor those of several other participant observers, such as Kenneth Briggs of *The New York Times,* Kenneth Woodward of *Newsweek,* John Dart of the *Los Angeles Times,* J. Edward Dirks of the University of California at Santa Cruz, and Marilyn Ferguson of the *Brain-Mind Bulletin.* Each of these persons contributed heavily to the success of the conference and to the shaping of our future plans for research in the area of new religions.

We wish also to thank those persons who helped during the conference and initial phases of the program: Eric Evans, Paul Schwartz, Richard Payne, and particularly Betty Roszak, whose expertise enabled us to lay the foundations for a national documentation center on the new religions.

Claude Welch, Dean and President
Graduate Theological Union
Berkeley, California

PREFACE

Jacob Needleman

IN JUNE 1977, the Graduate Theological Union of Berkeley inaugurated its Program for the Study of New Religious Movements in America. The occasion was marked by the convening of a national conference of distinguished scholars and writers, with the aim of determining how the academic community can best serve the accelerating public interest in new religions. The present book is the offspring of that conference.

Until now, most of the information about the new religions that has been made available to the public has been highly colored by enthusiasm, hostility, exaggeration, fantasy, condescension, fear, or plain ignorance. In calling this conference and in establishing our program, we hope to respond in some measure to the obvious and pressing need for ongoing, impartial *thought* about these movements and what they represent. Our premise is that the new religions movement, in its broadest sense, far from being an aberration, is a crucial aspect of the profound cultural change through which the American civilization is now passing. It is one of the key elements in a widespread reaching out for new values throughout the modern and modernized world: in science, in the arts, in education, medicine, psychiatry, economics, in the life of the family, and of course within the established religious institutions of the West.

As I see it, the academic community—particularly scholars of religion and related areas—has a uniquely important role to play in this whole cultural drama. For quite some time now, inquiries have been coming to us from many different kinds of people: worried parents, schoolteachers, psychotherapists, lawyers, clergymen, and journalists from all around the world. The need for understanding is being felt everywhere. But this understanding probably cannot come only from those who, rightly or wrongly, feel threatened by the new religions or who, on the other hand, are devoted solely to advocating or promoting them in one way or another. Someone needs to step forward who can bring a wider perspective.

It is both an extraordinary opportunity and test for the whole academic enterprise. The subject is, of course, intensely interesting from the point of view of cultural anthropology, philosophy, sociology, comparative religion, and social psychology, considered as specialized fields of research. But it goes far beyond that. The courts are being asked to redefine "religion"; psychotherapists are being asked to say what goes on, for example, in the "conversion" experience; clergy are being asked whether these new teachings run counter to the value structure of our society.

And those who are being asked are in turn also asking—but asking whom? They are asking us. Through them large segments of our society are asking about the nature and significance of the new religions and everything that goes with them: new (and often ancient) views of the meaning of living, the structure of reality, the limits and powers of the human psyche.

Those who view the new religions as a positive development, as a corrective to the dead-end of Western materialism, often maintain that through these groups a spiritualizing influence is re-entering the American culture in the form, at the very least, of new metaphysical ideas. On the other side are those who condemn what they take to be the abandonment of the standards of rational, liberal inquiry, a movement toward pseudo-mysticism and superstition.

Again, the former group sees these movements—particularly the Eastern religions that stress "inner" practices such as meditation—as a force for the regeneration and transformation of the individual, by means of which a true moral agency becomes possible. And on the other side are those who attack the new religions as a "new narcissism," an indulgence in self-cultivation, and a retreat from commitment to the community.

There are many such polarities in people's views about the new religions. The point I wish to make here is that such large, fundamental philosophical and moral issues almost always are in back of the apparently strictly informational inquiries about these movements. People are seeking not only information, but vision.

As educators and scholars in this field, we now find ourselves in a situation that is as awkward as it is challenging. Whether we like it or not, and there are many reasons for not liking it, we are in a state of what one might call "acute inbetweenness"—in between the guru, the priest, the parent, the schoolteacher, and the therapist. Many of us have spent our lives studying the ideas, teachings, and practices that in one form or another are now— without our prior permission, so to say—entering the lives of people throughout the country and causing all sorts of "trouble." That is, these ideas are having real effects on people's existence: their marriages, their careers, their sense of purpose in life, their friends, their politics. There is thus an important, perhaps even decisive, place which scholars are being called upon to occupy in this whole aspect of the current cultural crisis.

But what is that place?

I would like to state how I see this issue from my own, admittedly very personal, perspective as a teacher of philosophy. And I would like to begin by relating an incident that took place during my undergraduate years.

It was at the start of my first philosophy class. My instructor was a well-known scholar and had handed out a reading list that made me tremble with excitement: Plato, Aristotle, Descartes, Schopenhauer, Nietzsche, Russell, Whitehead.

The opening class discussion began with the professor asking us what we expected from the course. I was the first to raise my hand and I said, as though speaking not only for myself, but for the whole of the human race:

"I want to know the meaning of life!"

I will never forget the silence that followed. At first, I simply did not understand it; I assumed the teacher was waiting for me to say more, and so I went on talking while vaguely beginning to suspect that something was not quite right.

I don't remember anything of what I said, only that it was all centered around the question "Why are we here?"

Suddenly, I noticed that the teacher was smiling. I almost said "sneering," but that would probably be an exaggeration. At the same time, I noticed my classmates shaking their heads and I heard some snickering as well.

I stopped cold.

"Go on, go on," I was told.

Bewildered and frightened, I did try to go on and speak about all the questions that had been troubling me, but my voice was hollow and I soon had to stop.

After another terrible pause, the teacher said (and this I remember precisely):

"Yes—well, that is exactly what philosophy is *not* about. You are not going to get psychiatric help here [great laughter], or religious guidance [more laughter]. No, you are going to be taught what it means to think clearly and well, to examine your presuppositions, to criticize and argue. That is philosophy."

In my opinion, such an answer and the attitude toward the fundamental questions of life that may lie behind it can no longer be given and must no longer be given in our academic work with young people. But what is the alternative? Are we instead to take up the role of preachers or gurus? Must we change from being representatives of intellectual discipline to being therapists of one sort or another, becoming more actively involved in the personal lives of our students? I do not think so. There is quite another alternative, a whole world of alternatives.

At this point I should state that, from the point of view of the subject of this book, I am not making a fundamental distinction between the teaching of philosophy and the teaching of religion. Having worked in both areas for the past fifteen years, I have found that most students come to these two fields of study with the same motivation as I had when I entered my first philosophy class: as part of the search for meaning in life.

The importance of this fact about the motivations of young students of philosophy and religion and the difficulty of a proper response to it were brought home to me the very first time I myself stood in front of a class of beginning students. Sure enough, as I was describing the various branches of philosophy, I was interrupted by one student who asked: "Which part of philosophy tells us how to live?"

To my surprise, I was myself reacting in almost the same way my own first professor had reacted. "I'm sorry," I said, "that's not what we're here for. You'll have to go elsewhere for that." It was the safe answer, sanctioned by all the unwritten rules of the modern academic transaction. And it was, I told myself, the only "honest" answer I could give. How could I tell him how to live, after all?

But this was San Francisco in 1962, not Cambridge, Massachusetts, of 1953. The class did not look askance at this young man. Quite the contrary; and he, for his part, simply refused to accept my answer. Instead, he replied: "Well, then, where *should* I go for an answer?"

I found myself saying:

"Well, if you are willing to stay with us a few months and work hard, you may find something happening. That does not mean that you will find your answer. But you may discover something happening to your question. It may begin to deepen, to be connected with many other ideas and aspects of life that you don't now see. But for that to happen, you will have to work hard both at thinking and also at holding on to your question at the same time."

I do not know whether this in fact took place with this particular student. But my reply was far wiser than I knew—perhaps because his question had found me unprepared and had produced in me the shock of seeing my first knee-jerk reaction of turning away from the really existential element in the student.

Under such conditions one sometimes does learn from oneself. Over the years I have come to see that this is exactly what can be offered to students whose motivation is in part (whether they know it or not) something that we might call "religious," in the sense of a search for answers to the fundamental questions of living.

What I am saying is that we who teach courses in religion and in certain areas of philosophy, whether we know it or not, are the medium by which special kinds of ideas are communicated to young people. Many of our students first encounter such ideas in our courses. And these ideas have a very distinct action on a human being. If I were to put it in one word, I would say of these ideas that their unique effect is to evoke and then to support the state of self-questioning. And to my mind this state is the very root and foundation of what could be called the religious impulse.

I would like roughly to characterize how I am using this term, "ideas." We need to make a sharp distinction between ideas which evoke self-interrogation and theories which offer explanations that satisfy the mind or open areas of external research by promising to bring a variety of phenomena together under one unifying concept. Almost every academic course deals quite naturally with theories—theories of economics, theories of perception, theories of biological process, theories of history—including theories about religion. Such theories—or theoretical ideas—are not intended by their creators to still the mind and awaken that special emotional intelligence that appears when one's sense of oneself and one's own existence is suddenly relativized, put into question. These theoretical ideas are a crucial element in the survival and development of any civilization—they are our great tools for organizing the world and living in it effectively. But the ideas I am speaking about, call them "contemplative ideas," do not have that aim, in my view. They were meant by their creators, or formulators, to guide an individual in the quest for real, not imaginary, self-knowledge, to help him discover directly for himself the truth about himself. They are not explanations. And historically they have been so formulated—for example in the language of myth and symbol—as to resist man's treating them as explanations and as to make them accessible only to an individual in the psychological state of spiritual need; one might say they are geared to what the Sufis call "the intelligence of the heart."

As educators in the field of religious studies, we are dealing uniquely in these contemplative ideas. When we teach courses involving the presentation of the contents of religion—whether in the form of metaphysical ideas, accounts of ritual practices, studies of scriptural texts and commentaries, studies of traditional forms of myth, art, architecture—we are, to some degree, exposing our students to such ideas. In this respect our situation could be likened to experts giving courses in the theory and practice of preparing the various foods of the world to students many of whom are desperately hungry, or in any case in a condition of malnutrition. I would prefer to use a less homely example, but perhaps this adequately conveys the point I am making—that, as educators in the academic field of religion, we are handling ideas which could be said to be the carriers of a special kind of energy, which has the power to ignite the heart and mind of any serious person.

Could there be any more significant goal of education than this "ignition" of the search for Truth? If someone objects that such ideas can be extremely disturbing to young men and women, may we not reply by asking: "Where is it written that real education is for the purpose of confirming the values automatically conditioned into us by our cultural milieu?''

It is clear that what we are speaking about here has nothing to do with persuading or preaching, nothing to do with our assuming the role of guru or therapist or priest. Nor are we speaking of imposing values on young minds. It is solely a question of recognizing that some ideas have a very special kind of power, and that these ideas have been the heart of human civilization since the beginning of history. If we send our children to be educated about human civilization, then we must be prepared for their coming into some kind of contact, at least from a distance, with the special energies that have in fact moved human beings throughout all time.

But having seen this, I am now brought, as an educator, to a new problem, and a very difficult and painful problem. What I wish now to say touches on the whole question of the origins not only of modern education and scholarship, but indeed of modern, Western culture itself and the crisis in which it now finds itself.

The present influx of Asian religious teachings into America allows us direct witness to a process that has been going on in the West for at least a hundred and fifty years. Anyone who has observed the new religious movement at close hand cannot but conclude that in many cases what we are seeing is a drama in which ideas and methods that in their original setting required extensive moral, social, and psychological preparation before being given out are now being made available to anyone simply for the asking. As a result, the question has arisen whether these ideas and methods are in fact being used for purposes that are even antithetical to the purposes for which they were originally intended. It is a question that is quite unavoidable, for example, in the movement among some modern psychotherapists to make use of Eastern spiritual ideas for purposes that could be characterized as strengthening something in human nature, the sense of social personality or ego, that these very ideas and methods were originally meant to weaken or even destroy. The problem facing our society with respect to certain new mass religious movements may also exhibit this problem from another side. Here it is a question of the emotional energy generated by bringing unprepared people together for long periods of time and under unusual conditions of living that have the effect of creating certain poorly understood states of consciousness by freeing a psychic energy which then combines with impulses of whatever sort—for example, loyalty to a leader. Of course, there are many sides to this particular issue; I mention it only as one example of the kinds of problems generated when fragments of a complete tradition are made available without offering people the necessary guidance and knowledge of what to do with the energy that these fragments generate.

In the West, the liberal education movement arose in the last century with the avowed purpose of widening the scope of human inquiry through making all ideas and teachings available to everyone. At a constantly accelerating pace, published material of every sort began to become available and the literacy level of modern man began its spectacular rise.

Prior to that time, the average person was considerably more in emotional contact with the specific traditional teaching in which his life was immersed. Although his acceptance of religious authority was perhaps uncritical, he nevertheless retained in some measure the *will*, the emotional force to live according to great ideals and values. That is to say, he was more in relationship to his body and feeling.

As the modern era progressed, such a state of affairs began to be regarded as constricting and blindly accepting. It was thought necessary to develop the intellect of man. But how to develop the intellect of man without unwittingly creating a buffer between the mind and the heart?

What was not seen was that for certain ideas a definite preparation of the emotions and the body is necessary if these ideas are to have their intended beneficial action upon a man. Nor was it considered that through this process of making all ideas available to everyone (without exact knowledge of the conditions under which such ideas need to be presented), men and women were being drawn more and more into their thoughts, and moving further and further away from the life of feeling and natural instinct, wherein reside the most powerful energies of the human being.

Widespread questioning of authority accompanied the stimulated appetite for mental information and explanations, having its immediate effect on political authority throughout the Western world, and soon reaching to the areas of religious and family life as well. Above all, this process was fueled by the development of modern science with its specific canons of knowing and its particular view of reality. Everyone can and should know everything, can and should pass judgment on everything—from the nature of the universe to the actions of the king to the decisions of the father and the mother. That this right and ability to know and evaluate demanded a harmonious development of all the parts of the human structure was completely ignored—or, at best, acknowledged only in theory.

In our time this process has finally produced such massive dislocations of human life and such external crises that there is no longer much belief in external or piecemeal solutions to the problems of the world. It is clear to many that the only way out is to bring man back into contact with the sources of moral power within the self, and that this cannot be done in any of the familiar, conventional ways.

Nowhere is this need to bring values and great ideals into relationship with the life of feeling and action more apparent than in the minds of many, young and old, who are drawn to the new religions. Is this not what often lies behind the question about the meaning of life—how to transmit the great truths to the whole of our being?

This issue is the substance of the spiritual drama of the present era and underlies much of what is now taking place in the form of extraordinary changes and movements within the fields of religion, education, the sciences, art, and even, in part, in economics and politics. I have already mentioned one reflection of this issue in the field of psychiatry, but it is really quite pervasive, this search for a way to bring transcendent ideals and values into an active relationship with all the parts of human nature.

The question which we face, as educators and scholars in this area, is whether we will only be part of the process by which great contemplative ideas are turned into theories, or whether we wish also to be instruments by which the search for meaning is supported and strengthened. How to find our way between the scylla of pseudo-gurudom and the charybdis of bloodless intellectualism? How to recognize the special nature of the ideas we are dealing with without pretending we are able or obliged to create the conditions under which such ideas can be a guide to the spiritual disciplines in which they were originally embedded? On the other hand, how to maintain a sound, academic rigor in our research and teaching without crushing others' search for meaning by translating all contemplative ideas into theoretical concepts?

We need, I think, to be able to recognize two kinds of motivation in people that bring them to inquire about this material. On the one hand, they want information, theories. On the other hand, for some—not all—there also exists this other impulse to find a connection with something higher and more universal in life, call it "meaning." As educators and scholars in this field, our difficult and necessary task is to be able to distinguish these two kinds of motivation which correspond to the two natures of man himself, and to realize that it is only in the act of self-questioning that these two impulses are for a moment brought into relationship. The demand for academic rigor and impartiality in no wise contradicts or impedes this kind of self-interrogation; quite the contrary. However, the challenge we face is to satisfy the first kind of need without stifling the second kind, and at the same time to recognize that through satisfying the need for information and theoretical knowledge about religion, we are sometimes going to be instruments by means of which self-questioning arises.

Perhaps we need to understand more fully the nature of self-questioning in ourselves, that is, to see more clearly the twofold nature of our own relationship to great ideas. However, that is not merely an academic, professional challenge; it is the challenge of the meaning of one's own life. And it is in any case an issue which I am neither able nor expected to answer. Were I to attempt that, I would quite simply put the same question that I asked twenty-five years ago in my first philosophy course: "What is the meaning of life?" I am still asking that question.

INTRODUCTION

WHATEVER THEIR persuasion, that of religious aspirant or that of religious critic, persons that have taken the new religions seriously have been led to the question of context. Because both the new religious searcher and the new-religions researcher meet at the intersection of their respective questions, a relationship between them has taken form. That relationship in many instances has not been a cordial one.

The aspirant, seeing that the words of his spiritual teacher, or those of other followers of his movement, are about to appear in print in the report of an investigation, is apt to cry out that those words were taken out of context. If asked, What is the right context? the aspirant is faced with the problem of plausibly presenting the views and precepts of his church, and his answer may become that of an evangelist. The new-religions scholar, meanwhile, in preparing his report, is faced with the task of interpreting the transcripts of his interviews. He has to ask himself, In what context and form is a given quotation to be placed? The way he answers that question will be influenced by his own religious persuasion no less than by his scholarly background and breadth of understanding. For the researcher, the question, What is the right context? is as urgent as for the aspirant.

Although they come together on the question of context, the follower and the investigator of the new religions are apt to part company on the question, In what Age do we live? That question is not the same as asking for the year, decade, or century. Do we live in the Age of Abraham, Aquarius, Bahaullah, Christ, Mohammed, or the Lord of the Second Advent? Or do we live in the post-1960s, the postwar period, the post-industrial period, or as old-style Marxists used to say, the pre-historical period? The question of Age is important for both the aspirant and the investigator because the answer to that question will determine an important component, that of historical origin, in their explanation of context. Is one's explanation to start with references to the deeds and thoughts of Jesus Christ, Karl Marx, Max Weber, John Kennedy, Moon Sun-Myung, or Tarthang Tulku?

The question of Age leads to a related one, that of lineage. The intellectual and spiritual identity of both the aspirant and the investigator is a matter of what Buddhists call "dharma-lineage." The Sanscrit term *dharma*, as used by Buddhists, refers to the teachings of the Buddha. Because many schools of interpretation exist, a follower of the teachings of the Buddha is at the same time a follower within one of the schools the spiritual genealogy of which may be documented, from teacher to spiritual heir, as far back as a thousand years. In the West, only the lineage of the Roman Catholic Popes is well-known. Protestants, although they may have a clear idea of the teachings of the founder of their order, have little interest in a genealogically exact line along which those teachings were "transmitted" from the founder to the pastor of their neighborhood church.

Aspirants in new religions, no less than Ph.D. candidates in departments of religious studies, regard themselves as the representatives of their teachers; that is, they regard their work as a contribution to the tradition of which their teacher is the heir or heir apparent. At times, when aspirants in new religions are at the same time enrolled in an academic program of religious studies, a conflict of loyalty appears. That conflict may take the form of a "dharma battle" within himself, or it may take the form of a "dharma battle" with others. On the one hand, he is called upon by Conscience to represent the precepts and insights of his spiritual lineage, but on the other hand he is called upon by Intellect to carry out and defend scholarly rules for methodological purity. At times this battle may appear on the surface as a disagreement over the context and significance of data gained in field, library, or introspective research. The controversy over the nature, purpose, and benefits of meditation, transcendental or otherwise, is one such battle.

Meanwhile, the general reader has to place his own interest in new religions in context. What should that context be? Should it be that of the social critic who sees in the appearance of the new religions a positive or negative sign of fundamental change in society? Should it be that of parents who see in the participation of their child in one of the new religions a sign that the spiritual lineage of their family may be broken? Should it be that of the mental health professional who sees in the various ascetic practices of the new religious movements either a path out of adolescence and toward adulthood or a path out of normality and toward psychopathic illness? Should it be that of the interested shopper who is dazzled or baffled by the appearance of so many new religious products and services on the market?

For some readers the use of the word "should" in reference to their understanding of the signs of the present age may be premature. Such readers have learned from their preliminary reading of those signs that the primary question, What *is* the context of their interest in new religions? is more important than its corollary, What *should* the context of their interest be? Such readers will find in the following essays ample materials for the enrichment of their present, preliminary understanding.

A word about the documentation structure: Superscript numbers in the text refer the reader to substantive notes located at the end of each essay. Numbers in brackets, which are found both in the text and in the notes, refer the reader to the bibliographical references also at the end of each essay.

Part 1

New Religions in American History

INTRODUCTION

The essays in this section directly address one of the questions raised in the general introduction: What is the place and significance of new religions in the context of American history? When these essays are read in contrast to each other, and in contrast to the first three essays in Part Two, the thoughtful reader will probably ask, with Sydney Ahlstrom, What conditions have fostered America's "persistent inventiveness" in the area of religion?

Ahlstrom traces the way that the West's historic barriers to religious freedom and innovation have been overcome progressively in America. America's religious character and history are examined from other perspectives by John Dillenberger, Eldon Ernst, and Joseph Chinnici, who likewise seek an explanation for such unparalleled pluralism.

Other observers are fascinated, not by America's unique religious past, but by American life as a mirror to forces and patterns that transcend the cultural and historical boundaries of any one nation. Robert Wuthnow asks, in effect, What is the twentieth century? Most observers agree that the twentieth century is the history of large-scale changes, but they often disagree as to the scale on which the changes have taken place. Wuthnow says that there has been a major change in what he calls the "world order" since the nineteenth century. Dick Anthony and Thomas Robbins point to a change in what they, after Weber, call the "spirit of capitalism." In contrast, Theodore Roszak interprets the new religions as evidence of man's innate capacity for psychospiritual rejuvenation.

Behind many of these reflections is the residue of another question, one that was asked from the very beginnings of the

European colonization of *Las Indias,* as Spaniards used to refer to the American hemisphere. The question originally posed by the great Spanish theologians and jurists of the sixteenth century was, What is the spiritual place of America within Christendom? Francisco de Vitoria, the celebrated founder of international law, answered that spiritually America was an independent realm, and that the Catholic Kings of Spain could only lawfully extend Christianity by peaceful means.

Four centuries later Americans were asking, What is the spiritual place of Europe in the structure of American values and beliefs? President Woodrow Wilson realized that to answer that question was also to set American foreign policy toward Europe. In 1916 he argued, like Vitoria, for the spiritual independence of America, and, in promising to keep America out of the European war, he proposed that there be "peace without victory." In 1917, however, not only did Wilson come to regard Europe as an inviolable symbol of the integrity of American values, but he came to the painful conclusion that America morally was obligated to enter the war in order to make, not only Europe, but the world, "safe for democracy." Wilson's vision of America's moral role in international affairs deeply influenced American foreign policy for over a half-century. The Tet Offensive of 1968 forced Americans to recognize the moral independence of Viet Nam, and, by implication, of other nations as well.

Americans are beginning to recognize that Vitoria was right: The inhabitants of America, who now speak, not only Spanish, but almost every other tongue, Christian and non-Christian, known to man, have their own forms of spiritual life. At such a time, the appearance of new forms of religious expression is surely predictable. What remains to be explained is the reversal in the attitude of some Americans toward the spiritual traditions of non-European peoples. The East is often seen as intrinsically more "spiritual" than the West. Why? One reading is that Americans in general have entered a new phase of spiritual dependency. Another reading, one suggested by Anthony and Robbins, is that some of the new religions seem to offer ways to return to the moral security and purity of former epochs. A third reading, one offered by Jacob Needleman, is that some Americans have included in their reaffirmation of spiritual independence the right to search for truth wherever it may be found.

FROM SINAI TO THE GOLDEN GATE: THE LIBERATION OF RELIGION IN THE OCCIDENT

Sydney E. Ahlstrom

In a short parody of the consciousness circuit which appeared in a recent *New Yorker,* F. P. Ullius told of the new roads to richness of mind and spirit that he had discovered in his travels. In Sausalito, he had stood tête-à-pied with a man in the full lotus position and received instruction in the methods and disciplines of Tibetan lama calling. This was followed by an account of Cutical Awareness sponsored by a manicurist in the neighborhood of Bowdoin College in Maine. An adept in Japanese tool arranging was operating out of a repair shop in New York. In a Serbo-Croatian restaurant in Santa Monica, it was an advocate of Situational Ethnics who challenged the itinerant seeker. There was some sign, however, that his most satisfying experience had come through his training in Sufi Square Dancing.

The least that one can say of the article is that its author was aware of some changing patterns of religion in America. As if to highlight the newness, moreover, the magazine's editors had placed a cartoon on one of these same pages which depicted the passing of the old order. The scene was a tropical resort where an elderly gentlemen was ruminating out loud to his wife: "If I'm remembered at all, when I'm gone," he said, "I'm afraid it will be for what I did at that New Year's Party in 1953."

One can suppose that every reader is aware of the fact that with some slight but knowledgeable modifications of the movements depicted by the heavy-handed Mr. Ullius, his story could have been accepted as authentic. But we are less likely to realize that even the grandfather of Mr. Ullius could have been delivered from ennui and pointless living by a considerable number of very similar movements that arose in the Victorian era. "The Newest Consciousness," as it turns out, is not very new. Indeed both humorists and outraged establishmentarians of all hues have been ridiculing the American's penchant for religious novelty ever since a Puritan minister in Boston referred to Roger Williams' sect-filled commonwealth of Rhode Island as "the Sewer of New England." Henry Melchior Muhlenberg, the planter of Lutheran churches in eighteenth-century Pennsylvania, held a very similar view of the proliferating sects among the German settlers. He not only had to contend with a colony of hermits who had brought Rosicrucian Hermeticism to the New World, but with Count Zinzendorf, who wanted to bring most of these groups together under a single, rather flamboyant umbrella: his own Church of the Spirit. In the nineteenth century, John Williamson Nevin, who had translated himself from the Evangelical United Front to the more seriously theological confines of the German Reformed Church, was seeing the marks of the anti-Christ in the multiplying sects of his time. For a while, Nevin teetered in despair on the brink of Catholicism. Bishop George Washington Doane, the pro-Tractarian first bishop of New Jersey, became so disgusted with the country's numerous "dissenters" that he became the first American to utter the cry: "Back to the Dark Ages." Having recently made a preaching tour of the English Cathedrals, he was nostalgic for a unified Christendom and the days when bishops sat on thrones and wielded power. How Americans turned their backs on the bishop's dream of religious unity and moved instead toward the Aquarian Frontier will constitute the substance of what follows.

I

I have never counted all of the religious entities described or touched upon in my own *Religious History of the American People,* nor those described in various handbooks of American religious groups, but the basic fact is relatively clear, even though the attitudes of various observers differ sharply. Both Roger Williams and William Penn recognized this rampant pluralism and appreciated its epoch-making significance. Ezra Stiles in 1783 (the year of the nation's official independence) in his famous oration, "America Elevated to Glory," was confident and proud that America in due time would "embosom" all the sects and denominations of Christendom, and "give complete freedom to all." Phillip Schaff, in a mid-nineteenth-century statement, observed that America was already a "motley sampler of all church history," while Dietrich Bonhoeffer, almost a century later, reflected a more characteristic German view when he said of America that "it has been granted to the Americans less than any other nation on earth to realize the visible unity of the Church of God." All of these testimonies expose the vital fact about the country's life and culture. Pluralism in religion is an accepted fact despite the persistence of a certain ambivalence of view.

Our inquiry does not stop, however, with the recognition of great freedom and diversity. My task here is to place this fact "in an historical context." And I have never disguised my commitment to the view that the historian's office in such a situation is to provide an explanation in the form of an historical narrative, even though the achievement of this task requires one to stop the clock intermittently for sociological, theological, or speculative digressions. My chief purpose shall be to answer these questions: "How did this state of American affairs come to pass?" and "What are the generally prevailing conditions that have encouraged religious diversity and fostered the country's persistent inventiveness in the religious realm?"

Almost every historian of the American experience has somehow dealt with the topics of religious pluralism and diversity, and many have dealt with this people's propensity to spawn or support new religious movements. It thus goes without saying that my own awareness of the problem antedates the present discussion. But I will say that a major provocation to reconsider the problem came from an opportunity to discuss this and related problems in a series of lectures, seminars, and conferences in Australia and New Zealand. The general theme that emerged over and over again in those discussions was the comparative problem of understanding the religious differences of the several siblings of Britannia that are scattered around the world. More particular were the questions of similarity and difference between the United States and Australia, both of which are vast and affluent states of British heritage, but with populations which, though dominated by the native English-speaking majority, have been also shaped by an enormous flow of highly diversified immigration. In the face of these similarities, I was repeatedly asked to explain why, in sharp contra-distinction to the Australian experience, American religious life was in such a constant state of creative ferment. Discussants would note a dozen American innovations from Mormonism and Christian Science to Pentecostalism and Jehovah's Witnesses, and then ask, "Why has Australia shown almost none of these signs, even though the country's leading historian, Manning H. Clark, perceives the entire Australian experience as profoundly pervaded by a unique religious spirit?" Despite my heightened fascination with this comparative problem, however, I am referring to it here only by way of underlining the widespread recognition of America's religious fecundity. But let me stress the major fact again: American civilization from the beginning and in each passing century has been continuously marked by extraordinary religious fertility, and continues to exhibit this propensity to the present day. Indeed, one of the ironies of the 1960s was that just when many former Barthian theologians were proclaiming the death of God, other young Americans were kindling the fires of the new religious wave that we are now seeking to describe and understand.

Ralph Waldo Emerson observed, in his Divinity School Address (1838), that European civilization "has always owed to Oriental genius its divine impulses," and there is some truth in his claim. But we should recognize his limitations as an observer. In this same address, he was announcing the "death of faith" in the American churches at just the time when America's "Third Great Awakening," with Charles Grandison Finney as its most dynamic advocate, was reaching its revivalistic zenith. A new form of patriotic piety was also nearing its mature form. In other contexts, meanwhile, a dozen visionaries were ripening plans for communal utopias or for distinctly new religions. Indeed, Emerson and his "transcendental fellowship" were at this very moment developing yet another new religious impulse. The signs of the times were in fact suggesting that America was about to challenge the Orient as the fountainhead of new religions.

What needs to be examined, therefore, are the various dimensions of the American experience which help to explain that ethos, climate, or prevailing spirit which conduces to religious innovation despite the constant allegations by foreign observers and many Americans that this is the most materialistic of nations, and despite the further fact that Americans, generally speaking, have usually opposed these emergent faiths as dangerously subversive and have sometimes reacted with violence. Even today, Mr. Moon and the Unification Church is experiencing this tendency.

II

If we are to take these considerations seriously, it would seem necessary that we at least give brief consideration to the Judeo-Christian and Graeco-Roman sources of the Western religious tradition. It is in these dialectical relationships that we find both the roots of the search for human liberation and the roots of intolerance and persecution. At least since Tertullian, the contrasting implications of Athens and Jerusalem have agitated the conscience of Christendom. For reasons soon to be suggested, it is the Hebraic tradition which has been most decisive in shaping the American religious experience. Indeed, if one takes into account its relationships to Christianity, Islam, and Marxism during the last two millennia, the Hebraic tradition would seem to be the most consequential religion in world history.

Even so, however, we do well to remember that even Judaism was once a "new religion." It seems to have emerged from a form of nature-polytheism that is depicted in a fragmentary way in the Bible's oldest passages, such as the Song of Deborah in Judges and in other scattered texts. What one sees or hears is a storm god, whose spirit never entirely disappears from the tradition.

> O Yahweh, when thou camest forth from Seir
> When thou marchedst from the slopes of Edom,
> The earth quaked, and the heavens also shook,
> The clouds too dripped water,
> The mountains rocked at the presence of Yahweh
> At the presence of Yahweh, the God of Israel,
> Yahweh came from Sinai,
> And dawned on us from Seir;
> He shone forth from the mountains of Paran,
> And advanced from Meribath-Kadesh,
> With lightning bolts in his hand [1].

What this religion became over the course of centuries is disclosed in the Hebrew Scriptures, though I am not the one to arbitrate the vast scholarly literature that deals with its history and interpretation. Suffice it to say that the prophetic monotheism that took shape provided the decisive ingredients in the Western mind and spirit: its historical sense of reality, its profound insistence on covenantal obedience, its commitment to the scriptural word as the sufficient word of God, and a monotheistic strictness whereby every vestige of polytheism and every form of syncretism were to be repulsed and condemned. During the years of Selucid rule in the Middle East, Jewish intransigence led to conflict and war, and in the latter Roman years, to the drastic deeds of Titus and Hadrian. Among the Jews of the diaspora, however, many succumbed to the seductions of Classical philosophy, neo-Platonism, gnosticism, and other religious currents, with effects that reached from the age of Philo to the times of Maimonides, Spinoza, Moses Mendelssohn, and Freud. With regard to new religious impulses of a much later day, few writings would become more consequential than that strange body of biblical interpretation and esoteric speculation that came to be known as the Kaballa.

Most important for the fortunes of the biblical tradition and for Western civilization was the astoundingly successful evangelism of the Christian Church in the Roman Empire. By A.D. 311 this self-proclaimed "New Israel" had gained such importance that only a Christian could effectively rule the empire. What then ensued was a new age of orthodoxy in an empire that for several centuries had been remarkably receptive, not only to the Classical tradition of science, philosophy, and theological speculation, but also to many Eastern religious impulses and mystery religions. In the new age of the ecumenical councils, one beholds the rise of doctrinal conflict, acrimony, schisms, and competing anathemas. On every side theologians and bishops act upon the Pauline injunction: "If anyone is preaching to you a gospel contrary to that which you have received, let him be accursed." Under Theodosius the pagan temples are closed. Orthodoxy is hereafter enforced by imperial power.

During the long millennium which follows, the Roman Catholic Church dominated the religious life of Western Europe, bearing with it a powerful Graeco-Roman legacy. This legacy includes a strong juridical emphasis in church government, the assimilation of many patterns of Classical religious thought (from Plato to Plotinus), considerable syncretistic lenience, and a pervasive belief in the miraculous. All of these tendencies tend to mitigate the force of those Judaic themes defined above. There remains, nevertheless, an overarching insistence on subservience to Roman authority and to orthodox doctrine. Inquisitions, persecution, and the condemnation of heretics continued even in times of laxity and corruption. The extirpation of the Albigensian Cathari is perhaps the most outstanding instance. Yet the resort to coercion and intolerance continues even long after the Reformation. Due to the renewal of controversy by many of the great reformers, and to the territorialization of many Protestant churches, certain theological doctrines and scriptural interpretations became so refined and hardened that they perpetuated themselves in the twentieth century. Moreover, until the later eighteenth century, many of the churches supporting these rigid doctrines and interpretations could depend on the support of strong authoritarian governments.

The fact remains, however, that the Reformation was a momentous landmark in the history of toleration and the rise of new religious impulses. The sheer fact of religious pluralism was the most obvious effect, and probably the most important. It broke the power of the Pontifex Maximus, and shattered the ecclesiastical structures that had maintained the unity of Western Christendom. There is no need for a detailed description of the new confessional churches that were formed in many lands, or the many radical movements that soon made their presence known. More needful is it to recognize the way in which this process of division undermined the immemorial view of authority, relativized the idea of dogmatic truth, and opened the way for new religious leaders and disaffected groups to gather constituencies and to institutionalize some new-found consensus. This complex outcome is the chief event in Christian history since the time of Constantine the Great. The basis for making so drastic a claim is not so much the radical particularity of a certain number of sects, but the existence of several new magisterial churches. Luther's sensational unleashing of the Gospel, when placed over against the theology of Pope Leo X, must be entertained as virtually a new religion, especially if account is

taken of its long-term impact on piety and practice. And at least
as strong a claim can be made for that revolution perpetrated by
the various Reformed theologians who shaped the tradition we
call "Calvinistic." How in America today could we conceive of
an institutional dismantling equally thorough? And if that is the
case, what must we say of the revolution in Christendom carried
out by the Puritans in England? Due to the doctrinal conflict they
engendered, a wide spectrum of highly diverse sects and denominations was founded—from Presbyterians past the Quakers to the chiliastic Muggletonians. Yet out of what they held in
common came a social revolution that all but wrecked the old
order of church and state. And finally through their concerted
effort to demagicalize the "superstitions of Rome" and to see an
inward, subjective conversion experience as the chief mark of a
Christian, they opened the way for the rise of modern religious
ideas—including deism. As the effects of England's turmoil were
translated to the "free aire" of colonial America, the possibilities for religious innovation became almost unlimited. One
frequently ignored factor leading to this result was the increased
acceptance of the seemingly innocuous concept of "denominationalism," which is to say the almost revolutionary tendency of born-again evangelicals to recognize as Christian those
professed believers who witnessed to an experience of God's
redeeming grace, even though disagreements on issues, such as
baptism or predestination, made unrestricted fellowship impossible. In the long run, denominationalism weakened the hold of
strict confessionalism and encouraged departures from tradition.
These potentialities were even further enhanced by the fact that
in America the social order as well was shaped by the rising
spirit of political and economic freedom. One may wonder, in
fact, if anyone has described this new situation more
accurately—or poignantly—than Karl Marx in the *Manifesto* of
1848. By that time he can depict how remorseless change and
innovation is the only constant in the bourgeois social order
which has emerged. He can even lament that "all feudal, patriarchal, idyllic relations" have been "pitilessly torn asunder."
"Venerable opinions are swept away" as remorseless innovation
and change become the order of the day. It goes without saying
that the religious realm was as much affected as any. With the
force of tradition weakened both by Puritan principle and geo-

graphic distance, religious individualism quickly made itself manifest in America. By the time the earth tremors of the Great Awakening had subsided, the structures of the establishment, or of the "Standing Order," were crumbling, even in New England. And by the time of the American Revolution, religious freedom was largely attained and the separation of church and state was part of the nation's fundamental law. Finally, and perhaps as important as any development, the democratic idea had penetrated deeply into the life of the churches, giving confidence to the laity, and undermining the authority of ecclesiastical organizations, bishops, and clergy. The way was open for charismatic innovators, frustrated prophets, and dissident voices. So strong and pervasive was the spirit of religious independence that even in the Roman Catholic Church it took a half-century for the American hierarchy and the Vatican to quell the power of local parish trustees [2].

III

In the foregoing portion of this essay, our primary concern has been to depict the strenuously authoritarian notions of religious orthodoxy which have dominated the great part of Western history and to suggest some of the ways in which that tradition was mitigated over the passing centuries. We have sought to explicate the circumstances that made the United States the first country in the world to repudiate the Constantinian tradition of governmental watchfulness over the religious realm, to formulate constitutional guarantees of religious and ecclesiastical freedom, and most important of all, to shape a libertarian ethos in the religious realm that persistently challenged those persons, groups, and churches that sought by various means to limit the freedom of others. From earliest times, to be sure, there was a large Protestant majority that was hostile to Roman Catholic claims; and after the Revolution it often behaved as if it were in a privileged position. Sometimes its missionary activities were even overtly oppressive. On the other hand, the Second Great Awakening, which manifested itself after the century's turn, produced such a large degree of spiritual volatility that it encouraged sectarian and cultic secessions, and produced so strong a measure of religious individualism that its solidarity was impaired. (Which is why John W. Nevin found it so offensive.) By 1850, the Roman Catholic Church had become the largest denomination in the country.

In all of this discussion, however, the single most powerful element in this process has been purposefully ignored, namely, the fact that the American nation has been constituted by what is probably the largest and most diverse *Volkerwanderung* in history. It was a movement of peoples that began with the "swarming of the Puritans" in the 1630s and continues to this day. England alone of the early imperial powers encouraged its dissident elements to emigrate to the colonies. In contrast to the Spanish rule in America, English policy provided liberal naturalization procedures for the nationals of other countries. England thus set an important precedent which was continued after Independence. From the start, therefore, religious surveillance, coercion, and conformity were out of the question. The only major exception was the early shaping of a national civil religion in which the nation's providential destiny was proclaimed. Even this anomaly was mitigated, however, by the enthusiasm with which the poor and persecuted people who came to America overwhelmingly affirmed every major element of the national ideology. A patriotic tradition, of course, could not by itself eliminate the tensions of pluralism, or the ancient rivalries of various immigrant groups, such as those between Czechs and Poles, Catholics and Protestants, Jews and Gentiles. Yet even these hostilities were much mitigated with the passage of time. For present purposes, therefore, the chief remaining task is to consider the ways in which new religious impulses took shape in the various stages of the republic's history and how the opportunities for an increasingly wide range of religious expression came into existence. Under the circumstances this must take the form of a brief and rapid survey.

1. The age of the Puritan revolution has already been dealt with, but it is nevertheless essential that we recognize the powerful precedents for diversity and tolerance that were established during the early seventeenth century. It was then that various principled commonwealth founders such as Roger Williams and William Penn, along with other less principled colonial entrepreneurs, opened the new land to any and all who would come, and allowed freedom to them all. Also of great consequence in ex-

tending these liberties was the eruption of the Great Awakening and its spread into nearly all of the colonies. During this period new and more extravagant forms of evangelicalism appeared, as well as highly significant innovations in theology. Jonathan Edwards, in fact, added an element to the future civil religion of America. He saw fit to revise the more pessimistic view of the Puritans and declared these revivals to be a sign that the Kingdom of God was coming to America.

2. The Revolutionary Era which follows is pervaded by a very different spirit. Political concerns become dominant for one thing, but these are accompanied by very strong currents of rationalism and the rise of deism. It is also a time when enthusiasm in religion was coming under very heavy criticism. More important was the way in which many of the most honored Founding Fathers quite freely and very plausibly expounded and defended their religious radicalism. In so doing, they lent great prestige to an Enlightened outlook and emboldened others to unveil their own rationalism. The efforts of some to institutionalize deism were almost entirely unsuccessful, but within a decade or two both Universalists and Unitarians were making explicit denominational commitments to liberal religion.

Also, because many of the Founding Fathers were acknowledged Freemasons, they would in later decades be claimed as early leaders of American Rosicrucianism. In the broadest possible way, however, they opened the way for independent thinking in the theological realm and expressed their contempt for narrowness and intolerance.

3. The ante-bellum period, as already indicated, was to a degree darkened by the suspicions and counter-subversionary activities of the Evangelical United Front, notably in its attacks on the Mormons, the Masons, and the Catholics. But the overwhelmingly dominant tendency of those times was in the opposite direction. It became, in fact, the great seed-time for new religious impulses and communal experiments.

The most well-known of these undoubtedly was the Transcendental Fellowship that recognized Ralph Waldo Emerson as its leading spokesman. His romantic radicalism, however, reached far beyond Boston, and even beyond America. Furthermore, many of the most committed Transcendentalists not only founded a commune at Brook Farm but took the more radical step of transforming it into a Phalanstery after the designs of Charles Fourier, as did many other equally committed groups. Most radical, perhaps, were the Perfectionist followers of John Humphrey Noyes whose community at Oneida even practiced the principles of "complex marriage." The Universalists, too, were busy founding yet another perfectionist utopia, Hopedale, and also showing a remarkable interest in the esoteric views of Immanuel Swedenborg and the fully realized eschatology of the Church of the New Jerusalem, which his devotees founded. This led in turn to the Harmonial Philosophy of the "Poughkeepsie Seer," Andrew Jackson Davis. Emerson, too, deemed Swedenborg to be the "Last Father in the Church," and paid him the ultimate tribute of adopting in a qualified way some of Swedenborg's central ideas.

The sensational revelations and eschatological doctrines of Swedenborg also contributed heavily to the age's enormous interest in Spiritualism, and hardly less so to the widespread emergence of food and health cults. A surge of concern for time-specific doctrines of the coming millennium was another, somewhat contradictory, feature of the times. It was out of this enthusiasm over the triumphal return of Christ, or more accurately, the "Great Disappointment" which followed his failure to appear, that Ellen Harmon White appeared with revelations that corrected William Miller's calculations concerning the Second Coming. These revelations included a serious interest in dietary theories, healing, and above all a new doctrine of the Seventh-Day Sabbath, all of which would lead to the formation of a new Christian denomination of a very distinctive sort.

Still another innovative product of the pre-Civil War era were the four or five anti-denominational "restorationist" movements, the convergence of which emphasized the actual practice of the New Testament church and discounted the significance of the Old Covenant of Moses and the Jews. These disciples of Christ or "Christians" gradually separated themselves into three major groupings, but all of them maintain a distinctive group of concerns, doctrines, and controversies.

And so one could go on page after page identifying the dynamic qualities and novel proposals that characterized the age. In some cases the "newness" was syncretistic, while in other cases "sectarian" would be a more accurate term. In at least one case, however, no term is better than "new religion." This is the Church of Jesus Christ of the Latter-Day Saints which based itself on the *Book of Mormon* and the later revelations of its "proprietor" Joseph Smith. Despite widespread denigration and considerable violent resistance, or perhaps because of these, Mormonism became the most world-famous and successful new religion to emerge in the ante-bellum period.

During these same years Southerners may have been (in Sacvan Bercovitch's phrase) "the gentiles of God's New Israel in America," but this did not prevent contentions and religious innovations in that region. Especially after the Great Awakening, it was the Baptists who became the chief bearers of the Puritan impulse in America, and in the broad reaches of the rural South they became the predominant form of Evangelical religion, being almost twice as numerous as their Methodist rivals, both Black and White. In the region as a whole, non-Evangelicals (chiefly Catholic) were a very small minority. In their strict congregational separatism, Baptists had always resisted the attitudes of "denominationalism" and even the name of "Protestant." They regarded themselves as Baptists in an unbroken relation to the New Testament Church. They were not "Protestants." Late in the ante-bellum period, the Land-Mark movement made these distinctions clear and dogmatic as it gained force and influence. When the further issue of slavery and secession was added, the Southern Baptist Convention itself became doubly marked off from the nation's other Protestants. The result was by no means a new religion, but it was distinctive, and among the "Primitive" (strictly Calvinistic) Baptists and in the Two-Seed-in-the-Spirit Predestinarian secession these distinguishing marks were even more clearly marked.

It was in the South, too, that the unique and profoundly internal characteristics of Black Religion would emerge—first through its own very special forms of evangelical preaching and worship, and later in the twentieth century in a wide variety of new religions, among which are the Black Jews, the Moorish Temple based on Timothy Drew's *Holy Koran,* the Black Muslims, and several others.

4. The post-bellum period is often depicted as a period of declining religious enthusiasm, and the judgment is correct insofar as one compares it with the sense of manifest destiny that

dominated Evangelical thinking before the War. Yet the "Gilded Age," as this half century of massive and rapid change is so often called, became a time for grappling with a great many social and intellectual problems which the pre-war generation had evaded or not perceived. The many issues that arose cannot, of course, be described here, but they can be mentioned in no special order: Intellectual Modernism, Social Injustice, Urbanism, and Immigration. Taken together, they add up to drastic moral and religious disorientation in most of the churches and among most of the people. Everywhere there was felt a sense of old landmarks gone and of traditions in disarray.

Protestantism was riven by the Fundamentalist Controversy and by the closely related rise of dispensationalistic premillennialism of a sort that led to a whole new way of reading the Bible, as well as a distinctly pessimistic view of America's destiny in particular, and of the world's destiny in general. Dwight L. Moody, the age's most widely heard revivalist preacher, was declaring that the world was a "wrecked vessel."

Even more iconoclastic and time-specific in its millennial warnings was the Russellite movement, which later came to be known as Jehovah's Witnesses. So bold were its claims and so deviant its critique of nationalism, the business world, and all other "so-called churches," and so idiosyncratic was its theology that more than any other movement of its type it deserves the name of "new religion." Its growth throughout the world has been sensational.

Almost contemporaneous with the rise of Fundamentalism was a similar protest against laxity in the middle-class churches that stemmed from basically Methodist doctrine, namely the Holiness secession (or extrusion) which gradually led to the rise of several new denominations. It was largely in this context that Pentecostalism emerged with its special and more drastic emphasis on the Second Blessing, especially after speaking in tongues and the gifts of healing became prominent elements of doctrine. Its growth was precipitous despite the harsh criticism directed toward it by conservatives and Fundamentalists in the Reformed tradition. Quite aside from such criticism, however, most Pentecostalists were almost as deeply committed to biblical literalism and apocalyptic views as their critics.

At the far extreme from these new forms of conservative religion was the rapid growth of theological liberalism in the seminaries and the wealthy city churches of the Protestant establishment, as well as among many social critics who were deeply troubled by corruption in high places and poverty in the urban slums. During the 1920s, J. Gresham Machen of the Princeton Theological Seminary would declare that liberalism or the "new theology" was not only a different religion from Christianity, but that it belonged to another class of religions. In saying this, he at least described a common view of the rift. He also supports my conception of a *"new"* religious impulse. The fact is, moreover, that a great many Americans were seeking alternatives to a tradition they could no longer accept; and in the profounder forms of liberal theology they found an exhilarating and satisfying faith.

Equally important and even more revealing of widespread religious uneasiness was the emergence or revival during the later nineteenth century of a group of movements which were largely or entirely divorced from the Christian tradition. Most widely attractive was interest in mediums, seances, psychical research, etc., among people of all ranks and stations. To a small and ineffectual degree, spiritualism even took on the shape of a denominational organization.

More distinctly pointing to the future were movements stemming from the fascination with Mesmerism or Animal Magnetism (hypnosis) or more generally the mental and religious dimensions of disease, "neurasthenia," melancholia, and other "nervous" disorders. The close connection between religion and healing has a long history, but we can say little of it here except to note that the late nineteenth century saw a sharp rise of interest among Protestants who had hitherto linked such concerns with superstition and Catholic miracle-mongering. Among Swedenborgians there appeared a distinct change of mood and a new concern for nature cures, as well as a tendency to homeopathic medicine. This was no doubt a salutary change in a scene dominated by single-nostrum kooks and quacks. Among the many who moved more seriously in this area of psychosomatic concern was Phineas Parkhurst Quimby who had experimented with hypnosis but who turned to the question of a religious science of health and healing. He might well have been forgotten, however, if in October of 1862 he had not suddenly delivered Mary Baker Patterson (Eddy) from her infirmities.

Thereafter it was she, not he, who after single-minded and long-sustained efforts presented *Science and Health, with Key to the Scriptures* to an ailing world (1875). After still other adversities, she startled the world with a rapidly growing church—and a major new religion. Yet she was by no means alone, and around the Quimbyites and others a widespread movement of "New Thought" freed itself from Mrs. Eddy's authority and proliferated dozens of variations on the modern and ancient themes (gnostic, Swedenborgian, theosophical, and philosophical) that underlay the entire impulse. Before long and ever since, millions upon millions of Americans heard and read the message. One of the earliest to develop a mass audience was that fervent admirer of Emerson, Ralph Waldo Trine, whose *In Tune with the Infinite* (1897) may be considered a classic of the genre. Since then, of course, there have been many others from Emmet Fox to Norman Vincent Peale.

The successes of these counselors, in turn, have contributed to a parallel revival of interest in Christian healing not only among perfectionists, but in the churches generally. The questions of boundaries, distinctions, and overlapping theories cannot be unravelled here; but it is important to note the deep indebtedness that is expressed by the leaders of this impulse to the message of Emerson. As will soon be noted, he and the Transcendental Fellowship also put their mark on both the scholarly study of world religions and the positive evaluation of the religions of the East. Indeed, their work and advocacy carried the impulse down to that rather climactic event in 1893, The World Parliament of Religions, which was held in Chicago in connection with the Columbian Exposition. Some of these Emersonian vibrations even reached to Europeans such as Nietzsche and Hermann Hesse, and thus raised Emerson's capital among a younger generation of Americans during the 1960s.

More clearly out of the mainstream during the Gilded Age was the revival of interest in theosophy and the Hermetic (or Secret) Tradition that flowed into European thought through the Kaballa and a great many other Gnostic and neo-Platonic sources. Since Freemasonry in all of its bewildering array of organizations in Britain, Europe, and elsewhere was also a channel of Rosicrucian and Hermetic lore, there is no way at this stage of our historical knowledge to quantify its extent. Like Spiritualism, it appeared almost everywhere, often in utterly private forms. Indeed, due to its secrecy and privacy, it is almost impossible to estimate the size of its constituency. Nevertheless, one may say with great confidence that as a "new religion" it has had many revivals in America ever since the tradition was brought from Germany to Pennsylvania in the early eighteenth century. Due to its astrological interests, its devotees run to uncounted millions. On the other hand, there is a line of Hermetic thinking that includes some of the most exalted thinkers of the West, from Hegel, Schelling, Goethe, Maistre, and Balzac down to Nikolai Berdjaev. Especially during the 1940s, Berdjaev was being widely read in America in many theological circles, including the Roman Catholics, who published several of his American translations. Recently Theodore Roszak has given the tradition a rooting in American social criticism in his *The Unfinished Animal: The Aquarian Frontier and the Evolution of Consciousness* (1975). His brief accounts of Madame Blavatsky, Rudolf Steiner, George I. Gurdjieff, and P. D. Ouspensky serve an important expository purpose.

5. Given the extraordinary pluralism and, more importantly, the unremitting fecundity of the American religious tradition, the general observation is warranted that the appearance of many new religious impulses during the 1960s and 1970s can best be seen as a continuation of a venerable tradition—not only because they continue to be formed, but because they also maintain an explicit or implicit social critique. Perhaps the single most important near exception is the great receptivity that this more recent period has shown for religions of the East. In the past these have exposed a relatively low profile in America, despite the early enthusiasms of Emerson and others, and even though the World Parliament of Religions did give a formative impetus to organized Hindu and Baha'i movements, which endured. The basic fact is that the contemporary interest in various aspects of the Buddhist and Zen traditions are relatively new, and would, therefore, seem to require some special comment. Blanket "explanations" of deeply personal conversions, if we may call them that, are inevitably gross. Yet it was a sufficiently pervasive tendency to deserve a wider approach. It would seem that two factors were predominant. The first is negative. I refer to the "death of God" theologians. This is not to say, of course, that

the writings of a dozen or so radical theologians by themselves effected a change in American religious attitudes in a few years, though they undeniably did gain a large opinion-setting public. Far more important was the way in which the tumults of the time led to a widespread loss of confidence in the American tradition itself. These disruptive events had the effect of catalyzing the cumulative force of liberal theology and other modernizing and relativizing tendencies that can be traced back for a century or two. The ensuing crisis of religious credibility led many ministers and thoughtful laity to seek more meaningful forms of religious expression and more direct forms of social action than parish churches could mobilize. Underlying this search was the need for a religious outlook that was more consonant with the ways in which they understood the world around them.

In these exceptional circumstances, Dietrich Bonhoeffer's call for a secular interpretation of biblical categories, and, before that, Rudolf Bultmann's program for demythologizing Christian doctrine became very meaningful. Following the lead of Calvin and the Puritans, people of all ages seemed to be seeking a religion that was free of magic and superstition, and compatible with the existence of an orderly cosmos. As a result, Eastern religious impulses, whether learned from Hermann Hesse, Dom Aelred Graham, Daisetz T. Suzuki, or various other American gurus, satisfied the needs of many. These new commitments, moreover, had the further advantage that they functioned or could be interpreted as a repudiation of the American "System." They were seen as a critique of the dehumanizing, materialistic, and technocratic character of American life with its relative unconcern for poverty, injustice, and the forms of brutality being visited upon the people of Southeast Asia.

Beyond these critical responses was the *positive* fact that many Americans now repeated in their own lives the experience that had come to Freidrich Schlegel in 1803, after his studies of India's Sanskrit religious literature had led him to believe that India was the source of all wisdom: *"Alles, alles stamt aus Indien."* Such exaltation was hardly possible in the America of the later twentieth century, yet the cumulative impact of many personal conversions was very considerable. During the 1950s a distinct crescendo of interest was noticeable, and during the 1960s and 1970s the tempo of interest, as well as the founding of organized groups, increased in many unexpected ways. One of the most ironic developments of these times was the parallel revival of interest in the charismatic movement as well as in many forms of evangelicalism—which for many Americans was almost a new religion. Evangelical groups were by their own profession an American sub-culture—and in some ways even a counter-culture—and because they provided contexts for personal discussion and testimony, self-examination, and the opportunity for sharing moral and religious concerns, they answered to many of the same needs as the new religions.

IV

But to go beyond these brief observations on the contemporary scene would carry me beyond my present mandate. I hope, therefore, that I have shown how it came to be that this country could and did to a remarkable degree break down the West's historic barriers to religious freedom and innovation, and how, for better or for worse, it provided a climate in which these new movements could multiply and prosper.

It would not be right for me to conclude, however, without taking note that it has been suggested that my survey pays too little attention to the allegedly distinctive role of Californians in the later stages of my account. And as a mid-westerner who has spent the last half of his life in the East, I would admit that there are some grounds for the charge, though Californians have by no means hidden their light under a bushel, and I have taken account of the valuable studies of Jacob Needleman, Theodore Roszak, Robert Ellwood, and many others. Without being a professional Californiologist, I have assimilated these contributions to my overall interpretations of recent developments, both conservative and radical.

I would grant, however, that since the 1920s, when the great migration of Americans and others to this Western Eden began to accelerate (which is to say since the days of Aimee Semple McPherson's early triumphs), California has come to have the largest and most heterogeneous population in the Union. More important still, this rapid growth prevented the development of powerful traditions and restraints. It would thus be senseless to deny the frequently made claim that quantitatively speaking, California leads the nation in the proliferation of diverse religious movements. Perhaps one could say that just as the United States is an extreme form of Western civilization, so California is an extreme form of American civilization.

Yet, I would still venture the generalization that during the last two or three decades, the modulations of religious expression appearing in the urban North, east of the Mississippi, have been fully representative of the same religious trends. One could almost say the same of New Haven alone. If there is any part of the country that remains distinctive, it is still the South, though even this region is now experiencing a degree of social change that cannot but gradually alter its now-prevailing religious spirit.

REFERENCES

1. James Meek. *Hebrew Origins*, pp. 99–100. Harper & Row, 1960. A composite rendering of several texts.

2. A more extended account of the relation of the Puritan impulse to the rise of American religious liberty is given in my essay, "Diversity in Religion as a Force for Religious Liberty." In *Aspects of American Liberty: Addresses Presented at an Observance of the Bicentennial Year*, pp. 56–67. The American Philosophical Society, 1977.

ROOTS OF THE AMERICAN ETHOS

John Dillenberger

NEW RELIGIOUS movements have always been considered to be subversive, as Sydney Ahlstrom has said, and yet they have continued to emerge. Why? In the American scene, uniformity of opinion or practice has not been insisted upon; but conformity to some kind of ethos has always been central. This factor has bedeviled most of our history. Differences of opinion are acceptable, as are certain differences of practice. If a person does not conform to the major ethos, however, he or she is in trouble.

How did this arise? For a possible answer, we may compare the pre-Reformation and the Reformation developments on the continent with those of the English scene. The continental pre-Reformation period is far more diverse than we usually think. Culturally, continental Catholicism was never one church. It may have taken Vatican II for us to discover this fact. Catholicism had tremendous diversity. While there were attempts to enforce uniformity, such attempts never succeeded, perhaps because modern modes of communication and modern uses of power did not exist. Hence, the covert diversity was much greater than in our own time.

The continental Reformation was a series of uniformity splits, reflecting separately some of the previous, cultural diversity. These Reformation developments did not create new instruments and new institutions. In that sense, they continued the medieval tradition.

There is a great difference between what went on in the continent and what went on in England, and, of course, the English scene influenced the American scene much more than did the continental. Calvin or the Reformed tradition is not the spiritual base of English Christianity. English Christianity comes much more out of the spirit of the suppressed Lollard tradition: preaching is always more important than the sacraments; the Scriptures are the guide to thought, practice, and piety; predestination is strongly affirmed; society is to be totally ordered in the light of the Gospel; and in this way the cultural interests of the more established classes are to be rejected.

The English believed themselves to be the direct successors to Israel. Calvin and much of the Reformed tradition distinguished between the religion of Israel and the body politic that was also Israel. For the English, to be a successor to Israel is to have, by analogy, that religious interest, but, more importantly, to have religion enshrined in a body politic. That direct identification is implied in the term, New Israel, and, since England did not turn out to be the New Israel, as some thought it must, the identification of New England and New Israel resulted. But each claim of being the New Israel conflicted with others who made the same claim. Hence, if democracy came from this tradition—as it is usually claimed—it came not by design, but by accident or by necessity. Not a single group believed in it. They compromised on it only because nobody could win.

Until the modern world, all societies have felt that religion needed to form a culture. But in the English scene, "formation" is too weak a term. The English seized it, or, if one wants to use a stronger word, it "raped" the culture. The cultural domination of the English on colonial peoples was intense, whatever its benefits.

This English inheritance stands behind the American urge and impulse to form every segment of culture. Since a total single culture could not be formed, sub-cultures have evolved, each, however, claiming total truth. Accommodations were inevitable, but since, because of one's truth, one never trusted anyone else, the encounters were always negative, rather than positive. One had to come to terms with the fact of the existence of other groups, but such groups were always subversive.

This has been a long history, making it hard to accept pluralism in our bones. We do not yet know that divergences can also be convergences, that different traditions can enrich and fructify each other without loss of the self. There have been syncretistic developments, but they have scared those who do not want to be syncretistic. How can one learn and appropriate, without loss?

In the particular dominant English history here delineated, many of the ingredients of older Western Christianity were lost, which we are now rediscovering out of the East—mystery, contemplation, respect for nature, etc.

The Eastern religious traditions have been more prominent in the American scene than Sydney Ahlstrom has indicated. They have not always affected the religious traditions directly, but they have affected the culture in which they existed. There is hardly an American artist since 1860 whose life was not influenced dramatically either by Swedenborg, by Spiritualism, or by Eastern religious traditions and cultures. And this is true even today. Jane Dillenberger and I have just completed an exhibition and catalogue of twentieth-century American art, and it would be difficult to find more than a few artists whose basic perceptions come out of Christianity. For some, the perception comes out of Judaism in a direct, naive way. Mainly, however, the perceptions seem to be born out of Eastern concerns. Why is this the case? Many of the artists would love to be related to the church, but the church has forgotten them for so long that it would never occur to them that we live in a time of new possibilities.

The new religious movements are more dominant in the West, and in California particularly, than they are in other sections of the country. When I taught at Harvard in the 50s, whenever one wanted to do something radical, one found an old reason. And then one could get it approved. And if one did it once, it was tradition and nobody ever challenged it again. In California, creation starts over every day. One wins and loses one's reputation every day. Nothing carries over. So, in that sense, everything is equal. And that creates a different lifestyle, one in which the Eastern religions more readily take hold.

NEW RELIGIOUS MOVEMENTS AND THE STRUCTURE OF RELIGIOUS SENSIBILITY

Joseph P. Chinnici

SYDNEY AHLSTROM has placed the new religious movements in an historical perspective: the American experience has been unique in its openness to the future, and in its genius for the development of that which is revolutionary. This quality has nowhere been more evident than in the varieties of religious movements in the United States. In this area his analysis is sound. I shall mention only two places where I think his exposition is weak, but I shall call into question several of his assumptions. Afterwards, I shall propose a slightly different approach to the study of new religious movements.

Most of the time Ahlstrom talks in terms of North and South. We at this end of America think in terms of East and West. The American religious experience surely can be seen from the perspective of Puritanism and the Enlightenment on the East Coast. Yet on the West Coast, where the new religious movements have taken profound root, there exists a different cultural and intellectual matrix, one in which the Spanish Catholicism of mission padres and the Mahayana tradition of East Asian immigrants significantly appear. This difference deserves attention. To equate the American ethos with the Puritan or Protestant ethic is to fail to do justice to the complexity of the issue.

Ahlstrom's analysis almost exclusively deals with Protestantism. Yet a large segment of the proponents of the new religious movements comes from a Roman Catholic background. Ahlstrom's historical narrative does not illuminate the reasons for this. It does not address the issues of church authority, theological understanding, biblical criticism, and religious experience within Roman Catholicism. All of this would shed considerable historical light on the present crisis within American Christianity.

The underlying assumption in Ahlstrom's view is that "new" means "structurally different." A new movement is established only when there is a rejection of a previously existing body. Such an analysis stems in large measure from a sociological understanding. In this approach, for example, the "newness" of the sixteenth-century religious movements lies primarily in their structural and ideological elements. Lutheranism and Calvinism were new movements because they incarnated into a slightly different structure the key ideas of justification by faith alone and *sola Scriptura*. This went hand in hand with the rejection of traditional institutions of authority. One recent study of Calvinism in Geneva bears this out. Robert M. Kingdon argues that the reformation in that city was revolutionary since it dismantled and replaced the medieval papacy, monastic institutions, and legal systems [1].

Building on this type of foundation, Ahlstrom goes on to enumerate similar instances of "new" religious movements on the American scene. He invariably refers to departures from a given organizational model or a protest against predominant views of authority, God, and the church. There is a great deal of truth in this analysis. It indicates the close relationship which exists between ideas and institutions, and the interplay of both in creating new movements. But I do not think it penetrates deeply enough. It does not adequately explain "newness."

Ahlstrom presupposes uniformity in the old structure and stresses the comparative ideological and institutional discontinuity of the new. So, for example, he focuses too much on the legal, moral, social, and doctrinal unity of the Middle Ages. What happens then to the tremendous diversity of the religious movements of the thirteenth century, many of which were assimilated as diverse into the institutional structure itself? What does one do with the pluralism that is evident in the theological methods of Abelard and Anselm, Albert the Great and Bonaventure, Aquinas and Scotus, or the conflicting ecclesiological conceptions of the conciliar period? Again, although Boniface VIII's attempt to unite the spiritual and temporal in Unam Sanctam may stand today as a symbol of medieval Christendom, it did not have a uniform impact on either practical, everyday Christian life, or on the way the emerging nation-states saw themselves. It is too simplistic to define the unity of the Middle Ages in structural or ideological categories; the unity lay elsewhere. And if it did, then the "newness" of the reformation must be seen in a new light.

The presuppositions of Ahlstrom's view also emerge in his discussion of the Reformation. When speaking of the sixteenth-century movement, he defines it over against Roman Catholicism, the supposed cultural inheritor of medieval Christendom. Once again, this stresses the discontinuity between the "new" (Protestant) and the "old" (Medieval-Roman Catholicism) and the monolithic nature of the latter. Recent studies have broken from this view in two ways: (1) a whole group of French scholars have argued that Protestantism and Catholicism much more than defining themselves in opposition to each other, paralleled each other within the distinctive tradition of Western civilization [2,3]. For example, if Luther's understanding of faith was new, so also was that of Sadoleto or Contarini. If Calvin's recognition of the absolute sovereignty of God was new, so also was that of Pius V or Ignatius of Loyola. If the legal and administrative structure of the Reformation churches was new, so also was that of counter-Reformation Roman Catholicism. If John Bunyan's or George Fox's interpretation of interior religious experience was new, so also was that of Francis de Sales and Fénelon. (2) Studies in religious anthropology and psychology have acknowledged the underlying unity between late medieval and Reformation conceptions of reality and definitions of religious experience [4,5]. In many respects the sixteenth-century movement was not new.

All of this indicates that the analysis of what is "new" in new religious movements is largely determined by the level of reality which is examined. To see movements in basically structural or ideological categories does not do justice to the facts. It fails to acknowledge the diversity within the old and the influences of a given historical mentality on all denominations. Scholarly works have begun to detail the history of perception in the Middle Ages and early modern Europe [6,7]. A similar technique should be applied to the history of new religious movements. It seems to me that the historian should examine the ebb and flow of the inner life, the history of religious sensibility.

What is religious sensibility? I would like to define the term as the intellectual and affective perception which an individual or community has of the relationship between religious experience and the various dimensions of life. Religious sensibility is part of a broader personal sensibility. This latter is composed of the structural (e.g., legal and institutional), intellectual (e.g., philosophical), and religious ways in which reality is seen and experienced. Personal sensibility is usually presumed and rarely articulated. In any given historical period, it takes form within the structure of certain cultural givens, for example, climate, geography, material conditions of life, religious tradition. In this view, the history of religious sensibility is concerned with how the climate of opinion or "spirit of an age" or political institutions affect a person's religious self-understanding. How does a person experience the Ultimate Reality and perceive this to be related to the world? One of the church historian's tasks is to elucidate the relationship which may exist between the inner and outer modes of being, the integration or disintegration which may characterize a person's or community's faith experience, the union or disjunction which may be made in any given period between religion, legal forms, and intellectual currents. The history of religious sensibility is an attempt to correlate the social, intellectual, and psychological factors that encourage this or that type of experience. This can perhaps be clarified by the following example.

One major social and legal structure that has shaped American religious life has been the separation of Church and State and freedom of conscience. Together they imply the acceptance of religious pluralism. The incarnation of these principles in the first amendment was a total break with the European heritage of most Americans. It shattered both the medieval conception of Church-State union and the post-Reformation reality of a national Christendom. Focusing on Roman Catholicism, I would like to discuss the response of American religious sensibility to this reality and in this way shed some light on the emergence of new religious movements in our time.

Within Protestantism, the first amendment expressed a religious sensibility shaped by the eighteenth-century Enlightenment, evangelical pietism, and the practical needs of religious pluralism. For many Roman Catholics in America, it witnessed to the combination of the Gallican tradition of spiritual and temporal separation, the Jansenist emphasis on *liberté* and *verité*, the widespread acceptance of a Lockian political tradition, and the necessity of arguing for toleration in a dominantly Protestant state. In general, the religious sensibility that produced and accepted the first amendment was unique to the late-eighteenth century.

For some Roman Catholics, their religious sensibility, shaped by the forces of the eighteenth century, was uneasy. They found it difficult to accept the complete separation of Church and State. Religious pluralism implied for them the acknowledgement that "all churches are equal" or that "ultimate truth is relative." These people tended to accept separation as a purely pragmatic solution to a social problem and were unable to break completely with the idea of Christendom. Other Catholics took a more integrative stance. Distinguishing between civil toleration and complete liberty of conscience or religious indifference, they gladly adhered to the American experiment. In either case, the first amendment stood as a legal monument to one aspect of their religious sensibility. The fundamental tension between the approaches was never fully resolved: Did the acceptance of religious pluralism in the civil sphere necessarily entail the acknowledgement of the relativity of Ultimate Truth?

The religious sensibility of American Catholics towards the first amendment changed dramatically in the middle of the nineteenth century. For the most part, the integrative Enlightenment strain with its fine distinction between toleration and indifference disappeared. There was also a lessening of the uneasy tension which many people had experienced during the revolutionary period. Instead, American Catholics, influenced by the romantic concept of the organic state, the ultramontane movement, and the anti-popery campaign of the Protestants, began to argue from a position reminiscent of that of medieval Christendom. The American notion of separation of Church and State and of freedom of conscience was accepted as a purely pragmatic reality. Tension was relaxed by separating historical experience from dogmatic truth. The 1866 Pastoral Letter of the American bishops witnessed to the beginnings of this change in perspective [8]. Except for a very few people at the end of the century, this sensibility dominated. It reached final expression in the work of John A. Ryan on Church and State [9].

American Catholics of the nineteenth and twentieth centuries were incapable of reconciling American legal forms with the Roman Catholic position. They experienced a conscious tension between the Ideal (Christendom) and the Real (separation of Church and State). For this reason the religious sensibility of American Catholics was bifurcated. The absoluteness of religious experience was perceived to be incompatible with the relativity which the first amendment was thought to imply. There ensued an extreme split between the sacred and secular, the Church and the world, unchanging dogma and contingent historical circumstances. Faith and experience were compartmentalized. When people did attempt a more integrative approach (e.g., the neo-scholastic movement of the late 1920s and 1930s), they overtly espoused a new model of Christendom, a Catholic culture. This was imposed on the American experience and was essentially at variance with its legal forms.

Within Roman Catholicism, this religious sensibility towards the American proposition underwent a third dramatic change in the mid-1950s. Once again, there was a movement to go beyond the notion of Christendom and to distinguish carefully between a positive notion of toleration and a negative notion of religious indifference. This was based on a deeper historical understanding. The theory was elaborated by John Courtney Murray. It was later accepted as Church teaching in Vatican II's *Declaration on Religious Freedom* (1965). This document opened the door to the integration of the first amendment with religious sensibility. It indicated the compatibility between the American proposition and the acceptance of the ultimate nature of religious experience. To some extent, it was the revival of the enlightened Catholic position of the late-eighteenth century.

Now, given the emergence of this new religious sensibility towards Church and State and religious pluralism, it seems to me that there are three contrasting movements in American Catholicism today. The first responds to the situation by accepting the relativity of all religious truth, by subordinating religious conviction to legal form. Here legal pluralism necessarily entails religious indifference and both are acceptable. The second cannot adopt this solution, but it is also unable to distinguish legal pluralism from religious indifference. Compartmentalization follows. There is a search for an absolute experience, one which provides a stable point of belief in a world which has come to accept as axiomatic the principle of relativity. In a paradoxical way, both of these positions share Christendom's equation of toleration with complete freedom of conscience. Both are totalistic, either subordinating religious belief to legal form, or, since legal forms cannot be changed, withdrawing into a community of "absolute experience." The third position, one which Catholics are challenged to articulate, builds on the insights of the Enlightenment; it moves, in a definitive way, beyond the presuppositions of Christendom.

All three of these movements, it seems to me, are part of the religious sensibility which supports some contemporary movements in American Catholicism. From the perspective of Church and State, they account for the large numbers of Catholics who adhere to "new movements." The first leads to a canonization of cultural and theological relativism; the second to a retreat into an enthusiastic sect; the third into a hitherto undefined stance of integration.

This examination of the Church-State issue is only one example of how a history of religious sensibility could help to explain the rise of new movements. It attempts to get beneath structures and ideologies into fundamental perceptions of the relationship between religious experience and the world of culture. To understand any religious movement adequately other areas should also be examined. The history of religious sensibility should consider the conscious and unconscious bridges between history and dogma, political thought and ecclesiology, discursive reasoning and intuitive recognition. That task remains to be done.

REFERENCES

1. Robert M. Kingdon. "Was the Protestant Reformation a Revolution: The Case of Geneva." In *Church Society and Politics*, pp. 203–222. Edited by Derek Baker. Basil Blackwell, Oxford, 1975. Vol. XII in *Studies in Church History*.

2. Jean Delumeau. *Naissance et Affirmation de la Reforme*. Presses Universitaires de France, Paris, 1968.

3. Pierre Chaunu. "Le XVIIᵉ siècle religieux: Reflexions prealables." *Annales (Economies, Societies, Civilizations)* 22 (1967), 279–302.

4. Robert S. Kinsman, editor. *The Darker Vision of the Renaissance*. University of California Press, Berkeley, 1974.

5. Keith Thomas. *Religion and the Decline of Magic*. Scribner, 1971.

6. Carolly Erickson. *The Medieval Vision: Essays in History and Perception.* Oxford University Press, 1976.

7. Theodore K. Rabb. *The Struggle for Stability in Early Modern Europe.* Oxford University Press, 1975.

8. Hugh J. Nolan, editor. *Pastoral Letters of the American Hierarchy, 1792–1970,* pp. 147–148. *Our Sunday Visitor,* Huntington, Indiana, 1971.

9. John A. Ryan and Moorhouse F. X. Millar. *The State and the Church.* Macmillan, 1922.

DIMENSIONS OF NEW RELIGION IN AMERICAN HISTORY

Eldon G. Ernst

"WHAT IN God's name has happened to the Roman Catholic Church?" This question of alarm, asked in a recent *San Francisco Chronicle* advertisement under the "Church Notices" section, carries on the three-century-long American conflict over innovations within traditional religions. To exegete the list of complaints launched by the Orthodox Roman Catholic Movement, Inc., would be to uncover elements from a complex mixture of modern social-intellectual-spiritual movements of widely diverse origins, but with a peculiarly American flavor: "Hootenanny masses," "tables instead of altars," "words of consecration mutilated," "lay persons distributing communion," "reconciliation instead of penance," "altar girls," "charismatic movement," "situation ethics," etc. Readers are warned to be wary of "new-breed priests" [1].

Controversy over tampering with traditional religion is one of the constant themes in American religious history. One is reminded of John Williamson Nevin's famous mid-nineteenth century diatribe against the novelties of popular revivalism that had "infected" even Reformed traditions. According to this scholarly Scotch-Irish Presbyterian immigrant, revivalism was a superficial "whirlwind process" which produced "a sickly Christianity." He described "revival machinery" as "solemn tricks for effect, decision displays at the bidding of the preacher, genuflections and prostrations in the aisle or around the altar, noise and disorder, extravagance and rant, mechanical conversions, justification by feeling rather than faith, and encouragement ministered to all fanatical impressions." Better to maintain the traditional "system of the Catechism" than to succumb to the novelty of such "new measures" as "the anxious bench" for promoting Christian experience and life [2].

Apologists of tradition in religion always have provided a certain kind of documentation to the dynamic impact of newness in American religiosity. America, the new nation built upon the foundations of New Spain, New France, and especially New England (along with New Amsterdam, New Denmark, and New Sweden, etc.), and conceived in the imagery of a "New Israel," consistently has expressed an ideology and ethos of newness deeply infused by religious symbolism and energy. In a nation thought to be new in many ways—a new kind of society mixing peoples and cultures of the world, a social experiment in democratic institutions, a people putting-off the bondage of past traditions and oriented toward the future—it is scarcely surprising that newness in religious life and thought would become a peculiarly consistent theme.

If the new has penetrated American religion throughout its history, then the expanding dimensions of that newness also constitute a history. That is, whereas there are some constant themes in American religious history that focus on the new, such as pluralism and innovation, there also is a development of the boundaries of new religion in America. This historical religious development, so crucial to recognizing the significance of contemporary religious movements in America, participates thoroughly in the evolving nature of American civilization.

During the nineteenth century, the essence of newness in religion flowered fully and permanently in a pattern of expanding pluralism and innovation. In the twentieth century, however, the range of newness in American religious life and thought reached a fundamentally new dimension. The two periods must be seen together for their organic wholeness as well as for their distinctions.

I

The flowering of nineteenth-century American religious pluralism is an oft-told story. Constitutional religious freedom, immigration, geographical space, and the American ethos of "newness" all contributed to pluralism. European, African, Asian, and native American Indian religious orientations constituted the mix. First the Shakers, then the Disciples of Christ, the Mormons, the Black Churches, the Seventh Day Adventists, the

Jehovah's Witnesses, and Christian Science emerged as major new religious groups in most respects indigenous to nineteenth-century America. (After the turn of the century the Black Muslims would emerge as another new American religion.) The Religion of Humanity, Theosophy, Rosicrucianism, Vedanta, Baha'i, and Buddhism extended the range of religious thought in America prior to 1900. By then, also, there had appeared most kinds of European Protestant and Roman Catholic Christianity as well as three major forms of Judaism. Meanwhile the less enduring new small groups, experimental communities, movements and fads of religious character, as well as endless "come-outer" schisms from more established religions, flourished throughout the nineteenth century in America. In this sense the largest imaginable dimensions of religious pluralism existed rather early in American history.

Pluralism constitutes only part of the ingredients of newness in historic American religious life and thought, however. Of far-reaching significance to an understanding of the nature of American and of religion in our times is the sense of religious newness itself. This, too, has deep American roots.

In the face of traditions and status quo, American religious movements have expressed self-conscious newness. The Great Awakening revivals of the eighteenth and nineteenth centuries distinguished "new lights" from "old lights," "new sides" from "old sides," "new schools" from "old schools," and promoted "new measures." Eventually a "new evangelism" challenged the old in the midst of a new social gospel movement, and today we hear of "the New Evangelicals." Meanwhile movements of creative theology assumed such titles as the "new divinity," the "new theology," and "New Thought." Later pragmatism and process modes of thought presented new world views within which to reformulate traditional theology and ethics. Even the diverse restorationist (restitutionist) impulse in American religious life and thought stimulated innovative expressions of long-neglected or lost doctrines, experiences, structures, practices, or lifestyles [3].

Innovation is the key word. The innovative American expressions of old-world traditions have been a bone of contention in religious circles for three hundred years. Not only did European observers marvel and scoff at the unorthodox religious patterns among the Americans, but Americans themselves ceaselessly bickered over the legitimacy of innovations. Opposition came in the form of "conservative" ideas and institutions, of nostalgia for some "old-time religion," of repulsion at a popular "fad."

Immigrant churches especially struggled with innovations as their traditions faced the necessity of accommodation to the American environment. Most immigrant churches experienced some party or movement of "Americanism" in their midst, such as the "American Calvinists" within the (Dutch) Christian Reformed Church and the "Americanist Movement" in Roman Catholicism. The integrity of tradition was at stake as the churches took on American identity and competed in the smorgasbord of American religious free enterprise.

The apparent necessity of religious groups to be popular in order to survive in the nineteenth-century American environment of church-state separation, religious freedom, and pluralism contributed heavily to innovative tendencies. Church teachings, practices, and services that were directly relevant to people's felt needs secured voluntary support. Promotion of religion became standard practice early in the nation's history. Success came to those religious leaders able to adjust traditions, with imagination and persuasiveness, to popular demand. But religious popularity always has come under fire. Every popular religious movement in American history, from the Great Awakening to nineteenth-century revivalism, from post-World War II religious "upswing" to the present widespread fascination with forms of Eastern thought and practice, has elicited harsh criticism from those who feared that the depth and purity of the religion was lost.[1]

Concern about how innovation might affect the authenticity of a religious tradition helped to foster interest in the essential nature of the religion itself. In response to criticism of the novelties of popular revivalism, for example, Charles Grandison Finney defended his "new measures" on the proposition that throughout church history, renewal and reform came through innovation. Revival meetings, he thought, could be seen as the flowering of new spiritual life in the unique American environment. The Christian religion was essentially innovative. From vastly different sectors of American Christianity, Transcendentalist

Unitarians and Roman Catholics asked questions about, re-
spectively, "the transient and permanent in Christianity" and
the "accidents" and the "essentials" in Christianity [5,6,7].
What are permanent, essential elements in the Christian religion
that cannot be altered without losing the very nature of the religion, and what characteristics of Christianity are relative to time
and place? In other words, how far can innovation go?

In the constant grappling with this question of innovation, a
foundation was laid for later concerns of theologians about the
"essence of Christianity" and of scholars of comparative religions about the definition and phenomenology of religion [8,9].
Small wonder that the scientific study of religion would become
popular in twentieth-century America where religious innovation
and pluralism flourishes and continually forces the question of
the essential nature of particular religions and of religion-in-
general.

The range of newness in American religious life and thought
thus reached dimensions wide and deep during the nineteenth
century. Nevertheless, the implications of that newness are more
visible today than they were a century ago because the twentieth
century has ushered in a new stage in American civilization.

II

Historically, America has been a frontier of Western civilization. The dominant cultural heritage has been British and Northern European. The primary religious force has been broadly
Judeo-Christian. It is a story of conquest. The British came early
in the seventeenth century and conquered the Spanish, French,
and several native Indian tribes. Slaves were brought in chains
from Africa. In 1776, British colonists fought "for their rights as
Englishmen" and declared their independence from "the mother
country." Throughout the nineteenth century, immigrants came
to America from all parts of the world. The cultural establishment into which they were to be Americanized was heavily
white, Anglo-Saxon oriented.

At the dawn of the twentieth century, few questioned the fundamentally Judeo-Christian nature and destiny of the United
States. America was the frontier of Western civilization on the
move. Indeed, the assumption prevailed that the nation was es-

sentially Christian—a kind of voluntary Christendom. In 1892 the Supreme Court, ruling on *The Church of the Holy Trinity v. United States,* boldly declared America "a Christian nation" [10]. Religious leaders, politicians, journalists, scholars, and writers freely referred to the Christian identity of the nation. It was only in a slightly exaggerated tone that the racist and imperialistic provincialism of this widespread sense of American identity was expressed in the following excerpts from Associate Supreme Court Justice David J. Brewer's book entitled *The United States: A Christian Nation* (1905):

God's plan was first to evangelize the white Gentile world; to save our Teutonic forefathers as the most strategic thing to be done; to move toward the coming Anglo/Saxon civilization, and so to get His hands on the mightiest national life of the world. . . . The Spirit sought out the nation most capable of responding to the gospel, and by temperament, by instinct and by pre-eminent missionary genius qualified to give Christianity initiation in other lands and in other nations on its way to final and complete victory. . . . We may leave the Orient peoples their yellow skins, the African peoples their black skins, but we must create in them all the one spirit, a kinship of soul and a common national aim, and under the power of religious impulse rally them all to our standard in fulfilling our national mission. . . . This is a Christian nation, and we can all rejoice [11].

Language of this kind would seem absurd or repugnant to most Americans in the 1970s. It is true that racial and cultural provincialism and imperialism have survived two world wars plus military involvement in Korea and Vietnam. But the notion that this nation is destined to be the Anglo-Saxon instrument of Christian conquest of the world is not the general assumption of the bulk of American citizens today. The giant qualification of nineteenth-century American religious pluralism and innovation—the great boundary surrounding the range of newness in American religiosity—has been crumbling. "The long spell of Christendom," as Robert T. Handy called it, has broken; and it is neither misleading nor simplistic to describe twentieth-century America as "post-Christendom" or even "post-Judeo-Christendom" [12,13].

Historically, the forces of transition from American Judeo-Christendom to a larger range of religious pluralism began to be visible near the end of the nineteenth century. The rise of the

United States as a world power and its reaching out in economic and military ventures in Asia and Africa slowly began to open American eyes to formidable cultures other than European. In this context, the foreign mission thrust of American Protestants and (after the turn of the century) Roman Catholics took on added impetus. The romantic aura surrounding earlier nineteenth-century foreign mission adventures into distant "heathen" lands (serious as those missions were) gave way to a more militant and crusading apologetic to "Christianize American foreign relations" and to "Christianize the world." As the twentieth century wore on, foreign missions theorists and programmers debated over the possibility and desirability of combining Western culture with Christian evangelism in Eastern lands. Eventually some churches dropped the word "foreign" from their mission vocabulary, renaming their programs something like "world missions." Throughout this modern history of American Christian mission, despite glaring exceptions and constant conflict among missions leaders, there developed an increasing respect for the richness of the world's diverse cultures, plus a tolerance and even appreciation of non-Judeo-Christian religions.

At the same time that foreign missions extended American awareness and appreciation of Asian and African cultures, the massive "new immigration" from around the world between 1870 and 1920 radically altered the ingredients of the American population. The field of home missions acquired new dimensions. Pre-Civil War America was relatively homogeneous compared to the pluralistic domestic scene that unfolded during the following century. Unlike their European counterparts, who had to travel to distant lands to encounter religious cultures greatly different than their own, American churches found the world's cultural-religious varieties settling in nearby neighborhoods.

The combination of foreign and home missions, coinciding with American world expansionism plus massive immigration, may be viewed as American Christendom responding to forces that eventually would alter the nature of American civilization. With Christendom challenged, the range of newness in twentieth-century American religious life would expand fundamentally.

The World's Parliament of Religions that took place in Chicago in 1893 in conjunction with the World's Columbian Exposition represents an historical event symbolic of the approaching post-Christendom era in America. Representatives from the cultures of the world presented their religious traditions in Chicago. Debates over the value of such a display in "Christian America" ranged far and wide. In these discussions, one begins to feel the impending challenge to America's Judeo-Christian stronghold. Many persons were concerned about how Christianity should relate to other religions *at home and abroad*. Significant questions were raised about the nature of different religions and even about the essence of religion itself. Some spoke of what they felt to be a challenge of cultural and religious pluralism that might change the nature of American civilization. Despite an over-arching sense of optimism among American church leaders that Christianity was the superior religion and would reign victorious in free competition with other world religions, the sense of new challenge to the Judeo-Christian foundations of American civilization rang loud and clear [14,15].

In the World's Parliament of Religions, we can begin to see the combination of twentieth-century American Christian interests in mission apologetics, ecumenism, interfaith dialogue, and the comparative study of religions. All of these reflect the growing pluralization of religious life in America. It is also in this kind of atmosphere that one finds resistance to the emerging newness in defense of a more provincial past. Only in the context of the rapidly expanding pluralism in early twentieth-century America, for example, can we comprehend the widespread fascination with notions of racial distinctions and racial purity in public and popular literature as well as in scientific and political circles. From traditional "old stock" sources, one is struck by the extreme defensiveness of the Anglo-Saxon Christian nature and destiny of the nation. Clearly there was developing the sense that the Western European, Judeo-Christian core-ingredient in the American melting pot was being threatened by an emerging new cultural-religious pluralism, as can be detected in the following call to "old white stock" purity by a Presbyterian writer in 1919:

If the United States is to be one nation, with common feeling, language, habits, customs and moral and spiritual attitude, the Americanization must center around the largest racial group, the old white stock. . . . If American life is to have a tone, this tone must come not from the cities with their varied and heterogeneous racial groups, but from the villages and country districts. It is the task of the churches to see that this tone continues one of godliness and patriotism, high ideals and clean living [16].

How quaint, naive, and innocent this kind of statement, so common only a half century ago, strikes our ears today. We simply know today that religious pluralism is gaining the victory over the domination of any single religious tradition in America. The expansion of new religiosity in the twentieth century reaches beyond the imagination of Thomas Jefferson or James Madison, whose world was defined narrowly in Judeo-Christian and European terms. But is not the religious pluralism of modern America a new stage in the continuing saga of the revolutionary American religious experiment begun two hundred years ago?

Again we may view the mind of the Supreme Court as an expression of the movement of American religious history. In 1930, the Supreme Court, ruling in *United States v. Macintosh,* stated the following: "We are a Christian people, according to one another the equal right of religious freedom, and acknowledging with reverence the duty of obedience to the will of God." Since then, the Supreme Court has not described the nation as Christian. In *Zorach v. Clauson* (1952) the Court referred to Americans as "a religious people whose institutions presuppose a Supreme Being." In *Abington School District v. Schempp* (1963), the Court at great length described the role religion had played in American history. The decision concluded with a strong emphasis on religious freedom in American history and the resulting pluralism:

This freedom to worship was indispensable in a country whose people came from the four quarters of the earth and brought with them a diversity of religious opinion. Today authorities list 83 separate religious bodies, each with memberships exceeding 50,000, existing among our people, as well as innumerable smaller groups [10].

Finally, as American religiosity has explored new dimensions in recent years, the Supreme Court has felt it necessary to engage in the shaky realm of religious definition. How can the Court rule in cases involving religious freedom without normative guidelines for determining just what is religion in a particular situation? Traditional Judeo-Christian "churches" no longer automatically provide these norms. During the past twenty years, the Court has defined "religion" to include the following: beliefs, cultic association, a system of moral practice, and organization. Moreover, beliefs need not imply the "supernatural," but simply must be "sincere and meaningful" to the believer. Indeed, such belief need not even be claimed to be religious![2]

The confusion in courts of law over the definition of "religion" reflects the religious transition that has been taking place in America during the past several decades. The legal question of religious freedom and privilege in a post-Judeo-Christendom society becomes increasingly complex. Economics, for example, always has been a major issue. Originally the issue was over tax support of churches. Today the issue is whether or not churches should receive tax exemptions. Now that a "church" is no longer recognizable only within traditional Judeo-Christian boundaries, what is the scope of the definition of "religious organization" that would allow tax exemption? It may be that tax exemptions of religious organizations must cease in order for religious freedom to prevail.

Provincialism, bigotry, and oppression doubtless will continue to hinder the fullest expression of religious freedom in America. The African, Asian, Hispanic, and native Indian-rooted communities in America know that although they contribute to the authentic cultural pluralism of the nation, they continue to suffer as minorities in the power circles of white America. Similarly, non-Judeo-Christian religiosity still must contend with public attitudes that lack respect or seriousness at least, and express derision and discrimination at worst. For example, California Governor Jerry Brown, a Roman Catholic, has shown an interest in Buddhism and occasionally visits the San Francisco Zen Center on Page Street (formerly a Jewish residence club). Recently a front-page newspaper story described Brown's "Zen connection,'" noting that "it is here [the Page Street Zen Center] that he dabbles in Eastern thought and here that he meets the unorthodox peoples he has appointed to some of the most powerful positions in his administration" [18]. What major city newspaper would describe a politician's "Methodist connection" where the "dabbles" in Western thought? What, moreover, is an "unorthodox" person in modern religious America?

III

The range of the new in contemporary American religious life and thought has moved beyond the experience of earlier generations. The movement is away from the boundaries of the Judeo-Christian heritage of Western civilization. Whereas the religious diversity within that heritage continues to flourish in peculiarly American innovative forms, Eastern spirituality and third world religiosity also are profoundly and innovatively expressed in America. The American version of the Hebrew-Christian myth of a people called and set apart is being stretched by a larger world of equally chosen peoples. America's provincial past must be transcended in the more cosmopolitan future. To resist the unfolding of this new vision of American civilization would be to apply to the nation the kind of traditionalist reasoning so often applied to innovative versions of European churches. The expanding range of newness in American religious history is one major manifestation of the essentially innovative mixture of world cultures that constitutes the fullness of American civilization.

NOTES

[1] Popular Christianity has recently been criticised [4].

[2] John Richard Burkholder has analyzed these definitional concerns in recent Supreme Court decisions [17].

REFERENCES

1. *San Francisco Chronicle*, 15 October 1977, p. 38.

2. John W. Nevin. *The Anxious Bench.* In *Issues in American Protestantism: A Documentary History from the Puritans to the Present*, pp. 170–180. Edited by Robert L. Fern. Doubleday, 1969. Portions of the 2nd rev. ed. (1844).

3. Samuel S. Hill, Jr. "A Typology of American Restitutionism: From Frontier Revivalism and Mormonism to the Jesus Movement." *Journal of the American Academy of Religion* 44 (1976):65–76.

4. Murray L. Wagner. "Rinky-dink Religion Goes Big Time." *The American Baptist*, 30–31, October 1977.

5. Theodore Parker. "The Transient and Permanent in Christianity." In *Three Prophets of Religious Liberalism: Channing, Emerson, Parker*. Edited by Conrad Wright. Beacon, 1961. A sermon delivered in 1841.

6. John Ireland. "The Church and the Age." In *The Church and Modern Society, I*, 112–115. The Pioneer Press, St. Paul, Minn., 1905.

7. Thomas Preston. "American Catholicity." *American Catholic Quarterly Review* 16 (1891), 399ff.

8. William Adams Brown. *The Essence of Christianity: A Study in the History of Definition.* Scribner, 1902.

9. Henry Louis Jordan. *Comparative Religion: Its Genesis and Growth.* Scribner, 1905.

10. Anson Phelps Stokes and Leo Pfeffer. *Church and State in the United States,* pp. 563–564. Harper and Row ed., 1964. 1st ed., 1950.

11. David J. Brewer. *The United States: A Christian Nation,* pp. 18, 40, 66, 101. John C. Winston, Philadelphia, 1905.

12. Robert T. Handy. "The Long Spell of Christendom." *Soundings,* 40 (1977):123–134.

13. Eldon G. Ernst. *Without Help or Hindrance: Religious Identity in American Culture,* ch. 5. Westminster, 1977.

14. John Henry Barrows, editor. *The World's Parliament of Religions.* 2 vols. Parliament Publishing Company, Chicago, 1893.

15. Kenten Druyvesteyn. *The World's Parliament of Religions.* Ph.D. thesis, University of Chicago, 1976.

16. H. C. Reynolds. *New Era Magazine* 25 (1919):522.

17. John Richard Burkholder. "The Law Knows No Heresy: Marginal Religious Movements and the Courts." In *Religious Movements in Contemporary America,* pp. 46–50. Edited by Irving I. Zaretsky and Mark P. Leone. Princeton University Press, 1974.

18. *San Francisco Chronicle,* 21 October 1977, pp. 1, 6.

PART 2

Perspectives: The Nature and Significance of the New Religions

INTRODUCTION

The current religious ferment has many intriguing sides. It can be approached on religious, philosophical, social, and cultural grounds; and it is symbolic of profound changes and adjustments in both personal and social self-consciousness. It involves changes within the religious traditions themselves, as well as transpositions of the traditions to new places and contexts. "From all sides," as Walter Capps has written, "there is a prospect that something has been born among us that is genuinely new."

What is that new thing? For Theodore Roszak, it is a new chart by which many modern Americans are navigating their lives. For Robert Wuthnow, Dick Anthony, Thomas Robbins, and Harvey Cox, it is a new vision of the whole. They see human initiative embedded in newly recognizable, historical patterns. For Wuthnow, those patterns may be seen on a global scale. For Anthony and Robbins, those patterns may be seen on a macro-political and economic scale, and, in miniature, in the appearance of the Unification Church. For Cox, those patterns are visible in the way the Christian church has responded historically to the appearance of new religions.

Walter Capps shows how the academic study of religion has itself been a contributing factor in the rise of the new religions. Were it not for modern works of scholarship and translation, the heightened awareness of Eastern forms of spirituality would not have been possible. Bellah points to the religious underpinnings of religious studies, and suggests that the academic study of religion itself may be seen as a new religious enterprise. Goleman describes the transformation that is taking place in the minds of psychologists through their exposure to the ancient psychospiritual systems of Asia, especially Buddhism.

Theodore Roszak and Langdon Gilkey ask, What is the religious significance of cultural change? For Roszak, the new religions represent an improbable turning of the human spirit at a time in modern life when factors of production and appetites for consumption militate against spiritual regeneration. Roszak warns that foundation grants for the "study" of new religious movements in America are to be viewed with as much suspicion as hope; for there is no guarantee that new knowledge of these movements will redound to the benefit of the life of the spirit in America. Gilkey asks for a doctrine-free, religious criterion of religion that would permit a theological interpretation of culture in a way that would point beyond the embedded mind-body dualism of the Western spiritual tradition.

ETHICS, ECSTASY, AND THE STUDY OF NEW RELIGIONS
Theodore Roszak

WE MEET in a time of religious awakening. Yet I think we have as much reason to fear for the future of religion in this moment of rebirth as to celebrate its prospects. Because there are dangers in such a sudden efflorescence, whatever flowers so exuberantly in the public eye will be seen and judged. And I am far from certain that those who revive the spiritual traditions in our time are ready to stand judgment. I am even less certain that those who presume to judge them are qualified for that awful responsibility.

Yet, between these two—between the eager spiritual explorers of the day, and the stern secular humanism that dominates our intellectual and academic mainstream—we may yet see the life of the spirit ground to dust. It may be laid in the scales of history by those who cannot lend it the moral substance it must have if it is to address the great questions of justice and freedom that torment our age. And there, it may be found wanting by those who have been too lightly touched by the visionary powers to acknowledge the religious foundations of human conscience.

It is my own conviction that an air of terrible finality surrounds this confrontation of the new religious awareness and the humanist cultural mainstream. We live in the midst of a secular consensus that has very nearly reached the point of closure and monopoly. Science, technics, and social revolution—all radically divorced from religious tradition—sway the history of our time, and they do so globally, aggressively, militantly. They are fast taking over all the cultural ground, building a planetary synthesis that will soon bring our entire species within the urban-industrial dominance. We are very close to *Endgame*.

At the hands of social revolution, religion is treated as an object of moral scorn—an opiate of the people, the shield of injustice and class privilege. At the hands of the technicians—behavioral and pharmaceutical—it comes to be regarded as a quirky circuit of the human bio-computer, obviously in need of re-programming. Perhaps, most treacherously of all, at the hands of science and scholarship, it becomes (if its presence is acknowledged at all) an object of research—like some quaint fossil whose structure and uncertain function are now at last to receive expert analysis.

Once, no more than a few decades ago, religion held the most marginal and apologetic place at the fringes of the academy. Now, as a lively field of study, it is fast becoming a profession in its own right. It receives the concerted attention of specialists who can dissect their subject matter from every imaginable angle—psychologically, psychiatrically, sociologically, biologically, socio-biologically, anthropologically, neurologically. They can explain it, and explain it away—right down to its subtlest genetic and electrochemical vibrations. Or such is the prospectus.

No doubt, we who discuss these matters and indulge *our* academic fascinations are also part of the religious renaissance of the day. But is it for the better or for the worse that we now find religion so *interesting* that we rush forward to crucify it with questionnaires? What is our role to be? Will we become still another agent of the secular consensus or its Socratic gadfly? Let us bear in mind, before there are more foundation grants than gurus on the scene, how fragile and tentative this renaissance is. A few dozen imported and improvised cults, a minor immigration of swamis, shamans, and lamas (all of them endangered species, trembling on the brink of extinction), a scattering of mystical and psychotherapeutic experiments. It is enough to attract the bemused but always fickle attention of the media, enough to gain the sort of cover-story prominence that was given to last week's political scandal and which will be given to next week's "movie-of-the century." It is enough to generate some conferences and to inspire a few new journals. But, all together, it is a modest beginning, a *mere* beginning. And if that beginning should fail under the pressure of its abundant critics, if it should be weighed down by media-exposure and academic probing, I submit that we may see the advent of a permanent secular dominance, one that closes itself once and for all to our transcendent longings, allowing them to survive only as a sort of sub-cultural detritus left in the path of modernization. In that pathetic form, religious conviction of some description may linger on indefinitely as a colorful biographical detail of modern life—an item we take note of especially in the lives of presidents or celebrities.

In the books I have written, I have spoken of the visionary moment as mankind's generic cultural experience—that from which all else derives, by way of reflection, refraction, distortion, perversion. My argument is that culture is a splintered mirror coruscating that original splendor into a million variations, all bearing some trace of the divine light, some remote spark or glimmer. This is exactly what makes the secularization of culture possible—the presence in its every profane fragment of some sacred residue to which we can attach our passion for transcendence. Even in the depths, some reflected glitter beckons—just as our astronomers now tell us that, at the furthest, unlighted reaches of the universe, we still detect the expiring vibrations of our fiery genesis. Secularization is an idolatry of cultural fragments—the part mistaken for the whole, the lesser reality substituted for the greater. Our science is such a lesser light, brilliant by comparison with the brute superstitions to which people have often fallen, but nevertheless the downward translation of a higher knowledge. Our technology, too, with all the marvelous power it has given us to shape the planet to our needs, is the physical projection of that ancient magic which once obeyed the discipline of the sacred.

If there is any validity to this conception of visionary experience, then there is a sense in which human culture never stops being religious, no matter how "secular" it becomes. It will always be so many variations on the eternal theme. In the words of the ancient Hermetic teaching: "As above, so below." But—and here is the drama of our condition—the variations we guide our lives by may be moving out and away from their source, drawing us, luring us further and further into the surrounding dark—until, at last, we lose our sense of direction and cannot find our way home. That is what I mean when I speak of the finality of the world's spiritual crisis: that we may by now have wandered off after so many lesser reflections of the sacred, we may have lost ourselves among so many fragments, that we can no longer find our way back to the light even though it is only a trick of the mind that separates us from it. But those who know that trick of the mind—the cultures and teachers who hold the secret—grow fewer and fewer by the year. And how shall we make our way back once these bridges of tradition have crumbled?

So we may see all human culture as a confabulation with fragments of the divine. Even those things we name and identify as "religion"—the rituals, ceremonies, *sadhanas,* doctrines, disciplines—these, too, are apt to become partial realities that both delight and distract the mind. That, I suspect, is the major vice many of us might criticize in the religious renaissance of the day: that it, too, can become a fascination with fragments, each pursued and elaborated in isolation:

Religion as the promise of bliss, the gift of tranquility.
Religion as the portal to psychedelic splendors and
    amazements.
Religion as the ultimate form of mental health.
Religion as the panacea of all physical ills.
Religion as the gateway to erotic delights.
Religion as the secret of occult powers.
Religion as the Satanic depths.
Religion as the realization of personal divinity.

The psychospiritual explorations of our day take off in all these directions. And, of course, all these are or have been religion—in one degree or another, at one remove or another. Perhaps that is the greatest discovery which the current religious awakening—taken as a whole—has brought us: a sense of how much bigger and more grandly various religion can be than the narrow fixation upon Belief and Doctrine that has for so long preoccupied the major churches of the West.

But that is the collective image we can compose out of a hundred splintered preoccupations, each of which, on its own, may easily become an isolated island of private enchantment or personal consolation. The vices that ensue—the mindlessness and self-absorption—have been criticized more than sufficiently in the intellectual mainstream. The hedonism of it all, the narcissism, the escapism—the accusations are repeated so often by the press and pundits that they have become tough-minded mantras in their own right. It is already a journalistic cliche how frequently the new religions and therapies weaken toward privatism and withdrawal, how they become playthings of middle-class affluence, or havens of psychic desperation. Like all cliches, this, too, has a kernel of truth at its core. I do not wish to create the impression that I brush the criticism aside. If I spend no further time with it here, it is because the point has been abundantly pressed in recent years—indeed, to the extent of ignoring those religious groups that have shown how gracefully their spiritual calling can be broadened toward social responsibility (the Neighborhood Foundation established by the San Francisco Zen Center may serve as one example, the Humanity Foundation of 3HO as another), as well as the scattered many who have unobtrusively sought to create in the daily pattern of their lives some wholesome alternative to the waste and violence in which the dominant institutions of the world are sunk.

What takes my attention instead is the very fact of the indictment—how rapidly and how indiscriminately it has been drawn up in authoritative circles. My concern is that so many critics should feel licensed to characterize the entire spectrum of the new religions by the worst excesses of social unconcern and self-indulgence. For, in the ease and automaticity of that indictment, we have a telling measure of how morally suspect spirituality has become in our culture.

We have learned to mistrust the pursuit of ecstasy; we demand that its ethical credentials be clearly displayed. What secular humanism wants from religion is first and foremost a social gospel. And, having that, it looks no further. For, in truth, it believes that there is nothing more to be found there that is of historical and social consequence. The rest—the kingdom, power, and glory of awakened vision—it holds to be so much private fantasy.

Here, precisely, is where my own path parts company from that of the secular humanists, whose way I have myself followed through so many years. I have become convinced that in this relentless effort to divorce ethics from ecstasy there lies the whole burden of our alienation. We are the one people in human history for whom Enlightenment—"Enlightenment" with a capital E, the proud cause we inherit from Voltaire, Diderot, Jefferson, Paine—has come to be regarded as an anti-religious ideal, one that inexorably drives its champions toward a position of principled godlessness. In our society peculiarly, conscience has declared war upon the spirit and holds to its cause fanatically.

Here is the fact that makes me most fearful for the future of religion in our world—more so than the social delinquency of the swamis or yogis among us. At least, their dereliction has drawn heavy critical fire. But the angry separation of conscience from spirit is the least examined, the most militantly guarded article of our cultural orthodoxy. And, as the currents of contemporary history now run, this is the factor that works most persistently to exile the transcendent energies from our lives. If there is one thing in all the world that has the power to destroy religion, it is moral passion, which is religion's own fairest child.

Perhaps, at some point, those of us who busy ourselves studying the signs and symptoms of spiritual renewal should pause to ask: is this indeed what needs understanding—the fact that we see people reaching out for spiritual fulfillment? Is it this wholly normal, utterly natural human gesture that needs the benefit of professional investigation—as if it were such an oddity? Or is it perhaps our collective, cultural alienation from this level of being that needs study—our strange conviction that religion is the antithesis of truth and goodness?

I suggest that this is the most valuable lesson we can learn from the religion renaissance we are in. We can *use* what it tells us of human need and aspiration to question the assumptions of the secular consensus. We can use its conception of human potentiality to challenge the adequacy of our science, our technics, our politics. And from this encounter we may develop a new reading of the cultural history of the modern world, one that grants the humanist project its proper stature, but which also assigns it its proper limits.

The historical role of secular humanism has been to level all invidious hierarchies, to strike down all parochial loyalties that endanger the dignity of the person. Over the past two centuries, that heroic mission has pitted humanist forces everywhere against ecclesiastical privilege and sectarian violence; it has made humanism the punishing hammer of all the pious obfuscations that would legitimize social paternalism and civil persecution. At a critical juncture in the development of the modern world, humanism took upon itself the assignment of killing the old gods who had become so many oppressive phantoms of dogma and doctrine—the Word that had become mere words, and, as such, an apology for corrupted power.

Now, looking back, we can clearly see how wretchedly betrayed were all the spiritual traditions whose unworthy custodians forced that confrontation. Because Church and State had become partners in tyranny, it was left to elements outside the religious establishment—deists, agnostics, free-thinkers, atheists—to become "the party of humanity." Yet, perhaps we can also recognize that, far from being an inherently anti-religious mission, this defense of human dignity is the age-old task of prophecy. It is the vocation of Amos at the doors of the temple, unleashing the fires of visionary inspiration against priest and king.

But in the case of modern humanism, there was a crucial difference. The chosen weapons were not vision and rhapsodic utterance, but skepticism, mockery, social revolution—instruments drawn from another level of consciousness, and fashioned within the strictly desacralized worldview of modern science. *There* is the fateful connection: the moral passion of prophecy linked to the new sensibility of science and the new power of industrial technology. The cry for justice set adrift and howling in the infinite void of Newton's universe. That is the historical movement we see consummated in the revolutionary fury of Marx, Lenin, Mao, Castro, Fanon—prophets of the people who are driven to deny the sources of prophetical vision, and who finish with an image of human nature taken from Pavlov's laboratory.

Because the forces of Enlightenment mistook the ecclesiastical for the sacred, the tarnished vessel for the sacrament within, they were bound to overcarry in their assault. Once the humanist project blurred that crucial distinction, it lost all sense of discipline and limits, until, at last, it would turn back upon humanity itself to exercise its debunking talents. And what happens at that point? What happens when we seek to develop a science of human being grounded in skepticism and objective rationality? We finish with a nihilistic assault upon the personality, undertaken as a part of a principled effort to deracinate every claim to sanctity wherever it may be found hiding—even in the depths of the human heart. So, we find ourselves burdened with a humanism that again and again turns anti-human in its determination to expunge every trace of sacramental reality from the universe.

Over the past two centuries, the secular consensus has offered us many readings of human nature: Darwinism, Marxism, Freudianism, Behaviorism, positivism, existentialism, sociobiology. We have been told that we are "naked apes" and "meat machines," creatures "beyond freedom and dignity," governed by neural feedback or the reflex arc, by class interest or sexual appetite, by economic self-interest or genetic programming, by cultural conditioning or historical necessity. Curious, is it not, how all these images seem determined to root out our deep intuition of freedom and higher purpose—how none does justice to our yearning for completion at some higher level of being? None waters the seed within us that longs for cultivation.

But now observe a deep irony. There is a point at which this humanist compulsion to debunk and depreciate draws upon the very religious heritage it would reject and indeed reinforces its most unfortunate aspect. For can we not see in this reductionist assault upon human nature the same dark revulsion with our creatureliness, the same grinding discomfort with flesh and animal energy that has always haunted the Judeo-Christian tradition?

Granted that at one level—a high and unstable level—humanism celebrates our capacities for reason and decency (that is the classic humanist stance: proud, brave, Promethean); but delve only a little below that level, only as deep as Freud delved into the unconscious—only an inch deep—and what becomes of that fair image? It crumbles into the irrational and demonic. And what our culture knows of introspection carried to that level it has learned from a religious tradition that has always regarded the dark, swirling forces of the inner self as the mark of the beast and the sign of our fallenness. Consider the major forms of deep self-analysis we have invented in the Western world: the Catholic confession, the Puritan diary, the camp-meeting testimonial. In all these, the inward journey is undertaken in mortal terror and the dread of damnation.

Accordingly, the psychological literature of our culture has always doted upon guilt and self-loathing. What is Freud's psychoanalysis but—inevitably—an agonizing search for the guilty secrets: incest, perversion, patricidal fantasies, death wishes, the flight from mortality? So, too, the existentialist artists and philosophers of our time affirm the same image of the inner life as a private hell of nausea, nothingness, and self-reproach. Again and again, we confront the same annihilating lesson: the self as a chamber of horrors and den of iniquity. That is the experience of creatureliness that was once meant to drive us toward God in search of grace and salvation. First, unbearable guilt; then, the blood of the lamb.

In our time, the religious context and saving grace of this experience have fallen away for most, but the search for hidden terrors still stands as the criterion of authentic introspection. Self-knowledge is a hard road to guilty resignation. That, at least, has been our cultural orthodoxy. For most of us, I daresay, it is still the foundation of the personality and the basis of moral resolution. We therefore fear whatever weakens this ingrained sense of unworthiness. Moreover, I suspect that it is from this restless sense of guilty fear that much of the work discipline and entrepreneurial energy of our society derives. These are the displacements of a tormenting discontent into the surrounding world. We turn out and away from ourselves because inside is terror and the abyss. Our escape is into history; our penance is "progress."

This, I believe, is one of the principal discoveries of the new religions and psychotherapies. Somewhere, buried in the core of the Western conscience, there is a festering accumulation of "sin" that is simply unworthy of serious adult concern. It has nothing to do with justice, compassion, or good fellowship. Rather, it is the steady pressure of a guilt that arises from trivial childish fears, sexual hangups, thwarted familial anger, role-playing anxieties. Yet, this is the shallow ballast of our moral nature, and we let it hound us through a lifetime of "good behavior," "high achievement," "responsibility," as we try to prove over and again that we are pure and good and lovable. I often wonder how much of the moral scruple of ourselves and our ancestors has been grounded—sullenly and resentfully—in the guilt of infantile masturbation fantasies?

Now, the new religions and therapies bring us forms of self-examination that yield a very different understanding of our nature. They, too, deal with anxieties of guilt and inner terror, but they are not obsessed by them. Instead, they look beyond: toward higher potentialities and the prospect of growth, health, fulfillment. They may even make use of play, humor, pleasure . . . ecstasy. They invite us to relax, enjoy, unfold; they permit us to assert our essential innocence. Indeed, it is by now notorious that the imported Oriental disciplines teach our inherent divinity. From a traditional Western viewpoint, that is sheer blasphemy and the dissipation of all moral tension. But, from another perspective, it can be seen as the basis of a new moral authenticity, a sense of conscience that is not energized by guilt. That, at least, is the promise of these new explorations in the higher human potentialities: a morality born of innocence, a decency that springs from delight.

Of course, there are bound to be stern, censorious minds in our midst that fear the cultural disruption such as liberation of innocence might bring—and with good reason. Even more efficiently than police force, it is distrust-of-self that makes people vulnerable and obedient; it is self-loathing that opens them to emotional intimidation. These are the "mind forg'd manacles" of social domination. Beyond the use of naked power, society has very little leverage with innocent people. It cannot manipulate or mystify them into endorsing their own subjugation. It cannot make them despise themselves and so bow down to their prescribed duty.

We have seen what happens when blacks, gays, Latinos, native Americans, women, the handicapped, throw off their slave mentality and assert their natural identity in the full pride of their innocence. Is it not obvious that the new religions and therapies are yet another, more universal assertion of unashamed personhood? They are also teaching people that, if they look deeply enough within, they do not find guilty terrors but autonomous powers of growth, strength, and transcendence. I suspect that a society built upon that conviction of innocence (if there should ever be one) would lack all the psychic compulsions on which industrial discipline is based. Innocent people are not submissive people. They will not suffer the punishment of an alienated existence as if they *deserved* to be condemned to that death-in-life. They are apt to demand too many rights in the world, not least of all the right to know themselves and to be themselves.

A half-century ago, in the midst of the First World War, Freud raised the great question: What is the origin of the explosive discontent that continues to defeat the purposes of reason and to torment the course of human affairs? To raise the question is to ask, at the same time, what the essential energy of history is. What is it that drives us forward in this violent and unhappy adventure? In effect, Freud had issued an invitation to explore the demonic in our political life.

Answering Freud's question requires an archaeological study of human nature, a "dig" that will take us down and down through many layers of need and motivation. The uppermost layers are by now familiar: bread, justice, equality. These needs have long since been integrated into the dominant ideologies of the modern world. Freud, in his turn, added the sexual needs of the subconscious and the even deeper need to express aggression, which he wisely traced to the fear of death. The existentialist philosophers and psychologists have added the need for authenticity, for assuming full personal responsibility for one's ethical commitments and one's fate. The New Left of our own day has added the need of a humanly scaled community and of direct participation in political decisions.

Quite as important as the discovery of these many new needs has been the growing realization that they are *organically* and *hierarchically* related. They cannot be satisfied in a segmented and piecemeal way, any more than the human organism can be healed as a number of discrete parts divided up among specialists. The medicine of the body politic must deal with us as whole persons, or its best intentions will go awry. Yes, we must eat and be housed and clothed. But if these needs are met paternalistically and without respect for our individual dignity (as is the case with most American welfare programs), then the result is hostility and demoralization. Yes, we must participate in the politics of our community. But if that social responsibility crowds out our need for some quiet and private space in which to be uniquely ourselves (as is the case in most "people's republics" and totalitarian states), then the result will again be festering discontent.

The problem is this: we—by which I mean the intellectual consensus of the age—discover each of these needs on a different historical horizon. They seem to unfold out of one another sequentially. And as each is discovered, it seems to its finders to be the ultimate political value. So it is enshrined in an ideology or becomes the shibboleth of a movement, and is elevated above question. Anyone who then challenges the sufficiency of the ideology can only appear to be a traitor to the cause for having doubted the obvious truth that is here being championed. And none is more vulnerable to that accusation than those who speak in behalf of the spiritual needs. They must challenge what all the ideologies and movements of the past have in common, and that is their commitment to the great secular consensus which holds that all human needs can be fulfilled within the world of time and matter. All the dominant ideologies belong to that consensus; that is why their critique of the crushing dynamism and colossalism of modern industrial society is radically flawed. They cannot see how they, out of their own best intentions, have contributed to those life-denying forces.

This is no easy accusation to make when one is dealing with ideologies and movements that were created to serve mankind and whose adherents have sacrificed bravely and often. But the issue must nevertheless be joined. The needs of the person are held together organically; violate them at one level, and the result will be corruption and distortion all along the line, with the result that the worst evils—those which stem from deep and grievous discontent—will reemerge like a malignant growth whose root has not been found. This much we should by now have learned from the history of modern revolution. Yes, the revolution may redistribute the benefits of industrialism more justly. But the same tribal hostilities continue to flourish under its banner; the same diseased preoccupations continue to surface as if by iron necessity: the bomb, the assembly line, the mass market, the production schedule, the rape of the environment, the ministry of propaganda, the secret police, the power-political rat race. . . .

All is bound to go wrong with revolutions—with all political programs—that work within the secular consensus because, at last, the secular consensus is wrong. It does not go deep enough to touch what is most fundamental in human nature, and so it cannot understand our discontent or bring us fulfillment. Here is where the Aquarian frontier becomes an essential part of contemporary political life. Those who rise to this historical horizon have faced up to the demonic in human affairs; they have been willing to learn about its nature from traditions and sources long since dismissed by the tissue-thin psychology of the modern ideologies; they have plumbed the layers of human need and motivation that lie further down than bread, sex, justice, participation, and have learned anew a very old truth, the truth that Tolstoy asserted against Marx, the truth that Jung asserted against Freud: that we are religious beings down to our very core; that there is no wholeness, no sanity, for us until we make spiritual need even more fundamental than all the others.

Because the secular consensus and all the politics connected with it stop short of our spiritual needs, they progressively enlarge the spiritual void in our lives. And that void is the prime political fact of our time. It is the secret of our discontent, the anguish that animates our psychopathic conduct. The strenuous and foolish things that people in our time seek to do with history—to multiply thermonuclear overkill endlessly, to raise up economies of limitless growth, to build conglomerate empires that straddle the globe, to turn the planet into one, vast industrial artifact, to produce without limit, to consume beyond all sane need, to propagandize the world with one's ideology—all this is what people use to fill the emptiness inside them. So, too, the mindless mass movements to which they surrender themselves in desperation; these also are among the corrupted stuff they cram into the void.

But the void is too big to fill. It is an emptiness that can be occupied only by something greater than all history and material achievement can offer. We are in the position of someone with a teaspoon trying to fill the Grand Canyon from a child's sandbox. The task is hopeless; and because we know it is hopeless, we grow ever more frantic in trying to carry it through. Because we can see the thing we most dread and wish to bury—our own despair—rising out of the void like a man-eating monster. *Despair* . . . that is the demon of discontent within us.

Despair is what drives us into the maniacal history-making which is the hallmark of our age. No, not all the crusades and projects are to be condemned. Some achieve humane ends. But more and more they become desperate assertions of national egotism, collective power, aggressive arrogance. As if we wanted them to achieve more than they can. And that is indeed what we are after: a gratification of the spirit from that which is below the level of spirit.

Yet behind the fanatical bustle of the modern world, the simple truth stands firm: people are not power- and profit-seeking creatures. Not fundamentally. Power and possession are without significance for the whole and healthy person. They become goals only by default and to the degree that higher purpose withdraws from our lives. That is why, since time immemorial, people have treasured above all else the memory of their saints and sages—the gurus who have turned aside from money and domination as if these were the rubbish of life. By their very presence among us, they remind us of a greater project than the politics of civilized societies has yet embraced: to awaken the god who sleeps at the roots of our being.

RELIGIOUS MOVEMENTS AND THE TRANSITION IN WORLD ORDER

Robert Wuthnow

NOT JUST in the past few years, but ever since World War II, the United States has undergone a steady succession of religious movements. In the 1950s these movements included a broad revival in main-line denominations, a rebirth of pentecostalism and fundamentalism, and a renewed interest in ecumenism and church union. In the 1960s religious unrest became more pronounced. That decade witnessed a movement away from organized religion, especially among young people, many of whom defected from the churches, first to campus religious centers, and later from those, too. It also saw the spread of religiously inspired militancy among minorities and, in turn, of ethnic backlash. Among Catholics, it saw the initiation of the Vatican II reforms. And perhaps most visibly, the sixties gave birth to a host of new religious movements, many of which harkened to traditions beyond Christianity. In the seventies, these movements have survived, spread, splintered, and cross-fertilized to the extent that the number of local groups runs in the thousands and the number of followers ranges in the hundreds of thousands. Elsewhere [1,2,3] I have described the extent and nature of new religious experimentation in a larger setting.

Although many of the new religious movements have deep historical roots, the postwar period is unique in several ways. It represents a unique mixture of Judeo-Christian, Asian, tribal, cultic, and pseudo-scientific movements. It has produced no single philosophy or liturgical reformation, but a diversity of competing alternatives. Moreover, these alternatives have not, at least yet, crystallized into distinct, stable organizations, but have shown considerable fluidity in organizational style, teachings, and membership. For its part, the membership of these movements is also relatively unique in that it has included not only portions of the downtrodden, but substantial segments of the privileged as well. The religious unrest of the postwar period has scarcely been limited to America. If anything, it has been even more pronounced in Japan, Western Europe, and, though different in content, throughout large sections of the Third World.

A variety of social and cultural conditions have contributed to this religious unrest. But they do not explain it satisfactorily, either singly or in combination. The great increase in higher education since World War II has undoubtedly exposed people to new ideas, many of which have run counter to traditional religious beliefs. But there have been educational revolutions before, in the 1880s for example, without similar repercussions, and even the best statistical studies have failed by and large to pin down a direct causal relation between higher education and the present religious experimentation. The postwar period has contributed prosperity and affluence. But religious movements in the past have more often occurred among the less affluent and in times of economic uncertainty. Science has mushroomed in the years since Sputnik, undoubtedly with some effects upon worldviews. But the most dramatic scientific revolution in modern history, that of the late seventeenth century, did not produce such dramatic religious unrest. There has perhaps been enough tension and stress to inspire some to seek comfort in new religions. But surely this stress has been no greater than that associated with two world wars or the Great Depression in the last generation. Some have suggested that religious pluralism in America has itself been the source of ever-expanding religious experimentation. But this explanation fails to account for the parallel experimentation that has occurred in countries as different as France, Japan, England, and Denmark. Others have seen a connection between the present religious turmoil and the demise of the small business firm in favor of the giant corporation. But this connection fails to explain the relative absence of religious turmoil in earlier periods of this economic transition, notably during the age of giant trusts, nor does it account for even earlier periods of religious unrest, such as in the early nineteenth century. Still other explanations have been tendered, emphasizing professionalization, ecology, the mass media, urbanization, trade and technology. But they, too, fall prey to these limitations.

At its deepest levels, the taproot of the current religious unrest must be sought elsewhere. It must be sought in the fabric of social experience itself. For that is what validates (or undermines) our conceptions of reality, including our conceptions of ultimate reality. Peter Berger [4] has proposed the term "plausibility structure" to characterize the experiential *gestalt* that undergirds our constructions of reality. It is to this plausibility structure that we must turn if we are to grasp the deepest sources of our present religious situation.

In the modern world, there is but one plausibility structure capable of shaping the general contours of our religious consciousness. That plausibility structure is not that of the family, nor that of society. Both the familial microcosm and the societal macrocosm are embedded in a larger network of economic exchange, media communication, military contingencies, protective alliances, and resource dependency. The realities constructed in each are subject to the influences of international diplomacy, as the nightly news or any grocery shopper can testify. In the modern world, the plausibility structure that undergirds our religious consciousness is that of the modern world itself. If we are to understand the deep roots of our present religious turmoil, we must examine the current transition in world order.

THE TRANSITION IN WORLD ORDER

An understanding of the present transition in world order requires us to go back briefly to the nineteenth century. For it was in the nineteenth century that the world order we have inherited was constructed. That order rested principally upon the functioning of free trade within a self-regulating international market. From the middle of the century onward, the free-market system regulated trade, dominated international relations, benefited and maintained the power of principal interest groups, and provided unprecedented material welfare. Especially in Britain, where it was of obvious economic advantage, the free-trade system was looked upon with near-religious devotion. For instance, the *Economist* wrote in 1843:

Free trade is itself a good, like virtue, holiness and righteousness, to be loved, admired, honoured and steadfastly adopted, for its own sake, though all the rest of the world should love restrictions and prohibitions, which are of themselves evils, like vice and crime, to be hated and abhorred under all circumstances and at all times [5].

In addition to the free market, the nineteenth-century world order rested on three supporting institutions. The first was the British-dominated balance-of-power system, which maintained international peace throughout most of the century, a condition necessary for the successful conduct of international free trade. Second was the *laissez-faire* system of government, which minimized domestic interference with the free functioning of the market. And third was the international gold standard, which limited fluctuations in exchange rates, protected the value of foreign loans, facilitated the free flow of international commerce, and benefited the industrialized countries, mainly Britain, who were the leading exporters of goods and capital. These institutions, in turn, were legitimated by an underlying utilitarian philosophy that called for freedom of the will, freedom in trade, and freedom in civil matters, the combination of which were assumed to guarantee high levels of prosperity and social justice. It was under this system that nearly all parts of the globe were incorporated into the Western world-economy.

The free-market system operated as an integrated form of world order. Organized around a coherent philosophical worldview, the free-market system wedded the interests of dominant political and economic elites, provided stable assumptions for the governing of international relations, maintained the position of dominant nations, and effectively controlled the passions of subordinate nations and classes. It functioned effectively, however, only as long as Britain maintained the industrial supremacy that ensured it the advantages of open trade [6]. This advantage diminished greatly by the turn of the century, as other European nations, especially France and Germany, developed their own industrial capacities. The economic competition that resulted led the European powers increasingly to expand their trade and investments into the developing world, and ultimately to circumvent the free-trade process itself by partitioning the developing world into colonial enclaves.

With the outbreak of World War I, financial chaos befell the already weakened free-market system. Trade and investments were hampered by the war. Country after country repudiated foreign debts or declared moratoria on their repayment, and otherwise acted to halt international gold shipments, leaving the gold standard operational only in a trivial sense. The economic impact upon Britain was devastating. After the war, Britain was forced to borrow heavily from the United States and liquidated much of her investments abroad. In 1931, Britain abandoned the gold standard, devalued the pound, and adopted protectionist trading policies, signalling the collapse of the free-market era. Other signs of its demise included the launching of the New Deal, the Five-Year Plans in Russia, the rise of fascism in Germany, and the collapse of the League of Nations in favor of autarchist empires. Karl Polanyi [7], an economic historian, described the change in the international order in this way:

While at the end of the Great War nineteenth century ideals were paramount, and their influence dominated the following decade, by 1940 every vestige of the international system had disappeared and, apart from a few enclaves, the nations were living in an entirely new international setting.

The international gold standard had been displaced both in practice and, following Keynes, in economic theory. Throughout Europe, currencies fluctuated wildly, bringing concomitant unemployment and economic uncertainty. The hegemony of Britain, and with it Britain's peace-keeping capability, had been permanently destroyed. The liberal nation-state had temporarily ceased to function throughout much of the world, and was replaced either by totalitarian regimes or by new welfare-state economies. And while the ideology and tactics of free trade were far from dead, a profound ideological reformation had been successfully institutionalized in the Soviet Union, one which challenged the basic assumptions of the free-trade system.

By the end of World War II, the realities of global politics precluded any possibility of reconstructing an international order along the principles of the nineteenth-century free-market system. Western Europe lay in disarray, and the United States was still reluctant to shoulder the responsibilities of world leadership that Britain had carried. The lessons of international finance during the preceding two decades had shown the impossibility of any single country stabilizing international monetary arrangements in the way that Britain had done during the previous century. The communist bloc had succeeded in establishing itself as a significant foe of the free world. China had ceased to be a hinterland for Japanese and American investment. The preoccupation of Europe with its own affairs during the war had created opportunities for numerous incipient nationalist movements to emerge throughout the colonized world. As a result, the postwar period emerged as one in which repeated efforts to create a new world order would be made.

Such efforts have had to be made in the absence of an integrated system of international institutions, and in the presence of a world divided ideologically between the successors of utilitarianism and the successors of Marxism. As a result, national and international policy since World War II has had to be formed in the face of frequently incompatible objectives without the benefit of well-established policy guidelines. American relations with Western Europe, for example, have vacillated between a policy of bilateralism, designed to keep Europe divided and economically subordinate, and a policy of multilateralism, designed to strengthen Europe as a buffer against the Soviet Union. As international power arrangements have shifted, often from year to year, the United States has found itself favoring first one and then the other of these contradictory policies toward Western Europe [8]. United States policy toward former colonial possessions of the European nations has demonstrated a similar ambivalence: on the one hand American policy-makers have wished to erode the privileges of Europe; on the other hand they have wished to make sure that these possessions do not fall to hostile regimes, as in the case of French Indochina. In American eyes, Third World nations have appeared alternatively as little brothers ready to imitate the modernity of their more mature siblings, as junior partners capable of offering new markets and sources of labor, and as potential enemies ever waiting to remind Americans of their own guilty conscience. The political instability within the Third World has only added to the ambiguities of United States policy.

International economic arrangements have also been in a transitional phase since World War II. Chronic inflation, defiant of all Keynesian solutions, has dramatized the instability of the international monetary system that had been forecast by the economic planners from forty-four nations who participated in the conference at Bretton Woods, New Hampshire, in July of 1944. Rather than being guided by long-term policies, responses to economic crises, such as the OPEC price increases of 1973, typically have come forth on a case by case basis. Often, each nation has acted unilaterally to protect its own economy, through currency devaluation, for example, and in so doing has neglected the interests of international economic well-being.

At an even deeper level, economic policy remains ambivalently associated with the lingering principles of free trade. Given the changes in world economic conditions, a policy of free trade permits only two means of economic adjustment: (1) changing the level of domestic economic activity, or growth rate, and (2) changing the exchange rate, or productivity ratio, of currency. Both techniques are likely to have negative political repercussions. At the same time, economic policy is guided by principles of social planning, the application of which is likely to be perceived within the business community as restrictive of vital competitive prerogatives, as evidenced by the recent tensions between multinational corporations and their host governments. Of course, economic policy is a function of compromise in any era. But the capacity to achieve workable compromises in recent years has been complicated by the absence both of an underlying international monetary system and a coherent economic philosophy [9].

The construction of a stable world order has also been made difficult in the years since World War II because of (1) political problems associated with the management of large military forces and war-time economies in ways that are consistent with the prospects of world peace; (2) the fundamental instability of a nuclear weapons monopoly on the part of the superpowers as a key to world order; and (3) the comparative recency with which both the Soviet Union and the United States have assumed roles of world leadership. Despite frequent complaints about American imperialism, the United States has actually adapted slowly to its leadership role, lacking any deep philosophical rationale for taking an aggressive stance in international affairs, save perhaps the fear of communism. For having been critical of European imperialism and for having been economically self-sufficient throughout most of its history, America has remained deeply sensitive to accusations of imperialism. And yet, as further evidence of the ironies of world politics in the postwar period, some of America's most blatant imperialist activities, usually disguised as policies designed to protect national security, have been implemented by isolationists and internationalists alike.

In addition to the international uncertainties that these conditions have generated, an important consequence has been the politicization of domestic interest groups, including a nearly constant shifting of positions and alliances among these interest groups. The shifting state of world affairs has produced a proliferation of pressure groups to influence the domestic response. Labor has emerged as a politicized interest group, dependent upon government good will (again in the absence of a firm international monetary order) to go slow in the fight against inflation, rather than opposing it through recessionary policies that might reduce standards of living and create unemployment among workers. These concerns, together with fears of competition from foreign workers, have made American labor a generally protectionist, patriotic supporter of national government, contrary to labor's more general tradition of internationalism and class consciousness across national boundaries. Agriculture has also been politicized, but has found itself in an even more ambiguous position than labor. As political and climatic conditions fluctuate throughout the world, agriculture finds itself the supporter of protectionist nationalism in one instance and, in another instance, the supporter of open international markets. The professional and managerial staffs of large corporations dependent upon multinational markets have adopted a more consistent "live-and-let-live" attitude toward international policy, even toward Russia and China insofar as it has benefited trade, but have been less eager to take such an attitude toward left-leaning countries in the developing world, for fear of losing overseas investments. The universities have been placed in a similarly ambiguous position of benefiting materially from the development of advanced technology, including military and space technology inspired by the arms race and nationalist competition, while at the same time being committed to more humanitarian and universalistic values. Other examples could be cited, but the important point is that domestic interest groups have increasingly become oriented to the vagaries of international politics, finding themselves frequently in the position of having to adopt orientations internally inconsistent or contradictory to more traditional positions, and having to adjust these orientations with each new development in world affairs. The task of achieving stable relations among domestic interest groups, therefore, rests not simply on domestic political consensus, but is deeply conditioned by the affairs of world politics.

The relevance of all this to the recent religious unrest may in some ways be obvious, but it will help to see the connections in a theoretically more informed manner if we pause momentarily, before considering them explicitly, in order to examine briefly the religious response to two similar periods in Western history.

THE RELIGIOUS RESPONSE TO WORLD CRISES

There have been two previous periods in modern history bearing conditions structurally similar to the present one. The first was the early part of the seventeenth century. In these years, the European world lay in the midst of a deep social transition. The imperial order that the Spanish Hapsburgs had attempted to impose upon Europe during the sixteenth century had been defeated both militarily and economically by the rising states of northern Europe. The Reformation had played a significant role in undermining the universalistic assumptions on which the domination of the Hapsburg dynasty had been erected. In its wake followed a period of international wars through which most of the imperial possessions of the Hapsburgs had gained emancipation. The resulting situation in the early seventeenth century was a period of domestic tension and instability as the English, Dutch, and French sought to reconstruct a normative order along mercantilist lines. The civil war between crown and country in England reflected the adjustments that were being made among interest groups across Europe [10,11]. The second period was the early and middle years of the nineteenth century, during which the Western world was undergoing a transition from the mercantilist system to the free-trade system, of which we have already spoken. These years followed a period in which the sovereign ideals associated with mercantilism had led to increasing international conflict among the core European powers, drastically increasing the costs of maintaining the entire system. In addition, the Industrial Revolution had brought about new modes of economic production, the Enlightenment had done much to undercut the protectionist principles of international exchange, and the American Revolution had largely destroyed the prevailing pattern of colonial relations. By the early nineteenth century, the old mercantilist system had ceased to provide a stable normative order. The following transition period was accompanied by unparalleled conflict within nations. New interest groups arose and replaced old interest groups, while both looked to the polity for assistance, and the lower orders clamored for social reform. Between 1812 and 1865, Spain and Portugal (and their American colonies), Russia, Greece, France, Belgium, Italy, Poland, Germany, and the United States all experienced major revolts or civil wars [12,13].

What was common in both of these periods, as well as in the more recent period, was that the basic institutional structure of the prevailing world order had, for various reasons associated with the *expansion* of that order, broken down. As the core area of each prevailing world order was weakened, economic and political domination shifted to new areas formerly on the periphery of world politics. In each case, this shift was facilitated by a profound ideological reformation, which undermined the tacit sacredness of the dominant system of world order and gave legitimacy to its successor. But the transition to a new system of world order was not accomplished immediately or without difficulty. Each transition was followed by a period of domestic economic instability, itself the function of an ambiguous structure of international finance and exchange, and by a succession of civil conflicts brought on by the changing roles and strengths of nations and of interest groups within nations. Only gradually, through these series of domestic adjustments, were new patterns of world order forged and stabilized.

In the first two periods, historical hindsight has shown a close connection between the general crisis in world order and the prevailing religious response. Both periods were characterized by exceptional religious unrest and diversity. Rising interest groups developed new religious forms, often with strong moral and social welfare components which assisted in legitimating their new preeminence in social affairs, while declining interest groups were frequently led to reject prevailing values and to form splinter groups, often in response to changing relations between church and state. The rising power of the Puritans in England during the first period and of the New Light and popular denominations in America during the second period are among the best known examples of the former, while the latter are illustrated by the Oxford Movement, the Christian Reformed Church, and the secession of the "Old Lutherans" in Prussia. Instabilities in moral climates produced corresponding shifts in the popularity of alternative religious persuasions. And unsettled political conditions motivated religious protest, persecution, and emigration. The net effect in each period was a proliferation of religious movements throughout the international system.

In an immediate sense, the source of each period of religious unrest was domestic turmoil. But to understand the pervasiveness and the complexity of this turmoil, it must be viewed in an international context. We have come to recognize more clearly the profound connections between the religious convictions of a people and their sense of national purpose. But this sense is molded by the climate of world opinion and by the global milieu within which nations function. In times when there is an underlying structure of world order, national purposes are formed within a matrix of shared assumptions, whether these concern the defense of a universalistic religion and the authority of dynastic succession, as in the Hapsburg empire, or whether they concern the sovereignty and mutual antagonism of states, as in the mercantilist system. In times of deep polarization and conflict in world order, nations continue to be guided by prevailing global assumptions, either through strong reaffirmation of these assumptions, or in strong reaction against them. But in the aftermath of such polarization and transition, when the fundamental operating principles of world order are in question, the purposes of nations become subject to the vagaries of events and opinion. Interest groups adopt moral positions and root these moral positions in religious convictions. Religious bodies, in turn, derive moral positions in keeping with their role in society and that of their members. As political and economic conditions change, both domestically and in the larger world, the fortunes of those associated with these moral positions also change, and the relevance of the moral positions themselves may change. Religious orientations are likely to alternate, conflict, and multiply with each nation's efforts to find its place in the international order.

THE POSTWAR RELIGIOUS SITUATION

Since World War II, the multiplicity of religious movements that have taken place in America has been conditioned by the deep uncertainty of world affairs. Moral climates have vacillated in response to the changing circumstances of world politics, and with them the legitimacy of alternative religious orientations has risen and fallen. A few examples will serve to illustrate some of these relations.

The freezing and thawing of the Cold War and the uncertainties of detente have provoked direct religious responses from the American public. For we perceive rightly that communism represents not only an alternative political system, but a profoundly different interpretation of ultimate reality itself. As relations between the two superpowers have shifted, the plausibility of alternative religious positions has also varied. Whether we wish to acknowledge it or not, periods of moral conflict with the Soviet Union have always been associated with a reassertion of American religious traditions, while detente and peaceful coexistence have invariably required us to rethink those traditions. How closely linked our religious convictions as a people are with our sense of national purpose toward the communist bloc has been well-evidenced in recent years both in former President Ford's untimely remarks about Eastern Europe and in President Carter's campaign for human rights. Yet, the very reality of the Soviet Union and its growing importance as a vast export market for agricultural and industrial production have placed the religious convictions of many a farmer and factory worker at odds with their economic motivations. Is it not perhaps the accompanying sense of guilt and betrayal, however deeply subconscious, that has led to such violent denunciations of campus radicals and others who have openly admitted their Marxist leanings? The effect of a world divided between democracy and communism has not been simply to reinvigorate our civil religion, but to cast it into the depths of uncertainty.

The rise of China to world power has also contributed to the moral crisis in American religious culture. The case of China has been especially revealing of the precarious framework of world order that has been constructed since World War II. To a great extent, the postwar order has been predicated upon domination by the superpowers of the ultimate deterrent force, namely, nuclear weapons. When China exploded its own atomic bomb in 1964, a new reality was imposed upon the superpowers. Within both China and the Soviet Union, the process toward China's nuclear capability had been fraught with political conflict. Khrushchev fell from power the same day that China tested its bomb. For the United States, short-term alarm gradually gave way to long-term changes in foreign policy as the Sino-Soviet split deepened and as the United States became increasingly dependent upon China to assist in extricating itself from Vietnam [14]. Though the religious responses to these events were less direct than they typically have been to the activities of the Soviet Union, the consequences reverberated widely. No longer could the world be divided as easily into the Just and the Unjust. China's power represented an added peril, should its differences with the Soviet Union be healed, or a potential ally, should some common ground be found. Scholars and diplomats revived earlier reservoirs of fascination with the ancient culture and religions of China. Forward-looking American missionaries again began praying for the day when China's door would be reopened. "Yellow peril" fears that had crept into the churches during the 1950s (and before) came increasingly to be disrespectable and groups that had flourished in these fears, of which Sun Myung Moon's has become the most notable example, became increasingly sectarian and suspicious of the new mood of the United States government.

The absence of stable relations between the United States and the Third World, too, has deeply affected the moral consciousness of the postwar period, particularly when these relations have involved Americans in morally questionable positions, as in Vietnam, Cambodia, Chile, and Bangladesh. Each new failure to impose our American conceptions of stability and prosperity on the Third World has brought with it charges of imperialism and neocolonialism. Americans have been forced to reevaluate the moral basis of their motivations. The charges have come both from other nations and from domestic interest groups, and they have multiplied as policies are first initiated, then reversed, and then reinitiated. The effect upon religion has been that the plausibility of the whole Western tradition, with its emphasis upon modernity and rationality, can no longer be taken for granted quite as easily as it once was. This has not been the result of some mysterious philosophical reorientation, but the product of empirical relations between the West and the developing world. And in the *lacunae* of ultimate confidence, many have turned inward to reconstruct their own personal experiences of the sacred, often by borrowing heavily from the tribal, magical, and mystical religions previously relegated to the fringes of the Western tradition.

Because America has been a nation of immigrants, the frontiers of American religion have always been exposed to the influences of foreign affairs. But never before have these frontiers been as widely exposed as they have been in recent years. Not only has the postwar period suffered from the tensions of a world order in transition, but America's dominant role in world politics has exposed it on all fronts to world events. Accordingly, many of its new religions have been directly or indirectly influenced by America's foreign relations. As in the past, friendly relations with Britain and Western Europe have facilitated the import and export of new religions. Devotees of groups such as the Process and Scientology have turned from Britain to the United States when legal and economic restrictions have become oppressive. The Children of God turned to Britain when the same pressures developed against them in the United States. Transcendental Meditation found its way westward more easily because of the long-standing relations between India and Britain and because of the use of those relations by such prominent figures as the Beatles. Yet, the tensions that have existed between the United States and Western Europe since World War II as the United States has exerted its dominant influence in world affairs have made Americans somewhat less eager to borrow from the Europeans than they may have been in the past. Certainly there has been less fascination with European theology than with Asian religions. The protective and commercial alliances between the United States and Japan have made it as easy to import Zen Buddhism and Nichiren Shoshu as Datsuns and Toyotas. Similarly, the ease with which Tibetan yoga has been implanted, and the degree to which American youth have been able to make pilgrimages to the fountains of Divine Light and Hare Krishna, are partly a function of the United States' relations with Asia. In short, American religion has experienced the consequences of the United States' deep involvement in a global network of security and trade relations.

This network has created exposure to new religions, but it has ultimately been the transitional state of world affairs that has conditioned their legitimacy. Students, especially those on the nation's large cosmopolitan campuses, and young people more generally have grown up amidst competing conceptions of national destiny. Their futures have been much influenced by the demands of foreign wars, by the varied fortunes of the space and arms races, by academic preoccupations with international studies, and by the economic consequences of currency fluctuations, inflation, and energy embargoes. This has been as true of students in Japan and Western Europe as in the United States, and the religious consequences have been much the same. For the churches, it has been the liberal main-line denominations, those most capable of and most committed to speaking out on world affairs, whose plausibility has been undercut by the shifting contingencies of national and international politics. The effect upon these denominations was particularly evident during the 1960s when the rapid transition from support of the Cold War to protest against the Vietnam War gave rise to criticism and defection among both conservatives and liberals. Rightly or wrongly, the preeminent orientation in foreign affairs has been the amoral *realpolitik* of a Nixon or Kissinger, rather than the moral principles devised by the churches in their quest for public relevance. Thus, the churches that have fared healthiest have been the smaller fundamentalist and evangelical bodies which have sought only the salvation of souls and have skirted the practicalities of social policy pronouncements.

In the most general sense, the plausibility structure undergirding our religious consciousness is one that encourages diversity and change. The most powerful gods we experience in our everyday lives, the sovereign nation-states of the modern world, function within a transitional international order ideologically fractionated and institutionally precarious. Indeed, the precariousness of international affairs has made governments reticent to espouse irrevocable moral positions or to encourage the formation of overweening interest groups whose support today may become burdensome tomorrow. Particularly in the democratic world where public policy and public opinion are so closely linked, it has been in the interest of states to promote a climate of tolerance for diversity within broad limitations. This has redounded for the most part to the benefit of religious experimentation. As long as world affairs remain in their present transitional condition, there is no reason to suspect that religious movements and counter-movements will cease to be born.

Yet, it would be rash to conclude that the current unsettledness in world order and in religion is somehow an undesirable situation to be gotten through as quickly as possible. In the past, tightly consolidated world orders have been constructed only at a tremendous cost in human freedom and social resources. And when economic and political contingencies have gone beyond a certain point, the prevailing system of world order has itself given way to the challenges of new forces and new worldviews, as the failures of Spain, the Netherlands, and England have born witness. What is perhaps more viable in the long run than a tightly consolidated framework of world order is a loose confederation of local, national, and regional interests that can respond with flexibility to changing global conditions. Religious pluralism, diversity, and toleration could contribute much to the strength and adaptability of such a confederation.

REFERENCES

1. Robert Wuthnow. *Experimentation in American Religion: New Mysticisms and Their Implications for the Churches.* University of California Press, 1978.

2. Robert Wuthnow. "The New Religions in Social Context." In *The New Religious Consciousness*, pp. 267–293. Edited by Charles Y. Glock and Robert N. Bellah. University of California Press, 1976.

3. Robert Wuthnow. "A Religious Marketplace." *Journal of Current Social Issues* 14 (1977):38–42.

4. Peter L. Berger. *The Sacred Canopy.* Doubleday, 1967.

5. Julian Amery. *The Life of Joseph Chamberlain*, V, 221. St. Martin's, 1969.

6. E. J. Hobsbawm. *Industry and Empire.* Penguin, 1969.

7. Karl Polanyi. *The Great Transformation.* Beacon, 1944.

8. David P. Galleo and Benjamin M. Rowland. *America and the World Political Economy: Atlantic Dreams and National Realities.* Indiana University Press, 1973.

9. Fred L. Block. *The Origins of International Economic Disorder: A Study of United States International Monetary Policy from World War II to the Present.* University of California Press, 1977.

10. Immanuel Wallerstein. *The Modern World-System: Capitalist Agriculture and the Origins of the European World-Economy in the Sixteenth Century.* Academic Press, 1964.

11. Charles Wilson. *The Transformation of Europe, 1558–1648.* University of California Press, 1976.

12. Michael Kammen. *Empire and Interest: The American Colonies and the Politics of Mercantilism.* J. B. Lippincott, 1970.

13. Klaus E. Knorr. *British Colonial Theories, 1570–1850.* University of Toronto Press, 1944.

14. Franz Schurmann. *The Logic of World Power: An Inquiry into the Origins, Currents, and Contradictions of World Politics.* Pantheon Books, 1974.

THE EFFECT OF DETENTE ON THE GROWTH OF NEW RELIGIONS: REVEREND MOON AND THE UNIFICATION CHURCH*

Dick Anthony and
Thomas L. Robbins

THE TRADITIONAL "protestant ethic" and its secular counterpart, the Americanized "success ethic," implicitly legitimated small entrepreneurial capitalism. With the increasing domination of the economy by managerial capitalism, the "spirit of capitalism" has undergone a transformation [1]. Significant segments of the population continue, however, to socialize their children according to ascetic precepts intrinsic to the older economic style [2].

Erikson [3] has argued that the religious and ideological consistency of a society is very important for adolescents who are attempting to make sense out of the adult world. Part of the motivation for conversion to new religious movements, then, involves youthful dissatisfaction with the ideological and religious inconsistencies of the larger society. The symbol systems of new movements can fruitfully be viewed as attempts to replace an increasingly incoherent social philosophy with a more coherent one.

We have argued elsewhere [4,5] that Jesus movement groups and neo-Oriental movements represent opposed strategies for making sense out of the moral relativism associated with managerial capitalism. The Unification Church represents an attempt to resacralize the disintegrating moral and political order that differs substantially from either of these two main tendencies in new religious movements. This movement, because of its pronounced political dimension, can be viewed as a sectarian version of the disintegrating "civil religion" [6]. An attempt will be made here to clarify the relationship between American civil religion and the "spirit of capitalism" as it is understood by a self-professed "sacred remnant."

CIVIL RELIGION AND THE PROTESTANT ETHIC

The "spirit of capitalism" [7] incorporated a *dualistic* ethic which was especially pronounced in its American version. Such an ethic radically divided humanity into the saved and the damned in the moral realm, and into successes and failures in the secular realm. Key elements in this perspective included a system of dualistic moral absolutes "legislated" by a transcendent personal God which man could choose to obey or disobey by the use of his faculty of "free will."[1]

Given the process of rationalization—which Weber considered to be the central process linking modern religious and economic development—this ethical system in the United States at least acquired a specifically logical structure of the following form: dualistic morality was expressed in fixed negative injunctions prohibiting specific acts. Such prohibitions, however, had a latent "permissive" dimension. Within Aristotelian logic, all descriptive terms have logical contrast categories and a term and its contrary are assumed to be exhaustive with respect to a designated dimension. Thus, within the American system of dualistic morality, when the negative term was precisely defined, its contrary was assumed to have been exhaustively designated by implication. For instance, if "theft" was precisely and restrictively defined as the negative term within the dimension "property acquisition," other means of acquiring property were assumed to be *good* because they were "not-theft."

This orientation in the United States was used to "implicitly legitimate" *laissez-faire* economic entrepreneurial activity free from moral and governmental regulation. The concept of "equal opportunity" within the "free enterprise" economy provided a secular counterpart of "free will." Within this system of legitimation, as long as participants in entrepreneurial capitalism obeyed limited negative moral absolutes—primarily in the expressive realm—they received moral sanction for engaging in economic activities that resulted in social inequality.

This process of "implicit legitimation" integrates not only the religious and the economic realms, but also the political sphere.

Such a process has heavily influenced popular interpretations of "American civil religion." The United States has been viewed as a country in which equal opportunity is preserved by the structure of our political processes. According to our "myth of origin" [10], the equal opportunity democracy of the United States has been contrasted with eighteenth-century Europe, in which vestiges of feudalism allegedly resulted in political protection of hereditary privilege.

The logic of implicit legitimation argues that scrupulous adherence to moral imperatives will result in worldly success. However, within this framework, virtue results in success *only* in a country in which the political structure preserves equal opportunity and *laissez-faire* economic processes. Europe was viewed as more corrupt than the United States because the governmental protection of hereditary privilege was seen as stacking the cards against virtue.

The invidious comparison of American virtue with European corruption has been an aspect of the external contrast dimension of the civil religion. As such, it is part of the larger theme of God's favored people battling with evil adversaries. This theme is indigenous to Western dualistic religion, that is, to Zoroastrianism, Judaism, Christianity, and Islam. All of these traditions have emphasized their missionary role in forcefully opposing other nations and traditions which allegedly have not accepted God's covenant and which therefore do not obey God's moral rules. It seems likely that the obsession of Western capitalist nations with anti-communism since the 1920s represents in part a defensive amplification of this theme because of the increasing incoherence of the religious legitimation of their political and economic institutions.

The increasing domination of the American economy by corporate and governmental bureaucracies began to rupture the system of implicit legitimation between the religious, economic, and political realms in the early years of the twentieth century. As Daniel Bell [12] has argued, the protestant ethic's contribution to the "spirit of capitalism" has been in decline since that period. The advent of managerial capitalism disrupted religious social legitimation first of all by encouraging the development of a permissive "consumer ethic," which encourages violation of traditional ascetic moral absolutes regarding sex, use of drugs and alcohol, not squandering money, etc. The growth of bureaucracies has also disrupted traditional moral patterns by regulating the vocational realm with complex systems of rules and hierarchical authority relationships. Such controls violate free will and fate-control assumptions which are part of the traditional ethic [13]. Finally, the attempt to preserve equal opportunity in the economic realm through governmental action designed to curb the power of large corporations has created confusion about the role of the state in the American "civil religion."

Within traditional civil religion, the role of the state was largely a passive one. The virtue of good government was thought to be that it refrained from imposing inequitable penalties and privileges upon classes of society. The increasingly prominent role of the state in regulating the economy and in attempting various social welfare and "affirmative action" programs designed to compensate for the inequities of the "market" has created an apparent divergence between the traditional *laissez-faire*-limited-government-protestant-ethic form of the civil religion and contemporary social reality.

Arthur Vidich has noted that American capitalism has actually been insufficiently legitimated since the 1930s: "It was only World War II and the cold war that rescued capitalism from its ideological poverty. The ending of the cold war once again reopens this issue for the capitalist countries and their political systems" [14]. Since the late forties, then, legitimation and moral solidarity has been based in part on the pervasiveness of a highly dualistic and morally absolutist reinterpretation of civil religion, which has been elaborated around the symbolic polarity of democratic God-fearing America versus totalitarian "Godless communism." This "cold war" ideology has recently lost plausibility because of the impact of Vietnam and Watergate, as well as the longer range reality of detente[2] and increasing structural differentiation (which precludes the consolidation of consensual value-orientations for the total society [15]).

The erosion of Manichean[3] cold war absolutism is interrelated with the broader disintegrative process involving the decline of a whole American tradition of *dualistic moral absolutism* outlined above. In his essay in this volume, Wuthnow argues that religious change within nations actually results from shifts in systems of world order, and that the capitalism-communism cold war polarity constituted such a system. The transformation of that system by detente, according to Wuthnow, has motivated the present upsurge of unconventional religiosity. We will argue that young people unusually attached to the cold war version of American civil religion have joined the Unification Church because it supplies a sectarian version of that disintegrating meaning-system.

THE STRUCTURE OF MANICHEAN CIVIL RELIGION

According to Reverend Moon, America has a special role in God's providence and a special spiritual destiny.[4] This is illustrated in the following passage from a lecture at the communal workshop in Barrytown, New York.

During most of history America had not been involved in God's providence. God kept it in reserve. European Christianity went steadily downward. The Pilgrims came to America to serve God. This was parallel to Abraham leaving the security of his business and children to follow God's command and wander. European colonists in North America came to find God, while colonists in South America came to find gold. God is mentioned on American coins, which is true nowhere else. This shows that we view these coins as God's money rather than ours. God is central to our Constitution, which is also very unique. Thus, America is blessed and has accomplished great things. The 200 years of American history is a replay of the 2000 years of Christian history.

However, the Unification Church sees America as currently being in danger of losing her status as God's favored nation.

But today America is retreating. It's not just an accident that great tragedy is constantly striking America and the world, such as the assassination of President Kennedy and the sudden death of Secretary-General Hammerskjold of the United Nations, both in the same decade. The spirit of America has declined since then. Unless this nation, unless the leadership of the nation lives up to the mission ordained by God, many troubles will plague you. God is beginning to leave America. This is God's warning [18].

Reverend Moon and his followers perceive such imminent collapse as resulting from two general tendencies. The first is the abandonment of traditional patterns of moral absolutism (involving a strong emphasis upon impulse control and delay of gratification) in favor of a consumer ethic embodying a qualified moral relativism. The second tendency which Moon followers perceive as inimical to American civil religion is the current abandonment of uncompromising opposition to communism in our foreign policy: American virtue can no longer be legitimated by contrast to the evils of "Godless communism" if we adopt a policy of peaceful coexistence.

Riesman and his collaborators [19] have described the newly emergent bureaucratic middle class as "other-directed." They contend that the small-entrepreneurial emphasis upon invariant moral principles governing impulse control has been replaced by an emphasis upon the tailoring of behavior to fit the shifting nuances of peer-group expectations. Such expectations often involve gratification of impulses in leisure time activities in ways which violate traditional moral absolutism. In the following quotation, one of our subjects describes his view of the emerging relativistic society:

We've grown up in a society where no one knows a concrete plan, no one knows what the absolute standard of good and evil is, no one has the clear answers.

Moon followers perceive the deterioration in traditional moral absolutism as being caused by the permissive child-rearing practices, which have been described by Miller and Swanson [2] as characteristic of bureaucratic middle-class families. A Moon follower comments:

What is the family in America like today? Families have no meaning. And you can see that families don't have any meaning. Children have no respect for their parents because parents aren't showing them the clear way.

Moon followers believe, moreover, that such permissiveness has resulted in an increase in extramarital sex and a rise in divorce rates. Such violations of traditional moral absolutism—and the resulting deterioration in the stability of the family—are believed to be associated with the rise of a consumption ethic, which emphasizes personal satisfaction through leisure time activities rather than through work and the delay of gratification. A follower comments:

We in the United States have relative economic security and welfare, but God may abandon America in a few years unless we reform and create a spiritual revolution. If we can't give up our little things: our privacy, our apartments, our record players, all the big things will go.

This subject's emphasis upon the giving up of possessions, desires, etc., for a larger cause, is one which recurs throughout our interviews with Moon followers. In our view, such an emphasis results from childhood training in "worldly asceticism." Such training seems increasingly irrelevant in a consumer society and, therefore, people who are still affected by it defensively amplify this emphasis in reaction against permissive trends. In doing so, they exaggerate the traditional American concern with frugality and sacrifice. Reverend Moon writes:

The church must find individuals that will sacrifice themselves for their families, sacrifice their families for the American nation, and sacrifice the United States for the world. The ideal that can lead the whole world must come from the spirit of sacrifice for the greater cause. For the benefit of the whole world, one nation must really give herself to pursue the one ideal world [17].

As is the case with the inner-worldly asceticism of the "spirit of capitalism," such sacrifice is meant to be in accord with God's laws. An interviewer asks:

Interviewer: Why is it there's a stress over and over again about the need for absolute values? Why is it important?
Moon Follower: We all have, so to speak, an original mind, you know, stemming from God. We all seek for the same basic desires. So that because we have an original mind, the world can be united to discovering what is the value of God, what is God thinking, you know, what is God's plan for the world? What is God's idea for man? Without man's infinite interpretations, unless we understand what God's ideal for man is, what is in God's heart . . . then we can try to duplicate that.

The subject identifies absolute values with "God's plan for the world," which in turn is identified with "knowing what is in God's heart" without "man's infinite interpretations."

Bellah [10] has argued that American civil religion incorporated Puritan moral values. The Puritans emphasized—as does the Unification Church—moral absolutism based upon divine revelation. However, as Weber [7] noted, the Puritans also emphasized God's absolute inscrutability,[5] and probably would not have sympathized with the claims of the Unification Church to know beyond question God's plan for the development of contemporary history. Nevertheless, the Unification Church has articulated a prominent theme in the anti-communist Manichean form of American civil religion. Within this perspective, an element of God's plan is that America should sacrifice her material resources in order to more efficiently lead the resistance to communism. In a speech given in Washington, D. C., Reverend Moon discussed the origin of the political categories "left" and "right." When Jesus was crucified, two thieves were crucified with him, one on either side of him. The thief on Jesus' left reviled and taunted Jesus, while the thief on his right defended him.

At this moment the seed was sown by the left-hand side thief that the God-denying world would come into being—the communist world today. And the seed for the existence of a God-fearing world was sown by the thief on the right-hand side. The free world is in the position of the right-hand side thief. And America is in the center of the God-fearing free world nations. America has been chosen as the defender of God, whereas communism says to the world, "There is no God" [18].

This quote illustrates the legitimation of American civic virtue *by contrast* with the evils of communism. As such, it represents an explicit articulation in Reverend Moon's formulation of American civil religion of the "legitimation by contrast" dimension of the Manichean civil religion.

Laissez-faire capitalism was "implicitly legitimated" by reference to a system of moral absolutes. However, contrast categories within this system were not definitively identified with any specific set of moral exemplars. Good vs. bad people were provisionally identified according to shifting contingencies, and the ultimate judgment of the final worth of individuals—and nations—was left to God. However, with the rise of the relativistic morality associated with managerial capitalism, the domestic social system no longer provided a plausibility structure for moral absolutism. Consequently, an American populace which wished to hold onto the ideal of moral absolutism, without its substance, tended to erect a simplified system of moral reference which definitively contrasted American virtue with communist evil.

In order to thus define American civic "virtue" wholly *by contrast* with the "corruption" of foreign lands, the identification of America with good and of communism with evil must be unambiguous. Thus, moral absolutism is redefined as an *absolute contrast* between moral exemplars. A member of the Unification Church comments:

Well, in the Bible Jesus said, "I don't come to bring peace on earth, I come to bring a sword." And what that means is that what he is trying to bring us is a sort of *symbolic sword to divide good and evil*. You know, because the whole world is sort of in between. You know, sort of with one foot in the boat and the other foot on the dock. So for God to create an ideal world is for God to completely separate good and evil . . . so that, so that people can, you know, completely see the difference [emphasis ours].

Bellah [10] argues that American civil religion at its best has tempered chauvinistic themes by a willingness to subject America herself to moral scrutiny. Within this enlightened form of the civil religion, the dualistic contrast dimension consists in a comparison of the actual nation with a national ideal. The anti-communist form of the civil religion, however, identified all virtue with the United States and all evil with her competitors. We shall refer to this restructured ethic as "exemplary dualism."

The plausibility of exemplary dualism has declined as a result of detente. The Unification Church has constructed a sectarian version of this orientation which has amplified its basic features. These features are being utilized to motivate commitment to the Unification Church as they were once used to insure uncritical commitment to the nation. Members of the Unification Church use the dualistic framework to reduce the necessity for demonstrating positive features of their movement by their contention that: communism is the exemplar of absolute evil; the Unification Church is the exemplary contrast category for communism; therefore, the Unification Church is singularly and absolutely good. With this technique of identifying their movement as the vaguely formulated antithesis to an unpopular cause, the Unification Church converts the feelings associated with a negative stereotype into positive motives for commitment to their movement.

The Church argues that its version of the civil religion is the natural contrast category for communism because America is currently too corrupted by moral relativism to fulfill that role. If America does not adopt the improved civil religion of the Unification Church, then, communist atheism will triumph and meaning will be erased from the world. A follower comments:

If America doesn't fulfill its role, then it will make it much, much more hard for the whole world to, to unite behind the Divine Principle. If Rome, for instance, if we look at 2000 years ago, if Rome didn't unite with Christianity, Christianity could never have, have spread all over the world to the level that it's at now. You know, so that if America doesn't unite with the Divine Principle, then Divine Principle will find it very hard to spread all over the world and, therefore, if this is the one tool against communism, the world will be overcome, the world will turn communist and God will not have a foothold in the world anymore, and the world will go through terrible suffering.

Thus, God will retain an agent in the world through whom He can accomplish His aims only if America embraces the Unification Church. Church members believe that the power of this argument will cause all good people to convert to their movement soon. When this happens, the Unification Church and international communism are expected to have an apocalyptic "Final Showdown." A follower comments:

It's just that very quietly on campus communism is taking over. And America is still a free country, but it's not going to be for very long if this keeps happening. Because put into practice that's what happens. It just never fails. That's the way it goes with communism. And, well, also our movement is growing quietly in some places, not so quietly in others. The whole thing is that communism is saying, what it's saying is that there is no God and spiritual, that's ridiculous, and the whole bit. *And when it comes right down to it, it is going to come down to a point where either one or the other has to be on top.* Either one or the other has to be the one that everybody says "Hey, this is what is right." And, that is what is meant when it's said "The Final Showdown." It's going to be a question of, well, who wins [emphasis ours].

To the extent that prospective members accept the movement as the exemplary contrast category for communism and believe that communism threatens the fabric of their existence, they will be motivated to support it. The belief, then, that "one or the other has to be on top," suggests a simple formula for accomplishing their millennarian expectations: defeat communism and God's kingdom will be established. With respect to individual salvation, the formula is even simpler: work to convert others to the Unification Church and anomic ambiguity will be reduced. However, these stratagems have a cost.

The traditional civil religion regarded the moral worth of individuals and nations as ambiguous in principle. The moral tension resulting from such ambiguity motivated efforts to change society according to ethical principles. Within the exemplary dualism of the Manichean form of the civil religion, ambiguity becomes undesirable because it moderates the supposedly absolute contrast between concrete exemplars. Therefore, Moon followers tend to regard domestic and civil libertarian themes in the American political tradition as undesirable because they contribute to pluralistic ambiguity. They intend to eliminate them in the ideal America of the future. A follower comments:

We believe ultimately that, that neither communism nor democracy can work, you know, because democracy, the fallacy about democracy is, it says it is not an absolute system, you know, in that different peoples' opinions sort of balance, which is good in a sense, but also not so good if you're thinking about absolute values.

Moon followers also associate America's ambiguous ethical status with the heterogeneity of Christian denominations in America. America's pluralistic Christianity is viewed as inferior to Reverend Moon's new revelation, the "Divine Principle," because it is not monolithic. Its theology, therefore, has been neither uniform nor precise enough to protect America from relativistic corruption. The remedy is for all of America's Christian denominations to unite behind Reverend Moon. A follower comments:

There can't be 500 or 600 different denominations of Christianity because Christianity is collapsing now. There won't be any Christianity in ten years, if the standard of faith and the standard of spirit and Christianity today is kept at that level. So that the only way God can work through Christianity, so that God can, can create His kingdom on earth is through this absolute standard [the "Divine Principle" of Reverend Moon] so that the whole world can unite behind it.

We argued earlier that the key premises motivating commitment to the Unification Church are: (1) communism is a mortal threat to the fabric of personal and social existence in the non-communist world; (2) the Unification Church is the divinely designated (in that sense absolute) contrast category for communism. As we have seen, the Church would sacrifice religious and political diversity in its reformulated civil religion. The resulting religious and political uniformity—so the argument goes—would make the contrast between the Christian and communist worlds less ambiguous or more "absolute." (In other respects, of course, such sacrifice of democratic institutions would make the United States more similar to totalitarian regimes.)

The attempt of the Unification Church to shore up exemplary dualism by opposing pluralism has been practical as well as theoretical. A key element in Reverend Moon's plan to establish a more dualistic social order was his "God loves Nixon" campaign to save Nixon from impeachment.[6] Nixon was supported because he was "strong in his thinking in many ways, so that if he could have united with Reverend Moon he could have become a great leader" [interview excerpt].

Part of Nixon's "strength" was his perceived willingness to abandon civil libertarian principles to defend his view of the absolute good. A follower comments:

He [Nixon] is getting involved in all of these underhanded practices and we have no privacy and people are bugging the telephones and stuff like that. Yeah, but if that in the end leads to something even better then it's O.K.

On the face of it, it appears paradoxical that a movement dedicated to the resurrection of moral absolutism should advocate the use of political techniques which appear to contradict traditional civil morality. However, the Unification Church does not appear to define absolute values as universal moral principles. The Church, rather, considers moral absolutism to be a divinely inspired evaluative interpretation of history. As one follower said:

Sometimes when you follow absolute truth it's kind of a means to an end thing, where it might look kind of funny in the beginning, but if you can step back and see how it's put together, that's the difference between what we call taking God's point of view, an overall view of things, and taking a limited [human] view. . . . Again, the means to the end sort of thing.

Values, thus, are defined largely in terms of their historical exemplars and they are absolute in the sense that absolute certainty exists about the choice of examples. A follower comments:

It's very unusual to see that you have the truth, because no one has had anything as clear as Divine Principle throughout history, so that if you believe you have something that is universally true, which is universal cosmic truth, then it doesn't make sense to say, "well, you know, maybe this is wrong."

From this perspective, the United States, as God's principal agent in the world, may legitimately use force to suppress opposition. Members of the Unification Church affirm Reverend Moon's efforts to prop up United States anti-communist dictatorships in South Korea and Nationalist China. In commenting upon such efforts a member stated:

If you got the most authoritarian, totalitarian person, even President Park or Chiang Kai-shek, and if the people aren't being oppressed, if they've got enough food and they've got enough clothing and if they really care about each other, then you can't say anything about it.

As with their attempt to minimize domestic political dissent by supporting Nixon, Unification Church members believe that international actions may legitimately violate common assumptions of civil morality. Indeed, such actions may be a higher expression of absolute morality because they are derived from Reverend Moon's "divine revelation." The Unification Church supported United States involvement in the war in Vietnam on the grounds that this war was absolutely necessary for "God's plan." A subject comments:

War is sometimes necessary, you know, the principle of the family should sacrifice for the nation and the nation should sacrifice for the world . . . if by this war [in Vietnam], which was absolutely necessary for the plan that God has, that maybe, oh, say that 10,000 people would be killed so that eventually we can have peace and we can set up the right kind of government, the right kind of world, it's better that that should happen.

Dissent from the aims of the Unification Church should, therefore, be overcome by force both domestically and internationally when this is considered necessary to further God's will. Reverend Moon and the Unification Church make "infallible" political recommendations because Reverend Moon is God's preeminent prophet and God is speaking through him.[7] His primary prophetic duty is to stamp out atheistic communism and to lead the United States to the institution of a worldwide benevolent theocracy.

CONCLUSION

According to Eliade, religions establish and support values by formulating cosmologies which structure space and time. Such cosmologies can be understood on a primarily symbolic level, but they also tend to be interpreted in mundane terms. At the mundane level, the cosmological structuring of space and time influences a culture's attitudes toward territory and toward history.[8] Eliade has written that "every sacred space implies a hierophany, an irruption of the sacred that results in detaching a territory from the surrounding cosmic milieu and making it qualitatively different" [22]. The conquering and cultivation of territory repeats "the act of the gods who had organized chaos by giving it a structure, form and norms." The contrast between citizen and foreigner then becomes representative of the contrast between good and evil within the structure of norms. Good people are citizens because they obey the norms of the culture and foreigners are evil because they don't.

Dualistic religions, e.g., Zoroastrianism, Judaism, Christianity, and Islam, tend to affirm the contrast between concrete exemplars of good and evil as a metaphysical principle. The contrast between the citizen and the foreigner is replicated in a world beyond the world (which is entered after death), where good people reside eternally in a heavenly territory and bad people in a hell.

The attitude towards space in the Western religions, which Eliade refers to as a "geometric" one, tends to be associated with absolute conceptions of morality. The contrasts effected by morality are given an ultimate status by their literal location in sacred as well as mundane space. Eastern religions, on the other hand, tend to interpret their own conceptualizations of space as symbolic. According to Eliade, "all the oriental civilizations— Mesopotamia, India, China, etc.—recognized an unlimited number of 'Centers' " [23]. This relativistic conception of space is duplicated in their attitudes towards morality and towards salvation. Normative conceptions are binding only in the mundane world and do not have ultimate metaphysical significance. Salvation, then, does not apply only to members of the civilizations structured by "monistic" myths, but is awarded ultimately to foreigners as well.

As with space, Western religions give ultimate status to time. Time is irreversible in Western religion, and history involves a theophany that is a manifestation of a deity in the world [24]. The moral contrasts established in the sacred geography are amplified in time as God's people battle unrepentant foreigners. In the West, history is a morality play in which salvation depends upon one's contribution to the battle. God ultimately rewards virtue, and a "good" people will inevitably triumph. (In Eastern religions, on the other hand, time is cyclic and salvation is ultimately afforded everyone.)

Christianity, moreover, represents the most extreme of the Western religions in the degree of its dualistic conception of history. The conception of Christ as a manifestation of God in human form amounts to an extreme or "absolute" identification of the deity with the creation. In this respect, Christianity may appear to be "an innovation in relation to all previous religious life" [25]. (In Eastern religions, the God-man appears in history as an Avatar, whose appearance is recurrent and thus cannot be used to reify particular normative orders.)

Because in Christianity history is literal and unidirectional, it must have a goal. The goal of Christian history is the end of history, when Christ will return, virtue shall triumph, and the Kingdom of Heaven shall reign on the earth. At that point, the sacred geography shall be abolished, all men on the earth shall be citizens in God's Kingdom, and the normative order will be adhered to without a sense of strain.

The cosmologies of Western religions, most particularly Christianity, have obvious implications for the development of ethnocentrism and for tendencies toward imperialistic expansion. However, according to Eliade, such tendencies involve a heresy, the idolotrous identification of symbols of ultimacy with the ultimate itself. Such misinterpretations result because "in certain cases the psyche may fixate an image on one single frame of reference—that of the 'concrete'; but this is already a proof of psychic disequilibrium. . . . The history of religion . . . abounds in unilateral and therefore aberrant interpretations of symbols" [26].

The replication of dualistic contrasts in metaphysical, theodical, and eschatological structures makes Christianity (and Western religions generally) prone to ethnocentric and chauvinistic idolatries. Nevertheless, "although Biblical and Christian symbolism is charged with a historical and—in the last analysis—a 'provincial' content (since every local history is provincial in relation to universal history conceived in its totality), it remains nevertheless universal like every coherent symbolism" [25].

Dualistic themes in Christianity, properly understood, focus the religious consciousness with great intensity upon the historical moment. However, such a focus is not inherently ethnocentric because:

The mystical experience of the 'primitives' as well as the mystical life of Christians expresses itself through this same archetype—the re-entry into the original Paradise . . . it is not any temporal moment that opens out into eternity, but only the 'favorable moment,' the instant that is transfigured by a revelation . . . it is not for its own sake that an event is valued, but only for the sake of the revelation it embodies . . . the Christian is led to approach every historical event with 'fear and trembling,' since for him even the most commonplace event . . . may have a trans-historical meaning. . . . And yet it must not be lost sight of, that Christianity entered into History in order to abolish it; the greatest hope of the Christian is the second coming of Christ, which is to put an end to all History. From a certain point of view, for every Christian individually, this end, and the eternity to follow it—the paradise regained—may be attained from this moment. The time to come announced by Christ is already accessible, and for him who has regained it history ceases to be [25].

Within this symbolic understanding of Christianity, moral action is necessary for salvation, but virtue and salvation are not definitively identified with a particular interpretation of history. "Judaeo-Christianity does not [properly] lead to historicism . . . [because] it is not for its own sake that an event is valued, but only for the sake of the revelation it embodies—a revelation that precedes it. Historicism as such is a product of the decomposition of Christianity" [25].

We would argue that the Manichean version of American civil religion embodies such a mistaken "historicist" interpretation of Christianity. Within this perspective, eschatological themes in Christianity are "univocally" identified with the historical destiny of the United States. This tendency was intensified by the process of rationalization intrinsic to modernization [16], in that rationalization, by definition, involves the imposition of univocal meanings upon multivocal symbolic structures. Bellah [10] has characterized the spirit of capitalism's identification of material consequences with virtue as "utilitarian individualism." Such materialistic idolatry may be the domestic face of the univocal rationalization of Christian themes, while ethnocentrism and chauvinism compose the international face. The erosion of the plausibility of moral and cognitive absolutisms under managerial capitalism appears to have intensified the need for a polarized foreign policy, which could compensate for the diminished plausibility of internal dualistic themes.

Eliade has argued [27] that a myth may be corrupted or "infantalized" when it is "taken in a childish way, over concretely and apart from the system it belongs to. . . . For the moment, let us simply note the fact of the coexistence in . . . developed societies of a coherent symbolism alongside an infantalized one." Thus, the ethnocentric and chauvinistic tendencies represented by the Manichean civil religion have coexisted with multivocal interpretations of Christianity throughout its history. However, we may be reaching a stage in world history where the univocal reading of Christian attitudes toward history is inherently unfeasible. Such a univocal reading requires the existence of a plausible opponent, an enemy, which can be regarded as the exemplar of evil.

If detente becomes an accomplished reality, the United States will no longer be part of a complementary opposition which can operationalize such meanings. From this perspective, the failure to win the war in Vietnam placed a significant strain upon the tradition of dualistic absolutism because it tended to force a choice between these interpretations: (1) the United States did not win the war because it is an embodiment of evil and God was on the other side; (2) the literal absolutist interpretation of Christian dualistic themes is incorrect.

The widespread acceptance of the latter interpretation probably contributed to the explosion of interest in multivocal mystical forms of religion in the latter 1960s. The growth of relativistic themes in physics, modern art, social science, and—associated with—managerial capitalism had previously eroded the domestic infrastructure for this meaning system. The American defeat in Vietnam and the increasing reality of detente battered the superstructure. American youth increasingly were forced to abandon literal objectivist religion, and they consequently sought meaning in tolerant experiential religiosity.

However, the ambiguity of multivocal symbolic orientations may be experienced as inherently undesirable by some people. Members of the Moon movement converted in conscious reaction against relativistic trends expressed in mystical movements [4]. Frenkel-Brunswick [28] found that intolerance for ambiguity was associated with ethnocentrism. It appears that the reification of metaphysical polarities as ideological oppositions, which is found in the Moon movement, satisfies such a need for clarity in its members.

NOTES

* The research upon which this essay was based was supported by the United States Public Health Service, Grant No. 5-RO1-DA00407-05. The authors thank Robert Bellah for reading and criticizing an earlier version of this paper.

[1] Weber emphasized the role of the doctrine of predestination, as expressed in the Reform Protestant tradition and most especially in the English and American Puritan traditions, in preparing the way for capitalism. However, in the United States, the emphasis upon visible manifestations of election to Heaven or Hell had evolved into an Arminian position emphasizing free will by the time of the nineteenth century heyday of the spirit of capitalism [8]. The contrasting doctrines of predestination and free will have enjoyed alternating ascendency throughout Christian history, although Campbell [9] considers free will to be the more fundamental doctrine in dualistic religions.

2 An American consensus on the long-term significance of detente has hardly been reached. However, the emerging "anti-Sovietism" of the late 1970s differs sharply from the Manichean anti-communism of the 1950s. The latter was preoccupied with the "communist conspiracy" as an almost metaphysical category. The "conspiracy" was seen as an embodiment of evil that transcended the nationalistic policies of the communist-bloc states. Negotiation or compromise, therefore, was impossible. Indeed, McCarthyites, like members of the Unification Church, often seemed more concerned with internal purification, than with international relations. The decline and consequent "sectarianization" of Manichean anti-communism is the context for the growth of the Unification Church and current, militant, right-wing fundamentalism in general.

3 Manicheanism is the name of a syncretic middle-eastern religion founded by Mani in the third century A.D. [11]. It incorporated elements of Gnosticism, Christianity, Buddhism, and Zoroastrianism. The term is used generally to refer to the notion that absolute good and absolute evil are battling for the future of the creation. Within Christianity, Manicheanism is considered a heresy, although Weber [16] has argued that it is a recurrent theme in all the ethically dualistic religions.

4 In Reverend Moon's vision, America is not the "New Israel" in the strict biblical sense. According to *Divine Principle*, Korea has replaced Israel as the "land of the Messiah." America, however, is given a special providential role leading the free world against satanic communism in numerous speeches by Reverend Moon in America. This theme is not highlighted in *Divine Principle*, which does, however, depict an apocalyptic struggle between atheist-totalitarian "Cain-type democracies" (communist nations) and God-fearing "Abel-type democracies" epitomized by the United States and Great Britain [17]. In Reverend Moon's September 18, 1974, address in Madison Square Garden, he argued that Jesus originally intended to utilize the economic and political might of the Roman Empire to establish the Kingdom of Heaven in the world (John the Baptist failed to lend his anticipated support and so Jesus failed and was crucified). The implication seems to be that America is really the New Rome providentially designed to provide the material strength to exalt the new messiah and establish the new kingdom.

5 Weber [7] focused upon the Puritan's doubt and anxiety concerning God's judgment as a key element in the development of the "spirit of capitalism."

6 See Wills [20] for an interpretation of Reverend Moon's support of Nixon as straightforward celebratory success worship. According to Wills, Moon's real attitude toward Nixon was "Isn't he powerful? He leads the world's greatest empire. What further sign do we need of the heavenly favor?"

7 At gatherings of disciples, Reverend Moon is capable of making his Messianic status quite explicit (e.g., referring to his wife as "the bride of Christ" and plotting out how all contemporary history is centered on him). Such references are avoided in public meetings and speaking engagements and in street level proselytization, presumably to avoid alienating other religious leaders and political figures who have given Reverend Moon's mission qualified support. It is worth noting in this connection that the Christology of the Unification Church identified both Jesus Christ, the original Messiah, and the second Messiah, or "Lord of the Second Advent" as perfect men used by God to lead mankind to redemption. Trinitarian doctrines are rejected. The first Messiah, Jesus Christ, was betrayed by John the Baptist, and hence was not accepted by

the people of Israel and could not establish the Kingdom of Heaven on Earth, which awaits the Lord of the Second Advent.

[8] George Baker [21] has suggested that conceptions of history differ in Western and Eastern religions, and that these differences are important for understanding the recent appeal of Eastern religions in the West.

REFERENCES

1. Alan Winter. *Continuities in the Sociology of Religion.* Harper & Row, 1977.

2. David R. Miller and Guy E. Swanson. *The Changing American Parent.* John Wiley, 1958.

3. Erik H. Erikson. *Identity, Youth, and Crisis.* W. W. Norton, 1968.

4. Dick Anthony and Thomas L. Robbins. "Youth Culture Religious Movements and the Confusion of Moral Meanings." In preparation, 1976.

5. Dick Anthony and Thomas L. Robbins. "A Typology of Nontraditional Religious Movements in Modern America." *Journal of Social Issues,* in press.

6. Thomas Robbins, Dick Anthony, Madalyn Doucas, and Thomas Curtis. "The Last Civil Religion: The Unification Church of Reverend Sun Myung Moon." *Sociological Analysis* 37 (1976):111–125.

7. Max Weber. *The Protestant Ethic and the Spirit of Capitalism.* Scribner ed., 1958.

8. Sydney E. Ahlstrom. *A Religious History of the American People.* Doubleday, 1975.

9. Joseph Campbell. *The Masks of God: Occidental Mythology.* Penguin, 1964.

10. Robert N. Bellah. *The Broken Covenant.* Seabury Press, 1975.

11. Jerald C. Brauer. *The Westminster Dictionary of Church History,* p. 522. Westminster Press, 1971.

12. Daniel Bell. *The Cultural Contradictions of Capitalism.* Basic Books, 1976.

13. C. Wright Mills. *White Collar.* Oxford, 1950.

14. Arthur Vidich. "Social Conflict in an Era of Detente." *Social Research* 42 (1975):64–87.

15. Richard Fenn. "Towards a New Sociology of Religion." *Journal for the Scientific Study of Religion* 11 (1972):16–32.

16. Max Weber. *The Sociology of Religion.* Beacon ed., 1964.

17. Reverend Moon. *Divine Principle,* pp. 458–530. Holy Spirit Association for the Unification of World Christianity (HSA-UWC), 4 West 43rd St., New York, N.Y. 10036, 1973.

18. Reverend Moon. *Christianity in Crisis: New Hope,* pp. 61–62. HSW-UWC, 1974.

19. David Riesman et al. *The Lonely Crowd: A Study of the Changing American Character.* Yale University Press, 1950.

20. Gary Wills. "Piety in the Bunker." *Harpers,* October 1974, pp. 18–26.

21. George Baker. "Silence in Japanese Policy Toward Korea." *Journal of East and West Studies* (Seoul) 7 (1978):39–62.

22. Mircea Eliade. *The Sacred and the Profane,* p. 26. Harcourt, 1959.

23. Mircea Eliade. *Myths, Rites, Symbols: A Mircea Eliade Reader*, II, 370. Edited by Wendell C. Beane and William G. Doty. Harper & Row, 1975.

24. Mircea Eliade. *The Myth of the Eternal Return*, p. 102. Princeton University Press, 1954.

25. Mircea Eliade. *Myths, Rites, Symbols: A Mircea Eliade Reader*, I, 74–77. Edited by Wendell C. Beane and William G. Doty, Harper & Row, 1975.

26. Ibid., p. 91.

27. Ibid., p. 112.

28. T. W. Adorno, Else Frenkel-Brunswick, Daniel J. Levinson, and R. Nevitt Sanford. *The Authoritarian Personality*, pp. 479–486. Harper & Row, 1950.

THE INTERPENETRATION OF NEW RELIGION AND RELIGIOUS STUDIES

Walter H. Capps

STEPHEN TOULMIN once wrote that "men demonstrate their rationality not by ordering their concepts and beliefs in tidy formal structures, but by their preparedness to respond to novel situations with open minds." The novel situation that faces students and faculties of religious studies programs is the appearance of new religions. Here I wish to ask: How will the study of new religions affect the academic study of religion as a whole?

One sees that religious studies has yet to develop the methodological apparatus to trace, discern, and understand new religion. Until this happens, new religion will be approached as though it were old religion or an updated version of old religion. My thesis is that in this way the significance and force of the new religions will be missed.

One also sees that religious studies itself has contributed to the formation and content of the new subject. New religion has come into being, at least in part, through the process by which religion has been studied in recent years within the academy. The corollary follows: the new creation has profound implications with respect to our understanding of the enterprise we call religious studies.

It is a radical suggestion to make, I believe, for it introduces some ambiguity into operational principles we had understood to be well set. Many of us have been laboring for some time under the assumption that religious studies and religion can be neatly and permanently distinguished. We have taken this as a programmatic fact. We believe religious studies to be thoroughly and unqualified analytical work. Above everything else, we aspired toward accuracy in reporting. We wanted the account to be full and impartial. We worked to avoid serious omissions. We tried to remove all biases from the reporting procedures. The penchant for objectivity regulated both the substance and temper of religious studies.

However, more recent awarenesses conspire to make us wonder if the earlier distinctions can be sustained with such clarity and simplicity. In the first place, a survey of the history of religious studies will show that the new discipline was fostered from the beginning by suppositions that a prevailing religious outlook could support. Religious studies, at least in part, was prompted and sanctioned by specific forms of religious self-consciousness. Faculty and students argued that the enterprise made demonstrable educational sense; but, for many persons, it also made considerable religious sense. The academic interests that initially appeared in religious studies curricula generally were congruent with the personal religious attentiveness of the scholars and teachers responsible for such academic programs. Religious studies faculties of America were staffed largely by persons originally trained in one or another branch of Christian theology, most usually of a Protestant variety. Many of these persons aspired toward a vocation in theology before the new academic possibility became a reality. For many of them (or us), the initial interest in religious studies was cultivated through exposure to theological forms of reflection. That many were able to move from theology to religious studies also suggests that the new enterprise provides a more suitable form of academic vocation for persons with updated religious sensitivities. It has created a profession through which new ideas and insights can be brought into line with on-going, longer-term patterns of personal religious conviction. In this way, religious studies has been a significant carrier of a particular kind of religious development. The fact that religious studies and religion could be neatly distinguished without being in conflict simply indicates that their relationship belonged to, and was supported by, a conceptual framework in which the mode of inquiry prescribed that all overt religious avowals be bracketed or suspended. But the religious quotient was nevertheless there. In the present time it is taking a new form.

It is evident that there are significant methodological shifts associated with the appearance of new religion. Because new religion is in process of formulation, it cannot be penetrated by methodologies trained upon the permanent and static. If permanence is regarded as being normative, the sense of new religion's protean, dynamic character will be missed. In the past, religious studies has been preoccupied with stable factors: essences, norms, rules, laws, patterns, and structures. The worldview of religious studies tends to exclude the phenomena of metamorphosis, transposition, transformation, and transmutation, and even finds borrowings and syncretisms difficult to work with. But new religion—because it includes the phenomena of old traditions in new places, traditions undergoing transformation, as well as the prospect of genuinely new religious possibilities—will force the methodological reconstruction. The very presence of new religion will encourage the older mind-set to disengage. A method trained on "what is the case?" will miss its emergent quality, creative tendency, and fluid malleable form.

There is still another intriguing dimension to this series of observations. The relation of new religion to the ideas and methods by which new religion will be understood is much closer and more direct than the relation stipulated by the traditional academic paradigm of religion and religious studies. The traditional paradigm was designed to make almost any subject accessible, and to treat it in an objective manner. By contrast, the methodologies by which new religion will come to be discerned *must be designed primarily for the purpose of studying new religions.*

It is a very small extension of this thought to consider the possibility that a revised methodology will also play a role in stimulating new religion. Paul Fussel, in *The Great War and Modern Memory* (1975), showed that World War I could not be fought with effectiveness until writers learned how to describe its nature and character. Based on this analogy, it may very well be that new religion cannot come into being until a way is found to talk about it. Finding a way to talk about it will assist its coming to be. The cultivation of a new methodology is symbolic: something is yearning to be born. Looked at from the other side, new religion stands as a sign that the parent methodological paradigm has run its course, and is making a transition to a new way of doing and approaching things. New religion illustrates that religion is being perceived via new interest spectra.

The larger historical note is that the appearance of new religion, stimulated and given content, in part, by religious studies, is a sign that the dominance of the scientific method, based on an Enlightenment mode of understanding, is being seriously and, perhaps, successfully challenged. It was within the framework of that approach that the fundamental operational distinctions could be certified. And yet, as resourceful as the approach was—and is!—it failed adequately to recognize that Enlightenment truth and the truth to which the religious traditions bear witness are not always equivalent.

Religious studies was constructed upon a set of interrelated Enlightenment convictions, which can be readily identified: (1) objects of investigation have essences, which are discrete and unchangeable; (2) religion can be routinely investigated by the scientific method; (3) an agreed-upon sense of "objectivity" makes truth publicly or commonly accessible, regardless of what the subject is; (4) analysis can be separated from attitude; and (5) dispassionateness is a fit mode of scholarly inquiry, most able to make truth accessible. All of these assumptions presume the cardinal one, which is that clarity appears through the process of breaking things down into smaller and smaller pieces, so as to be able to discover the irreducible core. In this way, through a process by which the symbols, beliefs, and ceremonies are to be disassembled, the essence of religion is to be discovered.

The methodological transformations now occurring are challenging the assumption that Enlightenment methods offer the highest yield of truth about religion. They attest that the monopolizing compact between the Enlightenment and religious studies may need to be broken because of the nature of religious studies' subject. The Enlightenment made the subject manageable, but Enlightenment-influenced approaches deal only with religious studies' manageable aspects. It is one thing to exercise intellectual discretion, to deal with those aspects of a subject which are methodologically accessible. But it is something else to suggest—if only by example—that the subject has no additional accessible aspects. This is the impression that has been left. Religion has been translated into religious studies so that a certain kind of mapwork might be invoked. In being translated, the subject has also been pared. Increasingly, we are seeing the ramifications.

The new mood has no interest in removing all canons of objectivity, or in staking its claim against the older methodology in radical, blatant terms. Rather it offers an alternative to the dominance of the detached retrospective posture. It expands the range of methodological possibilities. Instead of believing that all truth can be found, it says that some must be made or won. There is no intent to create *ex nihilo,* however. Rather, it knows that the materials it has to work with can be nuanced in ways that give distinctive configurations. In giving shape, it also brings things into formation. In bringing into formation, it is also lending constitution. In lending constitution, it is also calling into being.

Thus, religious studies has come to the place in its own development when it no longer need restrict itself to studying fundamentally already-happened phenomena. I am not wishing that religious studies would abandon this objective: indeed, I would hope that it might do what it has been doing even more effectively. At the same time, there are other goals and services within its grasp. As with many of the sciences, religious studies is in position to be more constructive and creative with the phenomena it studies. It can lend new formation in seemingly countless ways because of the immense body of materials at its disposal. Simply by putting these materials together in different combinations, it will encourage patterns and formulations which have not surfaced before. Faculty members do this routinely in the way they organize curricula and classes. Students do it with the use to which they put course content, indeed, with the interests through which they select which courses to take. Both faculty and students do it repeatedly in the most common processes of pattern-formation by which they seek to make the results of their intellectual work cohesive.

And one of the products—it is both product and catalyst—is new religion: new religion as conceived within academic programs in religious studies, stimulated, in part, by the objective study of religion.

The transformation of religious studies is still in process. This process, in turn, is part of a larger transformation that is taking place in science and society. Religious studies is moving beyond the dogma of the Enlightenment. Its new place in the academic enterprise cannot yet be forecast, but its new office will appear as the methodological weight of scientific inquiry shifts from the eighteenth century toward the twenty-first. In this way, religious studies may come to offer a view of human life that looks out beyond the gates of our present understanding.

RELIGIOUS STUDIES AS "NEW RELIGION"

Robert N. Bellah

I BELIEVE that every young person arriving at college bears somewhere on his or her soul the questions Jacob Needleman brought to his first philosophy course at Harvard. The experience of higher education will necessarily be, in some form, religious. The question is, then, not *whether* we teach religion, but what kind of religion we teach.

The harder we try to teach about religion, or teach religion as part of "secular" education, the more clearly we will be teaching the reigning orthodoxy. I refer to that orthodoxy carried forward by what Peter Berger calls the "cognitive elite." This elite represents a militant secularism that is particularly visible in the American Civil Liberties Union and its friends. To a considerable extent, the courts are, I am afraid, attempting to make this militant secularism the established religion in the United States.

Though our field has been criticized for being overly concerned with methodology, the need for ever-renewed methodological self-consciousness is constantly felt. Promulgation of a militant secularism still goes under the guise of objectivity among professionals of our field. I received a paper from a member of my National Endowment for the Humanities Residential Seminar which vividly makes the point. The title of this paper is "A Second Fall," and this is the first paragraph:

Somewhere Mircea Eliade speaks of the change from the sacred mode of being to its profane successor, from tradition to modernity, as a second fall. Unlike the fall of the first parents, this fall was historical, not mythical. One might also say that unlike that fall, this one was the beginning, not of religion, but of religious studies.

I would like, then, to turn to some of the basic issues involved in what we do and how we teach. Under this, I would like to develop three rather tendentious rubrics: first, the propagation of religion, which is not what we are supposed to do, but which, I think, we do; second, religious studies as the second fall; and third, religious studies as redemption from the second fall.

By propagating religion, I mean the teaching of religion in a way which is to be differentiated from teaching "about" religion. The teaching "of" religion—that is, teaching which starts from the *a priori* assumption that the material being taught is true— was what we were supposed to avoid in establishing religious studies. Nonetheless, such dogmatic teaching does take place in religious studies. Perhaps it inevitably and rightly should take place. Often the best person to teach a particular tradition is a devoted adherent to that tradition who cannot or will not conceal his or her adherence. Edward Conze, for instance, taught Buddhism dogmatically at Berkeley with marked success. He simply told you what the truth was, and that was that.

But the consequence of this kind of dogmatic teaching has turned out to be quite different from what the Supreme Court or the ACLU might have feared. Far from religious indoctrination, such teaching may actually undermine whatever faith the student has. For at Berkeley when religion is taught dogmatically, as when Edward Conze taught Buddhism, it is only one course among many; a student can learn sixteen other religions right next door. The significance of such teaching is very different from dogmatic teaching in an institution that is wholly and single-mindedly devoted to the teaching of one and only one faith.

But something approaching the latter can perhaps be observed in some Jewish Studies programs. There is considerable ambivalence on the part of those teaching Jewish Studies toward religious studies. The heavy requirements, linguistic and otherwise, of majoring in Jewish Studies make it very difficult for the students in such a program, who are often almost all Jewish, to do much else.

Such intensity and immersion in a religious tradition gives me no cause for worry. There may be political and legal problems in the long run, though they would probably be more likely to emerge if we taught Christianity that way. Such an immersion method is most useful in teaching a tradition as an organic unit. Unfortunately, most of our students have only the vaguest sense

of what a tradition is. For them to really begin to understand
what a tradition is—how it is formed, how it operates, the enormous density of a tradition—requires that it be taught to them.
What it means to take certain things as normative and apply
them over the centuries, which is precisely what a tradition does,
is something which would be of great value for our students to
learn. Exposure to this sort of teaching might well be the only
way in which they could learn it.

The necessity to teach a specific tradition reflects a basic assumption of religious studies: man is an inveterately traditional
animal. All efforts to undercut and deny tradition have resulted
only in a formation of semi-surreptitious new traditions. Indeed,
when each of us defines who he is, he does so by citing or
alluding to certain authorities. This involuntary intellectual
genuflection happens in spite of our notion of individuality, of
being free from authority and pursuing truth without presuppositions. For even in being free from authority, we indicate those
authorities who have helped us become free of authority. It is
therefore as impossible to be wholly untraditional as it is to be
wholly unreligious.

What we have currently in religious studies is mainly an education that does not teach a tradition, but an education that
teaches a vast cacophony of traditions. Perhaps we have not yet
adequately helped students understand the nature, necessity,
and modus operandi of tradition. Yet that is one of our primary
tasks.

I want next to talk about religious studies as a part of the
second fall. The critical approach to religion is often understood
as the forté of religious studies. This is the essence of teaching
"about" religion. The assumption here is that if one is teaching
religion "objectively" and "scientifically" then one is teaching
religion from a non-religious, i.e., secular, perspective. But this
"objectivity" turns out to be illusory. If one believes that the
critical theories with which one explains religion are truer than
the religious beliefs themselves, then one is opting for an ultimate stance which is at least quasi-religious. In this sense, what
is really being taught in religious studies is often positivism or
relativism or historicism. These are powerful modern ideologies
with spiritual, ethical, and political implications. They may accord so closely with the majority ethos, or, if not the majority

ethos, the influential ethos of the cognitive elite, what I have called "enlightenment fundamentalism," that they seem to be simply true rather than only one possible position among others. In the guise of teaching "about" religion, very powerful beliefs, even dogmas, are being conveyed.

I certainly do not denounce the scientific study of religion. I accept, utilize, and teach a great deal of what comes from the critical approach to religion. I cannot, however, affirm the ultimacy of social science as a framework in which knowledge and values are to be sought. Of course there are human factors which help us understand, and even to an extent, to explain, religious phenomena. The notion that there are pure spiritual expressions which exist wholly aside from questions of power, economics, class interest, etc., is absurd. If we have not learned that lesson from what Paul Ricoeur calls the "masters of suspicion," then we certainly are not educated adequately in our own field. But while I would be the last to deny the validity, power, and importance of the critical theories of religion, I cannot finally accept what I think is their reductionism, and their covert replacement of religion by other quasi-religious dogmas.

The assumption that the critical understanding of religion is somehow higher, or more in accordance with truth, than the benighted views of religious people whom we are studying leads to a kind of "museumification" of religion. Religion, then, is understood as a series of exhibits, butterflies pinned to the wall, which we study, compare, analyze, and explain. If education is formation of a total human being, this process of museumification says something very significant. It suggests that religions are "belief-systems" that can be exhibited side by side and described as "true in the minds of believers." The result may be the same as when a number of religions are taught as true side-by-side. These are both ways of making specimens out of religion, and both contribute to the spiritual confusion and chaos of our day.

Whether confusion in the minds of the students is to be wholly pinned on the professors is dubious. The capacity of students to be confused in quite original ways is very great. Yet, I cannot help but wonder if in subtle, mediated, refracted ways, the confusion in the minds of the professors is not an important part of the story. Perhaps even our unacknowledged confusion concerning what we really think religion is and how we stand toward it should be of great concern in this regard. We can see, then, another way in which the study of religion can be the source of what my NEH Seminar member calls "the Second Fall," however valid many of the problems are.

I would, then, like to turn very tentatively to a consideration of whether, if at all, religious studies might contribute to some way out of the second fall, though, admittedly, this is not the only contribution to be made. Perhaps this contribution is to be found in a third possibility in religious studies, distinguishable from both dogmatic and positivistic points of view. This possibility accepts the critical enterprise, but does not assume that its truths are ontologically superior to those of the religious materials being studied. Indeed, critical theories are seen only as ancillary to interpreting what is there, letting the symbols speak. All that is taught about religion is seen as valuable only in so far as it helps us to teach religion. This is to be understood in the same sense as that in which a good teacher of literature teaches literature, not about literature. All analogies are dangerous, and I certainly think that that one is; but I also think that, if used cautiously, it is an illuminating one.

This third possibility I will call the symbolic. The symbolic approach holds that religious truth is ultimately symbolic and not conceptual in form. In this, it differs from some dogmatic approaches in accepting critical approaches and in being pluralistic instead of exclusivistic. I think it is not relativistic, though that is another problem. It avoids the pitfall of those who remain devoted exclusively to the critical approach by moving beyond concepts to the interpretation of symbols.

I am aware that this third way of dealing with religion can, and most often does, simply compound the confusion which I see arising from the first and second ways. Nonetheless, it is a serious attempt to cope with the religious meaning of a world which is indelibly pluralistic, while denying neither religious nor critical truths. It is a step toward acknowledging the legitimacy of different traditional views of truth concerning human existence. It is also a ground for interaction between traditions. Any student of Asian religions knows how profoundly the major traditions there have been influenced by the fact that they live in a world with other traditions. To cope significantly with religious pluralism, as an intellectual and religious fact, is something which I think some people in religious studies are trying to do.

Over the last twenty years a major shift has occurred among religious intellectuals, at least in the United States. Twenty years ago, they would have been found overwhelmingly in the seminaries, and today they are much more likely to be found in departments of religious studies or in those seminaries which are really graduate departments of religious studies. This is a fact which is of great significance in the long run. It indicates that the religious intellectuals are, perhaps to a greater extent than ever before in American history, cut off from large religious bodies which, theoretically, represent the majority of the religious population. But that is another problem with its own set of sociological considerations.

Walter Capps has pointed to the great importance of two figures, Tillich and Eliade, who, to my mind, represent this third approach to the study of religion. I would today add Paul Ricoeur. These are thinkers who are clearly not traditional church theologians. The ambivalence of the community toward Paul Tillich is well known. Tillich was always making reference to the boundary situation. He was certainly always on the boundary, and was never a church theologian in the typical sense. This is obvious also about Eliade and Ricoeur. Yet, it seems that much of the most important thinking about religion has been coming from these figures, and from those deeply influenced by them.

I will here simply point to the schema of Paul Ricoeur's which lies behind my own tripartite formulations. Ricoeur speaks of a primary naiveté, when the religious symbols are simply taken as given, without critical reflection. This is followed by criticism, which is his word for that whole vast rise of modern scholarship which calls into question all assumptions, particularly in the area of religion. Marx, Nietzsche, and Freud are the main figures in this criticism of culture and particularly of religion. They are known as the great "masters of suspicion," and what they stand for is representative of this critical stance. Ricoeur then tentatively suggests the possibility of a second naiveté. This is not a denial of criticism, but, as Ricoeur says, occurs in and through criticism: a return to the possibility that the symbols might speak again, that the inexhaustible depth of meaning in the symbols can, in a new way, help provide some form of direction for us. Here, to slightly extend a Ricoeurian formula, one might say that experience gives rise to the symbol, and the symbol gives rise to thought.

To see the relation between the symbolic, as a kind of primary form in which religion comes to us, and reason, I think I can turn to a passage from Whitehead: "It is the task of reason to understand and purge the symbols on which humanity depends." A very suggestive sentence, but also full of deep problems. What are the criteria for purging? Jonathan Z. Smith has suggested that some kind of criteria are inevitably involved in our study. But here I want to emphasize the dialectic between the symbols and the critical intellect. To me, the second naiveté is in no sense a simple basking in the light of the symbols, but it involves a critical dialogue, reflection, in the deep philosophical sense of that word, on the symbols which can be the sources of terror and destructiveness as well as of light and hope. The important point is that the symbols themselves are not created by reason. I think the primary symbols arise from the immediacy of experience, in very complicated ways. They are discovered, perhaps revealed. They are *not* invented. Yet, not to use our reason to reflect, criticize, and even on occasion to purge, seems to me to miss the important critical side of the process.

If the thrust of the most seminal thinkers in the field of religious studies—thinkers like Tillich, Eliade, and Ricoeur—is neither dogmatic nor positivist but some new thing, can we say that religious studies itself is, in a sense, "new religion"?

THE IMPACT OF THE NEW RELIGIONS ON PSYCHOLOGY
Daniel Goleman

IN 1969 Ram Dass lectured at Harvard's Department of Psychology and Social Relations, where I was studying clinical psychology. Ram Dass had just come back from India where he had adopted the garb, lifestyle, practices, and name of a yogi. He sat on a table in lotus position, while he told the story of why he was no longer Richard Alpert, the psychologist, but was now Ram Dass, the yogi. The audience was spellbound; the evening began at 7 p.m. and ended at 2 a.m. The next day during lunch, one of my professors on the clinical staff asked me about Ram Dass's talk. I described Ram Dass and recounted the meeting. After hearing me out, he leaned toward me and asked in a confidential tone, "Just between you and me, is he psychotic?"

A WESTERN VIEW

Psychology, in a certain sense, is a secular religion: It has its own belief system, its own practices, its own rituals. Psychologists do not speak of "heresy"; they talk about "pathology." My professor's question came from this set of beliefs. Many of his clinical colleagues share his concern: Is mysticism madness?

This concern epitomizes what is occurring in the history of psychology *vis-à-vis* the "new religions." By the term "new religions," I am not referring to the new religiosity, such as the Charismatics, or the brand-new religions, like the Unification Church. Rather, I refer to old religions, notably Buddhism, Islam, and Hinduism, in new places. At the core of each of the old religions is a psychology. In Islam, one finds Sufism; in Buddhism, Abhidhamma; in Hinduism, many schools of psychology; and in Judaism, Kabbalah.

113

These psychologies are relatively little known at the moment in Western psychology, but there is a fast-growing awareness of them. In our ethnocentrism, we psychologists had assumed that "psychology" refers to something that began a hundred years ago in America and Europe. Suddenly psychologists are confronted with a set of living, non-Western psychologies, some of which have survived for more than fifteen hundred years.

Whenever a new paradigm enters a discipline, some adherents of the dominant school try to discredit it. And that indeed has been the initial reaction of many modern psychologists to these old psychologies. William James talked about this attitude in his own day. James's father was a follower of Swedenborg, the Swedish mystic, and James was keenly interested in spiritual matters. In his *Varieties of Religious Experience*, James [1] says:

We are surely all familiar in a general way with this method of discrediting states of mind for which we have antipathy. . . . Medical materialism seems indeed a good appellation for the too simple-minded system of thought which we are considering. Medical materialism finishes up Saint Paul by calling his vision on the road to Damascus a discharging lesion of the occipital cortex, he being an epileptic. It snuffs out Saint Teresa as an hysteric, Saint Francis of Assisi as an hereditary degenerate. George Fox's discontent with the shams of his age, and his pining for spiritual veracity, it treats as a symptom of disordered colon.

Romaine Rolland, the French poet and Nobel laureate, while in India as a student of the Sri Ramakrishna, wrote to Freud of having experienced a feeling of something limitless and unbounded. This experience Rolland saw as the physiological basis of much of the wisdom of mysticism. Freud commented that he had searched within himself, but failed to find any trace of such a feeling. He thought that

the idea of men's receiving an intimation of their connection with the world around them through an immediate feeling . . . sounds so strange and fits in so badly with the fabric of our psychology that one is justified in attempting to discover a psychoanalytic . . . explanation of such a feeling [2].

This, of course, is exactly what he went on to do, setting an example for his followers. For instance, in 1931, Franz Alexander, an eminent psychoanalyst, wrote an essay which was entitled, "Buddhistic Training as an Artificial Catatonia." The attitude embodied in the question "Is he psychotic?" is a hallowed tradition in modern psychology as it eyes the old psychologies.

Jung was a little more open, but he also had his hesitations. He said in his essay, "Yoga and the West," that the Europeans who study yoga could learn much from it, but he warned that one should not try to apply it, "for we Europeans are not so constituted that we apply these methods correctly, just like that" [3]. Jung offered a suggestion:

Instead of learning the spiritual techniques of the East by heart and imitating them in a Christian way, with the correspondingly forced attitude, it would be far more to the point to find out whether there exists in the unconscious an introverted tendency similar to that which has been developed in spiritual principles for the East. We should then be in a position to build on our own ground with our own methods [4].

Jung was more open than Freud, but even so, he spoke with the voice of someone whose paradigm was threatened by these ancient psychologies.

AN EASTERN VIEW

We can also stand in the other position and look from the East to the West. How does Western psychology appear from the point of view of an Eastern psychology? The Tibetan Wheel of Life, for example, lets us view Western psychology with an Eastern eye. The Wheel depicts realms of existence which are metaphors for different states of mind. In the Buddhist view, people experience these realms from moment to moment as their mental states shift. The realms are also metaphors for different planes of being—they have both a cosmological and a psychological significance.

The realms that the Tibetan Wheel of Life depict correspond roughly to the major branches of Western psychology. Psychologically speaking, what is called the "Realm of the Stupid Beasts" is the level at which we all act with conditioned responses. This realm of activity is what Skinner and the behaviorists have analyzed. The "Hell Realms" are states where a person is in the grip of aggression or anxiety. These are the states that psychodynamic clinicians like Freud and Sullivan have mapped. The "Realm of the Hungry Ghosts" (who are sad little figures with huge bloated bellies and tiny scrawny throats) symbolizes insatiable craving—what Abraham Maslow called "deprivation motivation," the state of never being able to get enough. The "Heaven Realms" are blissful states in which a person feels totally fulfilled—sensual bliss of the highest order. Maslow's term "peak experience" fits here. Another realm is that of the "Jealous Gods" who, lacking the bliss of Heaven, seek it. Their attitude is a competitive, striving one, such as David McClelland analyzed as the needs for achievement and power.

In the "Human Realm," a being can have an existential insight into his condition and thereby understand the human predicament. From the Buddhist point of view, the Human Realm offers the most promise of spiritual progress. A person is caught neither in a horribly negative hell nor in a wonderfully positive heaven. In the Human Realm, a person has the most potential for growth into what is called the "Buddha Realm," which is not on the wheel at all.

At the top of the Wheel of Life, a Buddha stands on a cloud with strands going down to each of the other realms. These strands symbolize the possibility of reaching the Buddha Realm from any of the others. The Buddha Realm is where the Eastern paradigms diverge from the Western, and so present the greatest challenge. The Buddha Realms represent the possibility of sainthood—that is to say a mode of being that transcends the human condition, an escape from the Wheel, the cessation of suffering.

Western psychological literature is silent on this subject, but Eastern spiritual lore is replete with descriptions. One of my favorites is in a rendering by Thomas Merton of the poetry of Chuang Tzu:

> Chu'i the draftsman
> Could draw more perfect circles freehand
> than with a compass.
> His fingers brought forth
> Spontaneous forms from nowhere.
> His mind was meanwhile free and without concern
> With what he was doing.

. . . No drives, no compulsions,
No needs, no attractions;
Then your affairs are under control.
You are a free man [5].

Chuang Tzu depicts a person who is without psychological conflict—something every psychologist knows is impossible. The best one can become, in the psychoanalytic view, is a well-analyzed neurotic. Even a "self-actualized" person will have his low moments. This conflict-free state has no parallel in Western psychology. It presents a strong paradigm challenge.

ABHIDHAMMA: AN ANCIENT BUDDHIST PSYCHOLOGY

The Buddhist psychological system known as the Abhidhamma is preserved today among Theravadin Buddhists. It has been fully formulated for at least fifteen hundred years, and perhaps for as long as two thousand years. The Abhidhamma is a phenomenological assessment of the mind and how it works. The Abhidhamma psychologists catalogued fifty-six states of mind. Fourteen of these states were classified as "unhealthy," while fifteen were regarded as "healthy." The list of the healthy ones includes states like insight, mindfulness, modesty, discretion, confidence, rectitude, composure, non-attachment, non-aversion. Each of these are components of mental states, moments of mind that constantly shift in their make-up. Each positive state has a corresponding negative state. The psychological opposite of insight, for example, is delusion. The unhealthy factors of mind include states like perplexity, agitation, greed, aversion, avarice, worry.

As a typology of mental states, the Abhidhamma is only mildly interesting, but what makes this paradigm a challenge to Western psychology is the applied technology that flows from this analysis of mind. The technique for manipulating and transforming mental states in Abhidhamma is meditation. The meditator's craft is detailed in the *Visuddhimagga* [6], a practical guide from the fifth century. This manual offers an operational definition of "sainthood": a saint is someone who experiences only positive mental states, never negative ones. If one wants to become a saint, the *Visuddhimagga* tells exactly how to go about it.

MEDITATIVE PATHS

There are two major meditative paths that the *Visuddhimagga* describes. The first is the path of concentration, where one brings the mind to a point of focus. The focus can be on any one of forty recommended objects of meditation, including ten different kinds of decomposed corpses, the loathsomeness of food, or the breath. There is a personality typology that matches the best objects of meditation with each kind of person.

When a meditator reaches the point where there are no distracting thoughts whatsoever, he enters an altered state of consciousness. This moment marks an actual break from his normal awareness. He enters a *jhana*, a state in which he is aware only of the object of meditation. In *jhana*, according to the *Visuddhimagga*, in addition to the object of meditation, the predominant mental factors are bliss, rapture, and concentration. Then the meditator comes out of the *jhana* again and reflects that rapture is relatively gross compared to bliss. So he re-enters and gives up rapture, leaving only bliss and concentration. Then he again re-enters and gives up bliss—and so on, to the eighth and final level. This last *jhana* is a sphere of awareness so subtle that it is called "the realm of neither perception nor non-perception."

In the tradition of the *Visuddhimagga*, the *jhanas* are useful, but they also are called "concentration games." The goal is not a static, altered state of consciousness. The goal is a change of being. While in a *jhana*, a person's negative mental states are only suppressed. When the meditator comes out of a *jhana*, he is the same person with the same negative mental states. Such altered states leave his being unchanged.

The *Visuddhimagga* advises the experienced meditator to follow another path, the way of insight. In insight meditation, the meditator lets his mind go as it will and develops a neutral "witness"—an awareness that stays free of the comings and goings of the mind. He simply watches it. As the meditator observes the mind (and if his attention does not get caught by passing thoughts) he starts to perceive smaller and smaller units of consciousness. He sees that what he had construed in his ordinary awareness to have been perfectly rational thinking is really a mosaic of random nonsense out of which the illusion of rationality is constructed. He witnesses the process of constructing a reality. As the meditator watches this mosaic of nonsense, he starts to see the individual tiles of awareness that compose it. And if his concentration and insight are strong, he will begin to see the arising and passing away of each discrete unit of awareness. This progression is gradual, and reaching this stage alone may take years.

At the next stage of insight, all the meditator sees is the passing away of each moment of awareness. He then becomes disenchanted by the uselessness of all these moments of mind, and he becomes extremely detached. He feels no affective coloring toward his own mind—just neutral. At this point, he is on the threshold of what is called "Nirvana," or *Nibbana* in Pali. This state is not a heaven, or Valhalla, as is popularly thought in Western culture. Nirvana is a state of absolute nothingness—in which neither subjects nor objects exist. There is a total cessation of any awareness whatsoever. Nirvana is defined only in negative terms: the "unconditioned, signless, no-occurrence." Nirvana has no phenomenological description, for there are no phenomena to be described.

The tasting of Nirvana is crucial for the change of being which the Buddhist "psychologist" seeks. According to Abhidhamma theory, once a person experiences Nirvana he is irrevocably changed. There is a four-step progression whereby the meditator experiences Nirvana at increasingly deeper levels of insight. At each level certain personality characteristics drop away. This transformative process ultimately reaches the root of one's being.

For the last fifteen hundred years, people have been using the *Visuddhimagga* as a meditator's handbook, and have followed its direction for reaching sainthood. It was indeed a surprise to me, as a psychologist, to meet in Asia people whom I would describe as "saints." I call them "saints" not because of any miracles (which I had always associated with saints), but because they seemed to have transformed their deepest being.

These saints had followed different spiritual paths, but these paths seemed roughly parallel to that spelled out in the *Visuddhimagga*. As a blue-print for transforming consciousness, the *Visuddhimagga* is typical of the spiritual paths mapped out in other Asian psychologies. Each path is different in detail, but all share a basic core.

EAST MEETS WEST

The paradigm embodied in the Abhidhamma, it seems, is about to enter the mainstream of Western psychology as a new school of thought. There are at present three broad schools in psychology: the psychoanalytic, the behaviorist, and the humanistic. Eastern psychologies feed into a fourth, called the "transpersonal" school. This fourth school consists of psychologists who take seriously Abhidhamma, or a similar psychology, and attempt to apply it to problems in living.

In mass culture, the part of the transpersonal paradigm that has caught on is meditation. Meditation is the technology of mind, or the "therapy," of Asian psychology. Western psychologists are forced to listen when they realize that a measurable neuropsychology of meditation exists. Meditation has proved itself to be real in terms of their own belief system. Meditation has met Western psychology on its own ground and been accepted as consequential.

Eastern psychologies are confronting our own in offering us psychological systems that deal with spiritual matters. They offer models of inner development over and above the psychoanalytic, behavioristic, or humanistic models of mental health. They present psychology with a vision that not only accepts, but coincides with, the visions of religion. This vision of human possibilities is described in psychological, not metaphysical, language.

There are dangers, of course, whenever a new paradigm enters any field: one danger is over-reaction, another is over-enthusiasm. Over-reaction is epitomized in the question, "Is he psychotic?" We are all familiar with over-enthusiasm—people who proselytize for a particular spiritual group or meditation as the single answer to all human problems. In a balanced view, these Asian psychologies will be seen as having their own appropriate domain: the intersection of the ego and the spirit.

REFERENCES

1. William James. *The Varieties of Religious Experience: A Study in Human Nature*, p. 29. Collier ed. 1961.

2. Sigmund Freud. "Civilization and Its Discontents." In *The Complete Psychological Works of Sigmund Freud*, XXI, 65. Edited by James Strachey. Hogarth, London, 1961.

3. C. G. Jung. "Yoga and the West." In *The Collected Works of C. G. Jung*, XI, 534. Edited by Sir Herbert Read, Michael Fordham, and Gerhard Adler. Translated by R. F. C. Hall. Pantheon, 1958.

4. C. G. Jung. "On *The Tibetan Book of the Great Liberation*." In *The Collected Works of C. G. Jung*, XI, 483. Edited by Sir Herbert Read, Michael Fordham, and Gerhard Adler. Translated by R. F. C. Hall. Pantheon, 1958.

5. Thomas Merton. *The Way of Chuang Tzu*, p. 112. New Directions, 1969.

6. Buddhaghosa. *Visuddhimagga: The Path of Purification*. Translated by Bhikkhu Nyanomoli. Shambhala, Boulder, 1975.

DEEP STRUCTURES IN THE STUDY OF NEW RELIGIONS

Harvey Cox

My INTEREST here is mainly in the response of main-line religious institutions to what we call "new religious movements." And my interest is a little peculiar because I speak as a theologian and, therefore, as somebody from the inside of one particular movement.

I

It is becoming increasingly evident to me that what I learned as a graduate student about the emergence of the Christian movement in a context of polemical interaction with other movements is truer than I ever imagined it to be. All of us learned that the various creeds, the Nicene Creed and the Apostle's Creed and the others through Western religious history, emerged at least in part as responses to challenges, "deviancies," and marginal groups, against which and in terms of which a movement had to define itself. Even as far back as and including the New Testament, this was the case. The Gospel of Mark, at least some of its scholars tell us, emerged in the early church as a polemical document designed to demonstrate that the apostles were not as bright as they might have been. Readers of the Gospel of Mark know that nearly every time one of the apostles says anything, it is a rather stupid statement, usually immediately refuted by Jesus. The disciples all seem like something very close to stumblebums in the Gospel of Mark. Why? Some people have theorized that it was a document circulated to undercut the growing authority of some of the apostles or claims to apostolic founding in some of the early Christian sites. My colleague Dieter Giorgi has done a lot of work on what he calls

"Paul's opponents," and thinks that he can put together profiles of the opponents of St. Paul simply by sorting through the canonical writings of Paul and, of course, some of the extracanonical material. Now, if this is the case, the documents that we now think of as fixed texts really emerged in a polemical, or at least "definitional" situation, in which one movement was defining itself with reference to other movements from which it wanted to be differentiated.

The same process may be studied right under our noses today. Yesterday there came to my desk the twenty-two page document which will be issued this month by the National Council of Churches, explaining why the Unification Church cannot belong to the National Council of Churches. It is based on a very careful reading of Reverend Moon's *Divine Principle,* and explains why, on the basis of the *Divine Principle,* this church fails to qualify for membership. In defining what it means to be eligible for membership with reference to the Unification Church, the National Council of Churches is engaging in the same process we see in the Epistle to the Corinthians, in the Gospel of Mark, in the Nicene Creed, in the various confessions that have emerged in the course of Christian history.

This provides a fascinating vehicle for students of Christian history to learn some methods for examining the interaction of religious movements "on the spot," as it were. It will then enable them to "de-rigidify" or historicize the texts which are often appropriated in a more wooden and less historically sophisticated way. It is often said that in any period in history, Christianity defines itself with reference to two poles: the received tradition and the intellectual, cultural, and religious challenges that come into its ambience. What is often forgotten is that both poles are in fact quasi-polemical poles, that even the text that we use as the solid grounding, the "faith once delivered to the saints," is in fact a faith which was defined in the crucible of polemical interaction with other movements.

It could well be that since archeological discoveries in the last fifty years have contributed so much to our knowledge of Christian origins, we are now in a position to know more than almost any previous generation about the beginnings of Christianity. I refer here especially to the Qumran and Nag Hammadi finds, which tell us a lot about the environment in which Christianity emerged. Also, I think some psychoanalytic and psychological categories have become increasingly useful in the study of religion. Similarly, I would hope that the careful training of students in the examination of the interaction of the religious movements which have appeared on the turf, so to speak, of the existing movements will be equally valuable. For example, Jacob Needleman has referred to the enormous amount of misunderstanding about current religious movements. Oddly enough, this confusion persists despite the fact that people are right here, alive and well, to refute these beliefs. What chance does a Hare Krishna or a "Moonie" have to be understood? To make a comparison: what chance does a Montanist or a Marcionite have of being understood eighteen hundred years after the fact, if we cannot even understand people who are right there to talk with us and to explain what it is they believe? This is an especially difficult question when one remembers that many of the movements about which negative judgments are made in Christian history are movements about which we have no evidence, except the negative evidence of those who were refuting those movements.

This year we have a course at Harvard Divinity School, in which I am working with Helmut Koester of the New Testament Department, on "Heresies, Ancient and Modern." In this course we hope we can expose students to both the interaction of the early Christian movement with the movements about which it took some sort of self-definitional stand, and to movements we can study in other ways since they are living, breathing entities in our very midst. We hope this course will help us develop new ways of understanding a distant period in Western religious history.

This poses a question within the sociology of knowledge: why do scholars become so interested in new religious movements *now?* Why not ten or twenty years ago? Certainly part of the reason is that these movements, many of which have existed for a long time in a less visible way, have now come onto the turf which has generally been claimed by the main-line churches. An analogy may be made to the history of marijuana in the United States. While it was being used across the tracks and by marginal groups, nobody was terribly interested in it, but when it began to appear in middle-class white suburbs, it suddenly became an issue. When the Hare Krishnas were mainly providing an alternative to the hippie drop-outs in the Haight Ashbury, there was one understanding of them. When they began providing an alternative lifestyle to finishing medical school, for example, then a different kind of interest emerged. When the recruits to movements like this come from people who would not have become Presbyterians or Unitarians anyway, there was not much interest. Now there is. So in effect, it is the confrontational or interactional context which makes these movements more interesting to us. Since they are no longer out of sight, they are no longer out of mind.

A question that Jacob Needleman might want to ponder would be this: what is the religious significance of this discussion? Are we inadvertently providing a certain kind of legitimation here for movements who will gladly point to the fact that they are being studied by the Ford Foundation and the Graduate Theological Union, and therefore there must be something good about them?

II

When I began to read some of the attacks on the new religious movements, I became interested in the history of mainstream attacks on marginal, deviant, unhealthy, heretical, and schismatic movements. The literature is ample. One discovers, for example, in the stacks of the Andover Library at the Harvard Divinity School that most of the books on Mormonism treat the "crimes of Mormonism," and present exposés of life in Utah. There are actually fewer objective, scholarly, to say nothing of sympathetic, treatments. So one does not have to go very far, as any American church historian knows, to discover reams of material by mainstream religious writers about deviant or marginal movements. It makes wonderful reading.

At the same time that I was reading some of this material, I came across the paper in which Dick Anthony suggests the possible application of a modified version of Noam Chomsky's structural linguistic distinction between deep and surface structures in a religious movement. This suggestion provided me with a handy way of looking at some of the recurrent themes in mainstream polemics toward marginal movements. What I began to notice was that there are recurrent "deep structures" with which mainstream writers and critics characterize, caricature, and condemn marginal movements. The themes are repeated, as though the same scenario were there, and only the names of the actors needed to be changed.

Here I wish to outline four such themes. A useful term to refer to these themes is "myth."

(1) I call the first theme the "subversion myth," according to which a movement, whatever its religious intentions, is thought to pose a threat to the civil order. Sometimes these movements are seen as mainly religious fronts for politically subversive movements, or as movements that will endanger the civil authority. Other times they are seen as having at least secondary characteristics along this line. Time after time, polemical writers say that the main problem with "these people" is not what they teach, but what would happen if their movement were to become widespread. It would somehow undercut the fabric of society. Civilized life itself would be endangered. Sometimes the taking of oaths by "these people" is suspect. For a long time it was thought that Catholics could not take oaths to a Protestant sovereign, and therefore could not be accepted as a part of the commonweal. A similar argument was leveled against the Quakers: they refused to take oaths at all, and they refused, moreover, to take off their hats to magistrates. Quite apart from their religious perspective, they were seen as a danger to the civil community. In fact, Kai Erickson, in his little book on the *Wayward Puritans,* points out something that I had not noticed before, that in interrogating Quakers in the Massachusetts Bay Colony, the magistrates had no real interest in finding out what the Quakers were teaching. Simply being a Quaker was enough to get someone deported or, finally, hanged in the Boston Common. The recurrence of this myth may be seen in the current polemical literature. The threat to civil order is touted again and again.

(2) The second myth, i.e., accusation, that comes up, although again the faces and the actors are changed, is this: behind the walls of these movements exists a form of sexual or behavioral deviancy. How often has this accusation been heard? One remembers Maria Monk and all the babies born in the convents and buried in the basement. One hears stories of Reverend Moon's sexual prowess, and one used to hear similar stories of Father Divine. Sometimes the polemic is directed to the alleged orgiastic behavior, and at other times to the excessive sexual stringency of these movements. In this example, the mythic

power of the "deep structure" may be seen as the cause of allegations that appear contradictory at the surface level.

(3) The third theme one notices frequently is what I call the "myth of dissimulation." It runs this way: "You can't talk to these people because they are taught to dissimulate. They are carefully coached in not telling the truth and in misleading you. Because of this, any communication with this group is impossible, fruitless, and misleading, because their doctrine itself teaches them to lie to you."

Of course, the best example of this myth is the Jesuits. There are many other examples, but we still have the term "jesuitical" in the English language to refer to devious reasoning, mental reservation, or that kind of pseudo-communication that occurs when one partner in the dialogue is serious and the other is not. When it becomes widespread, this idea functions as what logicians call "poisoning the well." Communication becomes impossible because "I can't believe what you are saying from the outset," and since this kind of underlying myth structures the perception that one has of a movement from the outset, it tends to be self-reinforcing. In any religious movement somebody occasionally fibs. With regard to most movements, an instance of dissimulation is not taken as evidence of an underlying principle or teaching. It is seen as a temporary deviation. In other movements, though, dissimulation is understood to evidence refusal on principle to enter into real communication.

(4) The fourth myth is what I call the "myth of the evil eye." It is thought that no sane person could possibly belong to a movement "like this," and therefore the participant must be there involuntarily. The existence of some kind of coercive, manipulative, or magical activity—or witchcraft—is inferred. Unfortunately the term "brainwashing" has come into currency recently as a more psychologically acceptable way of expressing what was expressed previously in other ways. The brainwashing version of the evil eye myth holds that "these people" are the victims of prophets, spell-binders, witches, or hypnotists. There is a voluminous literature about how all of the Mormon women were being kept captive in polygamy by the brutal charismatic charm of the Mormon leaders. According to this material, there were no women living in Salt Lake City in the middle of the nineteenth century who were there voluntarily. This myth is expressed in much of the exposé literature that usually comes

with a title that includes the phrase "I was a . . . ." These include a description of how the apostate had been "tricked" or "hypnotized" or "charmed" into it.

Persons that have had an unfavorable experience with one of the new religious movements tend to speak of their experience in a characteristic way: such persons try to prove that they were brainwashed by recounting their bizarre behavior. They seem to say, "the more bizarre I can tell you my behavior was, the surer the evidence is that I must have been brainwashed." I recall a conversation I had with a young lady who had been a member of a Christian fundamentalist group and whose only way of being able to talk about her experience was to say that she had been brainwashed. At first she described the process, but then she began recounting the "bizarre" things she did: she used to stay up praying for three nights in a row; she always walked around with her eyes on the ground, and so on. I was immediately re-minded of the witchcraft trials in Salem, in which the proof that a person was a witch lay in the behavior of a second person. This second person might fall on the ground, and froth, and scream, and use profane language. This behavior, then, would be attrib-uted to the action of the witch. The more profane, the more bizarre the behavior of the bewitched person, the surer the indi-cation that that person was under control of an outside force. The myth of the evil eye presents an intriguing problem in in-terpretation. And, at this stage, I do not want to dismiss the possibility of there being manipulative or coercive forms of per-suasion in these movements.[1]

These then are the "deep structures" that seem to be enor-mously persistent in the anti-cult literature that stems from the main-line churches. Let me illustrate their presence in one case. In 1839, an Ursuline convent was burned by a mob in the Charles-town section of Boston. (Imagine that, burning a Catholic convent *in Boston!* That was really the old days.) I have been looking into the investigations of that incident, what preceded it, and the kind of atmosphere that surrounded it. Sure enough, all four of these myths appear. First, Catholics as such were sus-pect as being a danger to the civil order. Especially suspect were people living in convents and monastic situations, since they were believed to be under some kind of even more pronounced authoritarian control and therefore not eligible for participation in democratic society. There is myth number one: the danger to the civil order. Secondly, the atmosphere had already been charged by the book, *Awful Disclosures of Maria Monk* (1836), with its story of illegitimate babies, infanticide, graves, and all the rest. It had become a widely read, if not best-selling, book. In this particular convent, there was a young woman whom the people in Charlestown believed was being held there against her will. She had been "religiously seduced" into this convent, it was thought, and was not there according to her own choice. The selectmen investigated. They were shown through the convent by the Mother Superior and talked with the lady in question, who assured them that she was there of her own free will, and had not been seduced or otherwise forced into it. They made a public report completely exonerating the convent of any malicious or criminal activity. And the next week the convent was burned down. Part of this, of course, reflects the dissimulation myth. Some people believed the selectmen were misled and that the testimony of the woman herself was not credible because, as a "brainwashed" person (or in this case a "religiously seduced" person) she was not in a position to assure anyone that she was in the convent of her own free will. Thus all four myths I have mentioned, i.e., endangering the civil order, sexual deviancy, dissimulation, and the evil eye, were present in Charlestown in 1839.

These myths express primal religious and spiritual fears. The fear of civil subversion expresses the fear of corporate chaos. The fear of sexual excess reveals a horror of personal disintegration. The fear of dissimulation suggests the terror of breakdown of communications. The fear of the evil eye is the fear of bondage to an alien power. You can find these four motifs as far back as Gilgamesh, the Tower of Babel, the Captivity, and Exodus. The rubrics with which mainstream religious movements make their judgments about so-called marginal movements themselves express a religious content which merits further investigation and thought.

III

As a theologian working mainly in the churches and concerned about the response of the churches to these movements, my major fear is that the churches may emulate the "surface characteristics" of these movements: yoga, meditation, etc. We may witness a kind of ransacking of our tradition, not for the deep structures, but for surface similarities which can be pandered at a superficial level. My own hope is that through the study of new religious movements at a level which incorporates some of this "phenomenology of religion" approach, one might even find a link to the current liberation theologies. At least that is my hope, and let me tell you why that is. The first reason is a very personal one: I find myself embarrassed, as somebody who has been interested in liberation theology, with my friends asking me, "Why are you so interested in these bizarre cults?" I think there is a link, however, and it has to do with a statement by none other than Karl Marx. In the same paragraph in which the phrase "opiate of the masses" appears, Marx says, "Religion is the cry of the oppressed creature, the spirit of a spiritless situation, the heart of a heartless world." I wonder if an expansive and less narrowly ideological liberation theology might in some measure see in the religious movements that we are about to study the "cry of the oppressed creature," or even the "heart of the heartless world." As Jacob Needleman said, these movements may raise questions that go far deeper than the religious sector of our culture, narrowly defined, to questions having to do with deep, pervasive, epochal kinds of pain which have motivated people to move in directions that are very costly to them. They have often moved toward religions that demand a good deal of sacrifice and risk, and which are viewed as deviant by society. When all religious movements are understood as expressions of deep questions, then the answers will extend beyond the boundaries of narrow religious conceptions. Therein lies a link to liberation theology.

NOTE

[1] The "brainwashing" accusation goes all the way back to the New Testament. In the third chapter and first verse of the Epistle to the Galatians, St. Paul says, "Oh you foolish Galatians. Who has bewitched you that you should not obey the truth before whose eyes Jesus Christ hath been evidently set forth crucified among you?" The term "bewitched" means to cast a spell over, as if by hypnosis. So even St. Paul, who in most things was fairly insightful, had to attribute deviation from his teaching to people who were using these methods.

TOWARD A RELIGIOUS
CRITERION OF RELIGION
Langdon Gilkey

IT IS no accident that theologians are barely represented in this discussion, and probably Harvey Cox
and I are not here as theologians. There are several good reasons
for this. In their work—so it is commonly reported—theologians
deal with, and master, few facts; and our present study is one in
which a knowledge of the facts is basic. Theologians are also
regarded as poor at building bridges, and bridges are here what
are desperately needed. Above all, as Frederick Bird pointed
out, most of the "new" religions with which we are concerned
are religions of experience, not of reflection.[1] Consequently,
theology has played a very minor role in their sudden rise to
prominence. Thus, even if he or she makes a precarious bridge to
the new religions, and so can think of them from the inside as a
theologian might ideally do, the theologian will not find much
reflective content that is of real significance to the group.

My own brief relations to various groups have indicated that
theological issues and convictions were important neither to the
individual's conversion to the community nor to his or her continued loyalty to it. Cosmology is possibly more important then
theology—surprisingly enough. Strange forces are at work in the
"worlds" of many of these groups; but a geophysicist probably
knows more about them than does a theologian. As Yogi Bhajan
remarked once in a lecture, we are moving into the age of
Aquarius. (Although I am Aquarian, and so perked up at this, for
an Aquarian theologian what he said was disappointing!) The
passing age, said Bhajan, was an age characterized by the separation of experience from the object of faith, and so one demanding belief, argument, and theology. The coming age is to be
one of experience, of immediate contact with the divine, and so
one indifferent to theology. The cosmology of moving from one

astrological age to another raised questions in my mind that Bhajan did not answer. Nevertheless, the character of present religious existence in the cults I am familiar with bears out his point: these are religions of direct experience, and only secondarily of reflection and understanding.

If Professor Needleman is right, however, there is one very important theological problem entailed in our projected work. If, as he said, our most pressing need is to find an adequate criterion of religions and so of the new religions, then the theologian may be of some help. A *non*-religious criterion of religions would move us back into the position of being subject to the prejudices about religion of a secular culture. Moreover, a secular psychological criterion may well regard the new religions as deviant and consequently psychotic; a moral criterion might exclude them as subversive of our common American values. Strangely, as this shows, an "objective" criterion, wielded by the children of the Enlightenment, in the end may represent a patently ideological set of criteria.

Despite the fact, therefore, that religious criteria of religion have been the mothers of ideology and the fathers of fanaticism, probably our deepest need at present is theological, namely a *religious* criterion of religion that is *not* ideological. At the moment I have none to offer. Several, however, come to mind—for example, that of Tillich: the final criterion of a medium of revelation is a person, symbol, community, or religion that negates what is particular in itself in pointing beyond itself and thus genuinely manifesting what is ultimate. The relation of this criterion to Christianity is crystal clear. One thinks also of the prophetic criticism and criterion of religion, for example, in Amos; but the Semitic presuppositions here are undeniable. The liberal criticism of religion turned out, too, to be not at all universal and to produce a pallid form of religion. This is a theological as well as a social problem of great depth and importance. It is by no means easy to find a religious criterion of religion that does not merely dispose of all alternatives to one's own religious viewpoint, be the latter officially "religious" or officially "secular."

In our present discussions, a question has arisen whether a *social* analysis of the religious cults (as arising out of a social and cultural matrix of factors) is antithetical to a religious analysis (one which locates their causes in strictly "religious" factors). I would like to argue that this antithesis is unnecessary, and that to interpret religious movements as related to, even as arising out of, a given cultural situation is by no means reductionist nor does it qualify their religious character. In the history of the church—one thinks, for example, of the Reformation or the rise of liberalism—religious movements have arisen as genuinely religious and yet as responses to new and threatening cultural situations. The reason for this correlation of culture and religion is that ultimate issues—that is, religious issues—are raised by historical and social changes, and especially by historical and social crises. Society, its structures and forms of stability, does protect us from the ultimate void of existence. When in some way that protection is removed, the ultimate is opened up, often in terrifying forms, and religious problems impinge on us. Ultimate questions grow out of the loss of proximate answers. Thus what is going on in culture—and, correspondingly, the work of sociologists and psychologists—is of immense religious relevance, and so is important to a theological interpretation of both culture and of the new religions—as, I believe, a theological interpretation is relevant to them. Thus, social and theological explanations of religious movements must be correlated if either is to be illuminating and intelligible.

In applying this "method," let me admit at once that, far from being able to marshal swaths of evidence, I am actually "sniffing about," "following my nose"—which is what a theologian mostly does anyway. (By that canon Harvey Cox is the best in our business!) My reflections are largely personal and autobiographical, the result of several years of contact with Kundalini Yoga and with a Zen fellowship and Zen philosophers, in Kyoto.

One of the most important things we have all felt in our cultural life—and know deeply its truth—is the loss of the self in modern culture, the elusiveness of a sense of identity and of personal reality, the vanishing of a sense of the creativity and effectiveness—and so of the "realness"—of the inward. Frederick Bird spoke forcefully of the identity of the contemporary self with its social roles, the radical emptiness of those same roles, and so the loss of the self within them. One can also point to the almost exclusively external orientation of recent and present Western culture: its concentration on the skill to manipulate objects and others; its penchant for organization of processes and persons; its vast delight in the spiritless consumption of goods and of services—all dealing exclusively with the external relations of the self and not at all with its internal relations to itself and to others. Consequently the West has learned amazingly how to manipulate, rearrange, and reform the external world: nature, productive processes, and political and economic structures. In the process it has forgotten, and so infinitely weakened, the inward life of the spirit. The autonomy for which it has long stood has been weakened by the very externality that this autonomy had itself developed. The self has become an elusive shadow, a hungry and lonely ghost, unrecognized and hidden, in a merely external process.

I take this cultural history to be a major cause or situation within which the "new" cults, especially those of meditation and self-awareness, have arisen to prominence. My thesis is that among a plural set of factors, one of the primary ones is that in these cult communities many persons, who in modern society find themselves unsure they exist or are effective, receive a new sense of the reality, value, and possibilities of the self—though in many cases *not* within the external world of street, office, and suburb. This is the most immediate consequence of meditation: when the eyes are closed, concentration is radically inward; it is a concentration on the body and so on the self, but both *felt from the inside*. (Usually, the self is motivated, watched, and judged from without.) At such a moment of inner concentration, the equal, if not greater, reality of the *inner* world impresses itself deeply. The discovery of the self is the initial gift of the Oriental religions of meditation in our midst.

Concurrent with this is the discovery that the body is the self and the self its body: the unity of body and spirit. We in the West are, despite what we tell ourselves, incurably Hellenistic and Cartesian as a culture: the self *is* its thoughts, and it *has* a body; and the problems and crises of each are related only indirectly, so to speak by "alliance" alone, to those of the other. Calisthenics and medicine are for the body; thoughts, therapy, and contemplation are for the spirit. But here (in Yoga for example), all is a unity; it is *through* exercising the body, and feeling it from the inside, that the reality of the inward—and so of the self—appears. When, through exercising myself, I feel my body from the inside—is *that* spirit or matter?—both the "I" and the body are relevant, active, and united. Both for me make up *together* the newly discovered reality of my being. Thus I learn that the self is quiet and contemplative—and can lose itself!—only if first the body is quiet and under control. The self can transcend itself and its body in meditation and ecstasy *only* if that unity of the two has been realized and apprehended. Finally, there is no question that equally important in the long run—though possibly further down the road for many persons—is the experience of the relation between the newly rediscovered, inward self and the deeper sacral dimension of ultimate reality—or "nothingness"—itself. In a time when the self has been weakened and rendered almost unreal, experiences of the inwardness, the unity, and the transcendent rootedness of the self are, I am suggesting, important factors in generating the wide appeal of many of the "new" movements.

There is a deep irony in all of this. More than any other culture, the West has been responsible for the development and nurture, both on a felt and a theoretical level, of the consciousness of the reality, value, autonomy, and effective power of the individual self. On this score the Orient was apparently more ambiguous, less sure, if not downright negative. And yet so overwhelmingly have we emphasized the external, objective character of all reality and the manipulation of that objective world, that this treasured tradition, as felt and as thought, has had to find in the Orient a new basis for the return of the inward!

That in many profound ways this move "East" represents a gain, my remarks, I hope, clearly indicate. It seems to me, however, that it may not in every case or *in toto* be a gain. Concurrent with their traditional emphasis on inwardness and the transcendent, in many of these groups there is a tendency to qualify, and in some cases, eliminate, personal and individual autonomy. I find this tendency astounding. Even where the leaders do not welcome it—and more surely do welcome it than do not!—the drive of the new devotee to place his or her destiny solely in the hands of the guru seems to have irresistible force. A deeply weakened ego can only thus find help charting its precarious course in life. I recall the way a young, thoroughly educated American couple in a Yogic community described the grounds for their own recent marriage: "We wished to have a marriage based on *reality,* not only the unreality of mere individual choice. Thus when Yogi Bhajan informed each of us separately (we did not know each other at all) that we were destined for each other, *and* when our charts fitted perfectly, we knew this was to be a real marriage!'' After centuries of involvement in the search for and achievement of autonomy in such matters, a search prompted by the Enlightenment and its liberal offspring, such a witness bespeaks a very new consciousness—and a problematic one.

If this be so, a new question faces us on the deepest level: how can we accept these genuine benefits from the East and yet preserve some, at least, of our traditional values? Let us note that while it is new for us—since when has Western Christian culture had to accept *any* benefits from another culture?—this problem is not at all new under the sun. This is precisely the deepest spiritual, social, and political question which India, China, and Japan have increasingly faced for the past three centuries *vis-à-vis* the Christian West: how are we to accept their technology, science, industrialization, democracy (or socialism), their views of individual human being, of history, of morals, and of religion without losing all that is traditional to us? The search for a viable synthesis, and for identity within such a synthesis, as again India, China, and Japan each vividly show, represents a long, tumultuous, historical process. We, too, can expect that. It is also a process into which social, economic, legal, political, moral, *and* religious/theological elements are necessarily involved—if it is to be meaningful. There is no harm in our pondering its early issues and crises.

How might our own traditions, especially Christianity, view and relate to these movements, at least the older ones? Fascinating as I find Harvey Cox's evocation of the "polemical model" of interrelation, I prefer, I think, the "covenant" model. By that term—a patristic one—I refer to the concept of a "covenant of God with the Greeks" prior to the Christian revelation, a covenant that made legitimate a synthesis of Christian revelation with Hellenistic culture. One must, I think, also now speak of a "divine covenant" with modern culture, making legitimate our current theological efforts to reinterpret the Christian tradition in the light of modern science, modern social theory, modern psychology, and so on. In each case, let us note, the church felt free to use a culture essentially unrelated to Christian revelation (could anything be more "pagan" than either Hellenistic or modern secular civilization?) to reinterpret its message, to express it in new forms, and so to set it in a new light. As a consequence—in *each* of the above cases—it now saw some older elements that could and should be changed, and it discovered new elements, even some very important ones, in its tradition that it had never seen or guessed to be there (e.g., religious and theological tolerance and the social gospel). Buddhists have frequently witnessed to the fact that through their experience of the impingement of Christianity they have been sent back to their own tradition with new eyes and thereby been enabled to discover new and significant emphases in it. The same may be true for us!—for long ago a covenant unknown to us may have been prepared in the Orient as well as in Greece. I suspect that looking at our faith through the eyes of other religions, asking some of their questions, and receiving intuitions of their answers, we may be able to see creative elements in our own tradition we had not seen (new forms of meditation, a new view of nature?). Once again we may experience the gift of recovering, revivifying, and re-expressing our own tradition through this new and more universal covenant.

NOTE

[1] Many if not most of the so-called new cults are in themselves very old and are only to be considered "new" in relation to the American scene.

PART 3

The Phenomenology of the New Religions

INTRODUCTION

The phenomenology of new religions is often the phenomenology of culture in crisis. Joel Colton has observed that "one of the all-encompassing ideals of Western life, the idea of progress, is today being questioned more sharply than ever in the past. People ask, "Is growth progress? Are material advance, science, and technology to be equated with progress? What, indeed, is progress?" He calls for a "sociology of spiritual life, one that not only 'explains' the spiritual behavior of others, but explains our own innermost impulses."

The essays in this section may contribute to laying out such an outer and inner sociology of spiritual life. The essays are divided between first-order efforts, based on field research, to explain the spiritual lives of others, and second-order efforts, based on philosophical research, to explain the nature of the problems involved in understanding the new religions.

Three of the essays reflect both first-order, sociological concerns and second-order, "meta-sociological" questions. Emily Culpepper, Archie Smith, and Stillson Judah are concerned not only about carrying out an accurate description of the spiritual behavior of others, but also about the philosophical foundations of sociological inquiry. Ms. Culpepper, speaking as a radical feminist, surveys the lines of spiritual authority that are being followed within that movement. Smith, speaking as a student of the Black social consciousness movement, asks, Why, with few exceptions, are the followers, students, and critics of the new religions White? He argues that to regard White new religions as the true index of the new religious consciousness in America is to have a narrow conception of American spiritual life. Stillson Judah describes a proposed research project, the results of which he hopes will help to settle the controversy over what has been called "religious brain washing," and what Harvey Cox in his essay in Part Two called "the Myth of the Evil Eye."

In four of the essays the spiritual behavior of followers of new religious movements is examined. Charles Prebish discusses the historical development of American interest in Buddhism in relation to the cultural changes of the postwar era. Frederick Bird observes that by means of their ritual practices, followers of new religions seek to confer a hidden charisma upon themselves. Mark Juergensmeyer, who has carried out research on the Radhasoami movement in India, as well as in America, describes the movement as a "transnational" religion. Barbara Hargrove suggests that there are subcategories of new religions, and she contrasts "integrative" and "transformative" religious groups.

The remaining five essays furnish material for thought about an inner sociology of spiritual life. Donald Stone examines the problem of conceptual bias and offers suggestions that apply, not only to the scholar, but to the general reader as well. James Richardson describes how he and his associates had to reexamine their assumptions and views while under pressure to convert to the evangelical religion of the very group under study. Charles Glock allegorically describes his own misgivings and hunches about the whole enterprise of studying new religions. Robert Ellwood points out that it may not be helpful to think of the new groups as "new" in any historical sense; rather, they are new in the sense of being newly perceived. For this reason, he suggests that the term "emergent religion" properly points to the eye of the observer as much as to the new religion itself. Finally, George Baker argues that the comparative study of religious experience can lead to neutral ground on which impartial discussion of the new religions is possible.

ON KNOWING HOW WE KNOW ABOUT THE NEW RELIGIONS
Donald Stone

How do we know what to believe in the research reports on the new religious movements? Which of the diverse and often contradictory interpretations of groups, Reverend Moon's Unification Church, for example,[1] can be trusted? How is it possible that a Zen roshi's discourse makes no sense in one account, is enlightening in another, and sounds flat and banal in yet another? These questions indicate the problematic nature of understanding and interpreting the new religions.

Knowledge about the new religious groups is situational. It is produced by the interaction of the researcher with the focus and object of study. It is always an interpretation, influenced by the personal preferences, attitudes, and states of consciousness that the researcher (and reader) brings to the study. There are no immaculate perceptions. While bias is epistemologically inevitable, its influence on the interpretation can be gauged when it is made explicit. The greater the consciousness of possible bias, the greater the certainty about the foundation on which our knowledge of these new religious movements rests.

A number of research procedures can be used to correct for biases by making these biases explicit and by providing a variety of vantage points from which the new religions can be interpreted. These are procedures that the researcher might follow, and that the research reader might look for in a carefully executed study.

The classical conception of objectivity derives from early scientific investigations of things and objects. The objectivity that came when wishes and fears were excluded from observation—including the wishes and designs of a supernatural god—was a great step forward. Abraham Maslow maintains that this detachment gets more and more difficult as the object of study goes up the phylogenetic scale.

We know how easy it is to anthropormorphize, to project into the animal the observer's human wishes, fears, hopes, prejudices if we are dealing with dogs or cats, and more easily with monkeys or apes. When we get to the study of human beings, we can now take it for granted that it is practically impossible to be the cool, calm, detached, uninvolved, noninterfering spectator [6].

The problem of projection becomes even more problematic when dealing with religious and transpersonal realms [7]. Indeed, the new religious movements often serve as spiritual inkblots: reports of movements may tell us more about the observers than about the observed. Objectivity can thus be seen as the elimination of unconscious desires that influence observations.[2]

Personal preferences and value assumptions enter into the research process at many points. They occur in the choice of a research topic, the choice of research methods, and in the interpretation of evidence. As Abraham Kaplan says, "the problem for methodology is not *whether* values are involved in inquiry, but *which* . . . " [9]. Kaplan goes on to quote Gunnar Myrdal:

The attempt to eradicate biases by keeping out the valuations themselves is a hopeless and misdirected venture. . . . There is no other device for excluding biases in social science than to face the valuations and to introduce them as explicitly stated, specific, and sufficiently concretized value premises.

These issues point to the need for an interdisciplinary "psychology of knowledge" that deals with the varieties of personal bias and how they might be controlled. A psychology of knowledge would supplement the well-established perspectives in the philosophy of science, the sociology of knowledge, and hermeneutics in interpreting how we know what we know.

MAKING PERSONAL PREFERENCES EXPLICIT

In discussion with a scholar who had recently completed a book about the evangelistic Buddhist sect, Nichiren Shoshu, I asked how he felt about his account, now that it was ready for printing.

"In the book I'm too easy on them. I give them too much credit. I wonder if I was afraid they might be right."

I asked, "Right?"

He continued, "Yeah—that just by chanting in front of that *Gohonzon* [a scroll] you can get whatever you want."

I suspect that if this scholar had pursued his doubts surrounding the value of chanting, he might have written a different account. If a researcher does not carefully examine his attitudes toward the purported truths of a religion, the analysis may be full of unconscious hedging. This exchange suggests the need to be clear on personal hopes and fears, particularly prior to completing the research project. How is this to be done?

One approach to this problem in the psychology of knowledge has been suggested by anthropologists who have proposed that every ethnographer be psychoanalyzed, even that ethnographies be prefaced by psychoanalytic portraits of the author. While such a preface would carry with it additional problems of interpretation, the underlying idea is heuristic for how the researcher should proceed and what the research reader should expect: a disciplined method of uncovering and accounting for personal preferences germane to the topic of research.

Collaborative research would be another way of gaining awareness of personal bias that affects observation and interpretation. In the process of sharing findings with others in a research group (or in being "debriefed" when the research setting poses values in conflict with the researcher's), preferences and their impingement on the research come to the fore.

Another method to encourage this sort of introspection is the keeping of a research journal. Such a journal might include the following kinds of notes: likes and dislikes about the subject under study, the kinds of findings anticipated, the initial reactions to the findings, pressures to please funding sources, changing opinions about the subject, interpersonal problems in the research setting (such as obligation, gratitude, hostility), ambivalences, changes in research directions, differences between the researcher's view of human nature and the group's, ways in which any of these preferences may have been biasing the observations, ways to control bias, and, in general, ways in which the subject is both interesting and important to the researcher in personal and scientific ways.

In my own field work in the human potential movement, my notes on each consciousness training session that I attend include at least some of these items. Periodically, I make a more thorough accounting of "where I am at" in my feelings about this movement, and of possible biases. This alerts me to ways to correct for them, so my preferences do not blind me from other interpretations of what is taking place. A research journal of this kind is for the researcher's own use. However, some of the important preferences and the researcher's judgment of how these preferences temper the findings could be included in the research report, perhaps findings could be included in the research report, perhaps in a methodological appendix. Unfortunately this is rarely done.

Harvey Cox has a notable gift for including relevant personal detail in his writing. In *Turning East* [10], he conveys his attractions and skepticisms in a way that assists the reader in knowing how he knows what he is talking about. He is forthright about his limited contact with Tibetan Buddhism and his struggle to fathom sitting meditation. As a reader I am thereby warned that the author has a limited understanding of Buddhism, and I am encouraged to trust the author's observations on issues where he has expertise. Other examples of accounts that contain instructive autobiographical detail are Jacob Needleman's introductory chapter to *The New Religions* [11] and Robert Bellah's preface to *Beyond Belief* [12].

There are risks in this sort of self-revelation. Without grace and humor such accounts can be tedious. Preferences that an author has since shed may hang around to haunt him in print. Some readers will no doubt interpret the admission that research is a problematic interaction between self and subject as a failure to be "objective." Hopefully this is less likely to occur in the field of religion, where Berger and Luckmann [13] and Buddhist epistemology remind us how reality can be looked at as socially and personally constructed. Another danger is that readers may use their disagreements with the *content* of the author's preferences to dismiss the findings. And it may be that, in fact, preferences were not very well controlled for, and the research is of low quality. As a reader I want to know this and I am suspicious of any research accounts that do not pay attention to these issues of bias.

Another means to make preferences conscious and encourage fair-mindedness is to let the subject under study react to the findings.[3] This can be done in several ways. For instance, at the end of an interview with a participant or leader of a religious movement, the researcher can summarize what has been said, include an interpretation of it, and ask the respondent to comment. In my interviews with participants in *est*[4] and other human potential groups, I found that this interchange increased my confidence that I had an accurate understanding and in some instances was helpful in avoiding inferences that were not justified.

Showing first drafts of research reports to participants of a movement, particularly ones trained in the social sciences, can be another valuable opportunity for testing biases. If the researcher cannot account for the participant's objections that may be raised to the researcher's interpretations, the work is not done. Knowing that research reports will be reviewed by partisans, as well as by colleagues, stimulates more conscientious collection and interpretation of data. When objections to interpretation are mentioned in the research report, the reader's confidence in the research may be increased.

Reactions by the research subject can take a more formal form. One possibility is to print them in an appendix. In *The Road to Total Freedom* [14], Roy Wallis includes an appendix written by a Scientologist with a Ph.D. in sociology. Wallis offered to include the appendix and Scientology commissioned its writing. It addition to giving Scientology an opportunity to reply, I feel it strengthens the book. It provides dramatic tension, and generally confirms, rather than weakens, Wallis' analysis of Scientology. Publishers might encourage the inclusion of critical reactions in appendixes as a means of increasing controversy and raising issues of "objectivity."

VARIETIES OF RESEARCH STRATEGIES

Providing for a variety of vantage points is another means for becoming aware of the situational aspects of interpretation and correcting for bias. This can be accomplished in two ways: by using a diversity of research methods and a diversity of investigators in a collaborative effort. After years of controversy, social scientists now generally agree that no one method is intrinsically superior to another. Each has its strengths and weaknesses, and is appropriate for different purposes. For instance, content analysis of a theology misses important behavioral and organizational elements of a religion. Survey interviews tend to elicit responses in terms of the researcher's categories rather than the respondent's. Participant observation does not easily render the meaning of the actions observed, nor does it allow generalization of findings to those not directly observed. However, the use of multiple methods prevents the weakness of any single method from biasing the results. Borrowing from surveying technique, the use of multiple methods has been called "triangulation."[5]

In addition to triangulation by multiple methods, Norman Denzin suggests "theoretical triangulation," and "investigator triangulation." Theoretical triangulation involves the use of several different perspectives or theories in the analysis of the same set of data. Investigator triangulation is the use of more than one observer in the field situation.[6] "The advantages of multiple observers are obvious: Tests on the reliability of observations can be quickly made and observer bias can thus be judged" [16].

One vantage point that may contribute to bias is that of the covert researcher. Aside from the ethical aspects of dissembling—which federal and university guidelines are beginning to regulate—there are other reasons to be wary of its use. Covert research is likely to promote distorted observation by setting up a dynamic such that the continued secrecy has to be justified by finding reprehensible elements to justify the deception. The natural tendency toward selective perception is exaggerated in the direction of looking for absurb or evil elements in the religion.[7]

THE FURTHER REACHES OF PARTICIPANT OBSERVATION

In spite of his positivistic leanings, Emile Durkheim appreciated the need for intuitive understanding in studying religion. He recommended that researchers "confront religion in the state of the mind of the believer." On this condition alone could one hope to understand it:

Let him experience it as the believer experiences it, for it only really exists in virtue of what it is for the latter. Thus, whoever does not bring to the study of religion a sort of religious sentiment has no right to speak about it! He would be like a blind man talking about colors" [17].

One method that provides for this personal experience of religion is participant observation. There are many orientations that a participant observer can follow, each with its particular costs and benefits. For instance, the researcher can emphasize either the observer or the participant role. Participation can involve taking on social status within a group and identifying with its norms and values. The outcome of this kind of participation is often an apologetic. Participation can also involve entering into mystical experiences or altered states of consciousness provided by the group. While personal experience with these states of consciousness may not be necessary to report on them, any accounts of new religious movements that does not take note of them misses what is perhaps *the* essential feature that they all share in common. The provision of intense religious experience is what characterizes the new religious consciousness [18].

Psychologist Charles Tart has written on the value of researching experiential spaces by training investigators to enter these states and observe them. Some of the states appropriate to such "state-specific" investigations include auto-hypnosis, psychedelic-induced states, possession, and meditative states. Tart asks why science should have to rely on reports "obtained from untrained people, almost none of whom have shared the scientist's commitment to constantly re-examine observations in greater and greater detail?" Tart argues that observations made while in one state of consciousness will miss important features of another state. For example, subjects in LSD research may observe that "You and I, we are all one," while the researcher observes that the subjects are in a "confused sense of identity" [19].[8]

From my research on the *est* training, I am persuaded that the combination of my training as a sociologist and as an *est* participant sensitized me to psychological and sociological processes that are usually overlooked by researchers not exposed to *est*, and by *est* graduates not trained in critical observation. This was documented on several occasions as I served as a consultant to a survey of twelve hundred *est* graduates under the direction of Robert Ornstein (who is not an *est* graduate). Having been trained in the experiential spaces of the training and in the organization's ideology, I was more aware of the way to pose questions to respondents that would be valid measures of the dimensions the study was exploring. I was able to point out many alternative explanations for changes that respondents reported subsequent to the training that others on the research team had inferred were probably due to *est*.

Personal involvement has its drawbacks as well as its advantages. Tart warns of the perils of state-specific research. "In many altered states of consciousness, one's experience is that one is obviously and lucidly experiencing the truth directly, without question" [20]. Such an experience of "obvious" truth may undermine the desire for further investigation or consensual validation. The researcher may become attached to the good feelings experienced and refuse to consider alternative conceptualizations of them. Interest in analysis may be replaced by desire to re-enter the state and be uncritical toward the group that provided the trip. Thus, what anthropologists call "going native" may encourage either a research drop-out or an apologist.[9]

Another approach that involves the researcher personally confronting the religion under study is what Robert Bellah calls "symbolic realism." While Bellah does not feel previous personal experience is a necessary condition for empathic understanding, he holds that the "only adequate basis for the social scientific study of religion" is one that takes "seriously noncognitive symbols and the realms of experience they express" [12]. Bellah invokes symbolic realism as a way to avoid reductionism. He criticizes those who distort or ignore truth claims of a religion by portraying it as only compensation for personal deprivations or rationalization for ruling-class interests.

As with phenomenologists such as Alfred Schutz, Bellah approaches religion as one reality among multiple realities. But whereas Schutz brackets the question of religious truth and reality, Bellah asserts that the symbolic realist should be open to the possibility of religious truth. Symbolic realism assumes that in principle some religions may provide real and adequate answers to questions of ultimate reality. It may be that the religion under study does not provide what the researcher considers adequate answers. Or the researcher may consider the social sources of a creed or ritual as more noteworthy than its embodiment of religious truth. But a researcher who assumes *a priori* that there is no religious truth, or that it will not be found in the religion under study, will try to fit the religion into the form of a pretentious or misguided endeavor. Thus a participant observer with a symbolic realist perspective should affirm the possibility of a universal religious truth and be open to its manifestation in the setting under study.[10]

A distinction can be drawn between cognitive openness and experiential participation. Bellah's emphasis is on a cognitive rather than an experiential affinity for the religion under study. When both cognitive and experiential involvement is present, conversion with its attendant biases is likely. Bellah's cognitive approach is one way to guard against conversion.

The vantage points of a symbolic realist and state-specific scientist require skill in shuttling between immersion and analysis, and a high tolerance for ambiguity. Some of this psychic strain can be reduced through a collaborative effort where there is a division of labor. An example of such collaboration is the ten-year joint research of Dick Anthony and Thomas Robbins that has generated over thirty articles and book chapters on the new religions. Anthony, a symbolic realist with a direct experience of Meher Baba, has described his working relationship with Robbins, a secular-humanist skeptic, as one of creative tension. Together they produced a classic article, "Getting Straight with Meher Baba" (28). Over the years, each scholar has been open to the perspective of the other and the research has continued to generate some of the most interesting ideas in the field of new religions.[11]

Abraham Maslow suggests that "love" or "affinity" for the subject being researched may produce a special kind of objectivity which he calls "Taoist objectivity." Maslow writes:

My work with monkeys, I am sure, is more "true," more "accurate," in a certain sense, more *objectively* true than it would have been if I had disliked monkeys. . . . At the very least this kind of love produces interest and even fascination, and therefore great patience with long hours of observation. . . . My finding is that, that which you love, you are prepared to leave alone. . . . We do not wish it to be other than it is. . . . Which is all to say that we can see it more truly as it is in its own nature rather than as we would like it to be or fear it to be or hope it will be. Approving of its existence, approving of the way it is, *as* it is, permits us to be nonintrusive, nonmanipulating, nonabstracting, noninterfering perceivers.

Loving knowledge, Maslow concludes, has its particular advantages in particular situations for particular purposes.[12] If researchers are realistically aware that love of the object of study produces certain kinds of blindness as well as certain kinds of perspicuity, then they are sufficiently forewarned [6].

Research that includes participation and affinity is desirable, provided there are some other complementary vantage points. The viewpoints of someone experientially involved, of an empathic observer without direct experience, of apostates who no longer experience or identify with the religion, and even of true believers who are trained in research methods have valuable contributions to make.[13] There are no best methods. Whatever approaches are used, ingenuity and vigilance are necessary. In P. W. Bridgman's words, "The scientist has no other method than doing his damnedest."

NOTES

[1] A variety of interpretations, some of them contradictory, are presented by Cox [1], Judah [2], Lofland [3], Anthony, Doucas, and Curtis [4], and Sontag [5].

[2] Personal influences may also be seen in a positive light, as part of creativity intrinsic to breakthrough research. Philosopher of science Michael Polanyi has shown that "into every act of knowing there enters a passionate contribution of the person knowing what is being known, and that this coefficient is no mere imperfection but a vital component of his knowledge" [8].

[3] This assumes the account is not by an apologist—apologists might benefit from submitting their accounts to critics of the movements as well.

[4] *est* (Erhard Seminar Training) is a sixty-hour awareness training. Werner Erhard, the founder, states its purpose is "to transform your ability to experience living so the situations you have been trying to change or have been putting up with clear up just in the process of life itself."

[5] Eugene Webb, who introduced the term "triangulation," writes "Every data-gathering class—interviews, questionnaires, observation, performance records, physical evidence—is potentially biased and has specific to it certain validity threats. Ideally, we should like to converge data from several data classes, as well as converge with multiple variants from within a single class" [15].

[6] Fred Bird's research group on new religious movements (Concordia University, Montreal) is exemplary in making use of these three types of triangulation. They have provided a high quality data base resulting in prolific publication.

[7] I suspect that John Lofland's covert research on the Unification Church of the 1960s contributed to his portrayal of it as a kooky cult attracting lonely people and his neglecting its ingenious theology and experiential appeal. An epilogue to a recently enlarged edition gives a more balanced treatment of its appeal [3]. Among the most hostile accounts of *est* that I have read was one written by a covert investigator who went through the wastepaper bins at the *est* office to find a memo, which he proceeded to print, taking it out of context.

[8] The value of state-specific research has already been demonstrated in the findings of Lilly [21], Masters and Houston [22], Stanislav Grof [23], and Damrell [24]—all of whom have entered into the states that they have studied.

⁹ Charles Glock has quipped that research projects employing participant observers to study the new religions ought to take out "conversion insurance."

¹⁰ Bellah's treatment of symbolic realism is pregnantly ambiguous and is the focus of a forthcoming book [25]. Bellah introduced the concept of symbolic realism as a corrective to what he considers excessive reductionism, but he has not offered a research method to do this. The question of exactly what should not be reduced (or which religious truths should be taken seriously) remains. Drawing on symbolic realism as the basis of a research strategy, Anthony and Robbins offer the suggestion that "surface structures" of religions are appropriate for reductionistic analysis and "deep structures" are not. Deep structures of a religion point to a transcendental unity beyond the surface structures of particular creeds, rituals, and organizational forms. Thus the researcher should look for a core religious experience that is not determined by, or reducible to, other influences and is held in common across cultural influences [26,27]. The question of how these deep, non-reducible structures are to be identified remains. The criteria for what can be reduced perhaps may not be answered axiomatically. Keeping alert to the criteria in use may be the best that can be done.

¹¹ The collaboration between Bellah and Glock in directing the Berkeley New Religious Consciousness Project has been fruitful, though no jointly authored articles or common theoretical frameworks were produced. One of its greatest values was that of providing opportunities for conducting research amidst the ambiguity of respecting and doubting both religious and scientific viewpoints. Many of the points in this paper reflect my own research experiences in the project [29] and those of other participants as well.

¹² The attitude of "acceptance" in "Taoist objectivity" may be appropriate for scrutinizing *internal* states of consciousness, as well as external behaviors. With acceptance, where nothing is lacking or needs to be altered, the evaluative "chatter of the mind" is stilled. Attention may be directed toward observing the contents of states of consciousness, rather than trying to alter them into something "better." Buddhists, who cultivate this detachment, have developed incredibly detailed maps of many discrete states of consciousness. These maps are scientific descriptions to the extent that there is observation taking place which has been consensually validated over hundreds of years. These descriptions or "theories" have internally consistent logic that provides for prediction about what happens in these states.

¹³ Jeffrey Hadden has asked: Why should not religious adherents who are "passionately committed to their culture, be trained to do sociological observation? And why not give them full responsibility for a final product, respecting the integrity of that product? Perhaps we can learn more than is possible in the role of an aloof and detached observer. At least it is clear that we can learn something different" [30].

REFERENCES

1. Harvey Cox. "Something versus Nothing: The Real Threat of the Moonies." *Christianity and Crisis,* 14 November 1977.

2. Stillson Judah. *The Moonies: Conversion or Coercion?* In preparation.

3. John Lofland. *The Doomsday Cult.* Irvington Publishers, New York, 1977.

4. Thomas Robbins, Dick Anthony, Madalyn Doucas, and Thomas Curtis. "The Last Civil Religion: The Unification Church of Reverend Sun Myung Moon." *Sociological Analysis* 37 (1976):111–125.

5. Frederick Sontag. *Sun Myung Moon and the Unification Church.* Abingdon, 1977.

6. Abraham Maslow. *The Farther Reaches of Human Nature,* pp. 16–18. Viking-Compass Books, 1971.

7. Ludwig Feuerbach. *The Essence of Christianity.* Harper & Row ed., 1957.

8. Michael Polanyi. *Personal Knowledge: Towards a Post-Critical Philosophy,* p. xiv. Harper Torchbooks, 1964.

9. Abraham Kaplan. *The Conduct of Inquiry: Methodology for Behavioral Science,* p. 387. Chandler, 1964.

10. Harvey Cox. *Turning East: The Promise and Peril of the New Orientalism.* Simon and Schuster, 1977.

11. Jacob Needleman. *The New Religions.* E. P. Dutton, 1977.

12. Robert N. Bellah. *Beyond Belief,* p. 259. Harper & Row, 1970.

13. Peter L. Berger and Thomas Luckmann. *The Social Construction of Reality.* Anchor, 1966.

14. Roy Wallis. *The Road to Total Freedom: A Sociological Analysis of Scientology.* Heinemann, London, 1976.

15. Eugene Webb. "Unconventionality, Triangulation, and Inference." In Denzin [16], p. 450.

16. Norman K. Denzin, ed. *Sociological Methods: A Sourcebook,* p. 472. Aldine, 1970.

17. Steven Lukes. *Emile Durkheim: His Life and Work,* p. 515. Harper & Row, 1972; Penguin, 1975.

18. Donald Stone. "New Religious Consciousness and Personal Religious Experience." *Sociological Analysis* 39 (1978).

19. Charles T. Tart. *States of Consciousness,* pp. 210–212. E. P. Dutton, 1975.

20. Ibid., p. 223.

21. John Lilly, M. D. *The Center of the Cyclone: An Autobiography of Inner Space.* Julian Press, 1972; Bantam Books, 1973.

22. R. Masters and J. Houston. *The Altered States of Consciousness Induction Device: Some Possible Uses in Research and Psychotherapy.* Foundation for Mind Research, Pomona, New York, 1971.

23. Stanislav Grof. *The Realms of the Human Unconscious: Observations from LSD Research.* Viking, 1975.

24. Joseph Damrell. *Seeking Spiritual Meaning: The World of Vedanta.* Sage, 1977.

25. Dick Anthony, Thomas Robbins, and Robert N. Bellah. *On Religion and Social Science: A Non-Reductionist Approach to the Study of Religion.* University of California Press, forthcoming.

26. Dick Anthony, Thomas Robbins, and Thomas E. Curtis. "Reply to Bellah." *Journal for the Scientific Study of Religion* 13 (1974):493.

27. Dick Anthony and Thomas Robbins. "From Symbolic Realism to Structuralism." *Journal for the Scientific Study of Religion* 14 (1975):405.

28. Thomas Robbins and Dick Anthony. "Getting Straight with Meher Baba: A Study of Drug-Rehabilitation, Mystical Cults, and Post Adolescent Role Conflict." *Journal for the Scientific Study of Religion* 11 (1972):122–140.

29. Donald Stone. "The Human Potential Movement." In *The New Religious Consciousness,* pp. 93–115. Edited by Charles Y. Glock and Robert N. Bellah. University of California Press, 1976.

30. Jeffrey Hadden. "Review Symposium: The New Religious Consciousness." *Journal for the Scientific Study of Religion* 16 (1977):308.

REFLECTIONS ON THE TRANSMISSION OF BUDDHISM TO AMERICA

Charles Prebish

THE SCENE is a bright apartment in the "hill" section of Boulder, Colorado, near the University of Colorado campus. It is the occasion of a weekly "party" held by students who are enrolled in the first half of an intensive ten-week "module" in which they will study Indian Buddhism, live and meditate together, and otherwise partake of the activities that Naropa Institute has provided for the Summer Program of 1975. Only in its second summer of operation, this not-yet-accredited university has offered perhaps the most diversified curriculum of any alternative form of education since Esalen Institute first appeared on the American scene. The main focus of the university is Buddhist Studies, advertised in non-sectarian fashion in keeping with its founder's wishes, and this is what the party-goers are here to discuss: Buddhism. Seated on a sofa along one wall, two members of the experimental course are engaged in heated conversation. One is an instructor in the module, and the other is one of the students. Each of the two discussants normally teaches in a "regular" university during the academic year. With Coors in hand, the two figures debate the (Mahāyāna) doctrine of emptiness. After much talk, and little consensus, the module instructor asks the student to define "emptiness." The student replies quickly and with confidence: "Emptiness means that we don't exist. That's what Nāgārjuna said, and that's what I believe." Quick to respond, the instructor asks, "But does that mean that we are not sitting here having this discussion right now?" "Yep," notes the student, "no you, no me, no apartment, no Naropa Institute. That's what it means." "Then what's going on here? What about Nāgārjuna's two levels of truth?" asks the instructor. The student, sensing imminent victory, goes on, "Nirvāna and Samsāra are precisly the same thing, so nothing's going on here." "But isn't that a statement made from the standpoint of ultimate truth and doesn't Nāgārjuna also say, in the 18th verse of the 24th chapter of the Mādhyamikakārikās, 'It is dependent origination that we call emptiness,' thus stressing the *relational* quality of things rather than their non-existence?" the instructor answers. The student, now somewhat flustered, and becoming uneasy due to the little grin readily apparent on his interlocutor's face, says, "Look, you're just testing my faith." "No," says the instructor, "I'm just demonstrating how right Nāgārjuna is, especially when he says, in the 8th verse of the 13th chapter of the kārikās, that those who treat emptiness as a viewpoint are 'incurable.'" "Now wait just a minute," the student says, now getting quite angry, "you're just twisting my words." "Fair enough," quips the instructor, "How about if I demonstrate by pushing with no push the table which is no table into your non-existent knee and laugh no laugh while you cry no tears?" "Look, we're not getting anywhere," says the student, "Why do you suppose my teacher told me all this if it wasn't true?" The instructor, eager for an opportunity to change subjects, asks, "Who is your teacher?" "Why, Rinpoche, of course," the student responds. "Have you ever *met him personally?* By that I mean have you ever had a *private interview* with him?" the instructor asks. "Yes, once," the student retorts, "Not too long ago, when Rinpoche visited Chicago." Sensing a chance for some first-hand information, the instructor continues this line of questioning: "What was it like? How long did it last? How did you feel? What teaching did you get?" The student, now smiling, says, "Well, I was given five minutes with him, but actually our interview only lasted about three minutes. He was so compassionate that when he recognized my nervousness, he stared out the window the whole time." "You're kidding," says the instructor, "What did you learn from that?" The student: "I learned how terribly messed up I am, and how important his teaching was for me." At this point the instructor moved on to another conversation.

The foregoing is a mildly fictionalized account of a real conversation I witnessed in which the student was (by his own definition) a serious American Buddhist who devotes a considerable part of every day to Buddhist practice. Why do I start what I hope will be a reasonably sympathetic paper on Buddhism in America with such a profoundly disappointing demonstration? I do it because it must be clear from the outset that Buddhism in this country is a veritable "mixed-bag" of serious, mature, understanding students and practitioners, and a group of no less serious, but seriously limited students who understand little, perceive less, but are wildly vocal. I do not mean to imply by my example that all students of the teacher in question are like the one referred to above. Quite the contrary is true. Nevertheless, some Buddhist groups in America are growing so fast, with so little concern for the meaning of this rapid growth, that it is possible for one to follow a teacher that one has met only briefly, if at all, and to shape one's entire life around the supposed meaning of this teacher's pronouncements.

How did Buddhism in America grow from the simple beginning in the latter half of the nineteenth century to the mass movement that it has become less than a hundred years later? How did it come to the point which prompted Agehananda Bharati to remark:

Alan Watts once suggested that in another fifty years or so, people in India will drive around in cars, live in suburbia, and play baseball, whereas people in America will sit in caves in Oregon and in the Rockies and meditate on their navel and on ātman and nirvāna. This was meant to be facetious, but forensically useful exaggeration—still, the trend is certainly there [1].

I

With few exceptions, during its initial activity, Buddhism in America was represented by two essential sects of Japanese Buddhism: the Jōdo Shinshū tradition from Hompa Hongwanji in Kyoto and the Zen tradition, for the most part dominated by the Rinzai lineage of Imakita Kōsen of Engaku Temple. Apart from the almost exclusively Japanese communities that these traditions served, Buddhism was simply a curiosity for most non-Asian Americans.

A few Americans turned to Buddhism to quench an intellectual thirst, an inquisitiveness fueled by this seemingly exotic religion. In this regard, there is a striking parallel to the entry of Buddhism into China, probably in the first century A.D. With their Confucian and Taoist cultural patterns, the Chinese saw Buddhism as an overwhelmingly foreign and peculiar endeavor. Not only were Buddhisms's rituals and modes of religious practice strange, but its worldview and philosophical basis taxed the Chinese mind and temperament. To complicate the matter further, the language differences between the Indic and Chinese traditions were considerable. Consequently, during its first several hundred years in China, Buddhism made little meaningful headway. Its inertia was compounded by the fall of the Han Dynasty around 220 A.D. and the political confusion and instability that ensued. To be sure, the political dysfunction in China gave rise to substantial doses of social instability and the resultant anomie.

For Americans, Buddhism was no less foreign and curious than it was for the Chinese. America had its own variety of double helix basis for religious and cultural patterns in the Judeo-Christian tradition, and these are as anomalous with regard to Buddhism as Confucianism and Taoism were for the Chinese. Equally taxing for the American mind and temperament as it was for the Chinese was its attempt to understand a religious tradition that is essentially non-theistic, individualistic, apparently esoteric, mystical, and antithetical to social ethics. Not only is time construed in non-linear fashion, but we read of an endless chain of rebirths, suffering as the basic tenet of Buddha's preaching, and a meditational practice that many see initially as leading more to catatonia than to "enlightenment." Occasionally, too, we would hear of the ubiquitous doctrine of "emptiness," which seems to have been interpreted by many Americans to mean that nothing exists—not even America. Long before Buddhism's introduction, America had already built a powerful mythic history that was profoundly religious.

Although Americans during this period were likely attracted to Buddhism primarily out of curiosity or intellectual concerns (or perhaps even as a form of escapism), the American soil was fertile for further Buddhist development. The doctrinal basis for Buddhism has always been embodied in the teachings of Buddha's first sermon, a text which clearly espouses the Four Noble Truths of (1) suffering, (2) craving (or "attachment") as the cause of suffering, (3) the possibility for the cessation of suffering, and (4) the path to that cessation. America during the 1920s and 1930s was virtually the embodiment of, initially, the second noble truth, and then the first noble truth run wild. In the affluence following World War I, craving for material wealth in a rapidly changing world and society was rampant. The unrestricted fiscal policies quickly gave way to the deep Depression of the 1930s that scarred more than just America's economic foundations. And it is here that America, no less than India in the time of the Buddha, began to realize the truth of suffering. Out of the political, social, and economic instability, it might well have been possible for the American Buddhists to identify the rise of the Roosevelt administration with the third noble truth, and the New Deal policies of recovery with the fourth noble truth. In so doing, Buddhists in America would have been able to discern that life in America was not as incompatible with Buddhist teaching as it might at first appear. Since virtually all Buddhists in America were of Japanese ancestry, instead of remaining simply Japanese Buddhists in America, they might have approached the possibility of identifying themselves as Japanese Americans (long before this term was fashionable) who also happened to embrace Buddhism as a religious ideal. Nevertheless, these proto-American Buddhists either chose not to make this association or it simply did not occur to them.

To this point in American Buddhist history, its ritual life focused on the re-enactment of exclusively Asian (and to this point Japanese) mythic structure. Harvey Cox has noted that, "Rather than 'moving' people, a myth 'places' them in a universe of value and meaning" [2]. For early American Buddhists, the sacred center was Japan and not America, "placing" them more fully in that culture than the one of their residence. The temple was *in* America, but the sacred power in the ritual life enacted there, and the religious efficacy engendered by the powerful sounds of the ritual (especially remembering the importance of the repetition of the Nembutsu in the Jōdo Shinshū tradition) were all *of* Japan. Further, when Streng rightly notes, "In all major religious traditions there is a concern to make spiritual life effective in everyday social existence" [3], we must realize that social existence in America was a problematic area for the Japanese Buddhist. It was probably much more problematic for them than for non-Asian American Buddhists, since India has always been the *axis mundi* for Buddhists (as Jerusalem has been for Christians and Jews). Consequently, the lack of social identity confounded the problem of religious identity through this early period of Buddhist development in America.

Still, the identity problem might have been overcome had the Japanese Buddhists in America noticed some of the obvious parallels between avowedly American values and the enigmatic Buddhist practices noted above. On the one hand, the Zen tradition, like all of the meditative threads of Buddhist practice, emphasizes complete self-reliance in the attainment of religious salvation. No outside agency could produce the appropriate answer to the Zen practitioner's kōan; no outside agent could perform his zazen for him. Equally, this intense self-reliance was not unlike the so-called "rugged individualism" that Americans are so fond of citing as demonstration of their resilient nature and ability to overcome personal obstacles in the path to success. Yet only a few of the Zen teachers, and virtually none of the American Zen practitioners, ever seemed to have noticed the parallel. On the other hand, in more explicitly "religious" endeavors, the many practitioners of Jōdo Shinshū rarely (if ever) saw the parallel between the saving grace of Amida Buddha and the notion of grace in the Judeo-Christian tradition. Further, the usual reaction to social change on the part of the early American Buddhists was one of simple retrenchment. In other words, they seemed to opt for something less than the middle path.

A final handicap to Buddhist infancy in America was the lack of the Orient as a substantial "sphere of influence" in American political life. Unlike the post-1945 period, with Korea and Vietnam successively dominating the consciousness of many Americans, the Orient, before Pearl Harbor, was still regarded as the "mystical east" or the "inscrutable east," offering little fact or attention for the mind's eye of the public. To be sure, the war with Japan was a potential death blow to American Buddhism, with this period being particularly difficult for those in internment camps. Like the Buddhist persecution in China in 845, in which all the scholastic traditions faded to the background and only the predominantly practice oriented sects survived, World War II demonstrated the resilience of these same "vest pocket" traditions on the American scene. Instead of snuffing out American Buddhism before it had taken hold, the Pure Land and Zen traditions survived. At a time when Buddhism in America was so limited in scope, and with little diversity of traditions and sects, this survival was the foreshadowing of the great diversity and growth that was to follow.

After the Second World War, not only was the bitter taste of collective inhumanity (symbolized by both Pearl Harbor, and Hiroshima and Nagasaki) still souring the mouths of Americans, but also a profound awareness of the Orient in general and Japan in particular remained in our minds. Shintō in Japan had been disestablished. Buddhism, on the other hand, in spite of its support for the war effort, fared considerably better, both in Japan and America. American veterans, having returned to colleges and universities, were more aware of things Oriental. Also at this time, American universities began to expand their offerings on Asia, with courses on Asian history, politics, sociology, and religion. Just as today it is not unusual to find Vietnam veterans in courses on Buddhism, the precedent had been established by their fathers, the entire enterprise having been enhanced by the reappearance of D. T. Suzuki and others who pursued university lecturing with vigor and integrity. In addition, the study of Asian religions was finally emerging as an academic discipline in America, one that required serious and painstaking language training if the task was to be meaningfully accomplished. Like the coming of Kumārajīva to China, it was not long before scholars with more than appropriate credentials indirectly aided in the task of establishing Buddhism's first significant entry to America by providing excellent translations of Buddhist texts from virtually all the Buddhist traditions and languages.

By the mid-1950s, Buddhism in America was on the brink of several new developments. First, new forms of Buddhism were appearing on the American scene, particularly Sōtō Zen, Zen that combined Rinzai and Sōtō techniques, and the beginnings of Tibetan Buddhism. Second, and by far the most important development in Buddhism since its entry into America, was the emergence of "Beat Zen." Although the Beat movement had its official beginning at the now-famous reading at the Six Gallery in San Francisco in 1955, the movement had roots that went back considerably farther. The appeal of the Beats was founded on the basis of their American heritage, a heritage which they also, in large part, rejected. In building a myth of their own, the Beats replaced what they rejected of American culture with what they perceived to be Zen culture.

The parallels between Zen and what the Beats themselves

thought they represented are all too apparent. In the first place, the Beats identified with the spontaneity of the Zen tradition. Perhaps the most significant example of this, on the literary level, is Kerouac's "spontaneous prose," written on long rolls of paper, quickly and with no revisions. Just as Buddhists choose not to cling to a past that is already dead, Kerouac refused to polish his work. On the personal level, the Beats practiced a sort of perverted situation ethics. For them, the unifying character of this ethical system was (assumed) freedom, manifested in their blatant antinomianism. In addition, the Beats rather naïvely assumed that because some Zen monks wandered over the countryside, as apparent "lunatics," in a style consistent with their satori experience, *all* Zen monks followed this practice. In so doing, the Beats not only ignored the very basis of Zen monastic life and its incumbent discipline, but they used this assumption to form the basis of a normative model (and justification) for their own itinerant lifestyle. The Beats also prostituted the supposed ecstasy of Zen experience. Consequently, the erotic quality of life was overemphasized, as were their frequent excursions into the world of drugs and alcohol. Even in the musical styles favored by the Beats, they sought to convey the non-intellectual, intuitive style of Zen, exemplified by their fascination with jazz improvisation.

The Beats had come close, with their zany antics and the suppositions that they were founded on, to providing a real *American* beginning for Buddhism. Had they only understood more fully the Zen tradition they associated with, and incorporated an authentic Zen *lineage* into their tradition, genuine success might have been achieved. Of the lot, it was only Gary Snyder who had any acumen in properly understanding the meaning of Zen. Having studied Chinese and Japanese at Berkeley, he went to Japan (in 1956) to learn meditation from the great masters. As it turned out, Gary Snyder became the disciple of Sessō Oda Rōshi (who was a disciple of Sōkatsu Shaku's student, Zuigan Gōto), and he studied with Oda Rōshi until the master's death in 1966. It is curious and puzzling why the Beats did not adopt an approach more consonant with the one taken by Gary Snyder, apart from the fact that it may have required more responsibility than they seemed to possess. Whatever understanding Ginsberg may have attained seems to have come much later, and it is just not clear that Kerouac ever understood

Buddhism very well, in spite of the fact that several of his novels (e.g., *On the Road, The Dharma Bums*) were clearly Buddhist-inspired.

Frank Reynolds and Joseph Kitagawa have noted that, "throughout Southeast Asia modern reform Buddhism has been associated with the emerging urban elite" [4]. Equally, it could be argued that a similar claim might be made for "Beat Zen." How strange it is that none of the Beats ever sought to identify the city domain of the American Zennist's search for satori as the wilderness in which religious wholeness might be found. Had such a notion been propounded and accepted, not only would the superficial layers of the forthcoming "back to nature" movement have been seriously undercut, but also the city as symbolic of inherent evil and darkness might have lost some of its apparent support, all with the result that Americans of the 1960s and 1970s would not have incorrectly surmised that in order to practice Buddhism properly, they must desert the city and run to the naked wilds, raping it in the process.

If the Beats are reputed to have publicized Zen while possibly damaging it in the process, the other side of the proverbial coin was represented by the "Square Zen" of Alan Watts. Watts's influence has likely been more significant than the Beats (if only through his prolific production of popular books), and he certainly reached more people, but in his somewhat amateurish attempt to explain Zen in the context of modern science and psychology, he had neither the Buddhological sophistication of D. T. Suzuki, nor the deep, personal experience of Philip Kapleau (or a host of others). While Zen became a more commonplace word in America, it was wounded by the double-edged sword of America's inherent rejection of the Beats and their suspicion of Alan Watts's scholarship. My own suspicion is that movements like "Beat Zen" and "Square Zen" cause scholars to grossly underestimate the integrity of the Buddhist movement in America. Thus by 1960, Buddhism in America was still groping for leadership, a Western identity, and a solid community of participants.

II

In the decade of the 1960s Buddhism was to reap the largest, fastest, and most dynamic growth spurt in its short history on the

American scene. Concomitantly, its rapid rise presented Buddhism with as many potential liabilities as it did opportunities, liabilities which, without proper care and attention, could have fragmented Buddhism in America quite severely. The story of Buddhism's growth in the 1960s must be cast against the backdrop of two general, umbrella-like trends that were just beginning to come to full fruition: the rampant social and religious unrest. These two trends, in a country founded on social and religious freedom, were to interpenetrate in an exciting but disruptive fashion. The complexity of life in the 1960s must, however, be restricted somewhat so as to focus on those issues most relevant to the major concern of this study.

In the social domain, the most significant development for Buddhism in America was the emergence of a considerable counter-culture, from which Buddhism was to recruit some of its most ardent supporters. Nevertheless, the most immediate predecessors of the counter-cultural movement were the Beats of the 1950s. Kerouac himself conceded that the hippies were the descendants of the Beat Generation [5]. The hippies, however, unlike the Beats, intended to gain more than just a mere reputation as critics of society. They responded to technology run wild, to what Toffler refers to as the superimposition of the future on the present, in a personal active fashion. Here also one sees a clear affinity between the pure self-determinist notion of the hippie movement and the law of karma as stated in Buddhism. Despite a present shaped by past actions, freedom of action in each new moment persists, enabling the practitioner to claim complete responsibility for and control over the future, religiously and otherwise. Further, the practitioner is enjoined not to look outside of himself to any agency of control such as God.

In the 1960s the entire religious situation in America was in turmoil. There was a continuous drop in church attendance, possibly indicative of a declining faith in the value of religion or its importance in a secular society, and the "Death of God" theologians such as Thomas Altizer, William Hamilton, and Richard Rubenstein were creating a fuss in both the public and private domain. Given the intensified secularization of the 1960s and its attendant pluralism, America was ripe for Buddhism to advance. When Harvey Cox's *The Secular City* appeared in 1965, it made no less impact than John Robinson's *Honest to God* had two years earlier. When Peter Berger contends that secularization follows from modern industrialization, he also notes that, "secularization brings about a demonopolization of religious traditions and thus, *ipso facto*, leads to a pluralistic situation" [6]. If we follow Berger's argument to its conclusion, we learn that some of the results of this secular, pluralistic situation are *ecumenicity*, in which religious collaboration results, regarding one's rivals as "fellows" rather than "enemies," the elimination of the "supernatural" elements from the traditions (in extreme cases), and a new emphasis on the laity [7]. The demonopolization of (predominantly) Western religious traditions created an environment in which many persons saw Buddhism as a religious option which deserved exploration.

Thus the 1960s witnessed more new Buddhist groups, with a greater diversity of traditional and sectarian affiliations, than ever before in America. Buddhism's lack of a God concept to express ultimate reality made it attractive to those persuaded by the Death of God argument and those feeling the fallout of the declining supernatural thrust of traditional religion in America. Renewed interest in the laity on the part of Western religions only worked to Buddhism's advantage, since it has yet to establish a significant monastic community (or even a large community of religious officials) on American soil. A corollary to this last point is that unlike the Hare Krishna movement, conversion to Buddhism did not entail "an emphatic rejection of conventional affluent America" [8]. Rather, Buddhist laymen searched for a Buddhist way to live within such a context, just as earlier laymen had sought in their Asian homeland.

A consideration of the Drug Culture brings the hippies, once again, into immediate view. Roszak sees what he calls the "psychedelic obsession" as a symptom of "cultural impoverishment" [9]. Just as the hippies' concerns with social evils have their basis in a culture that has always noted civil disobedience as a valid form of dissent, their concern with drugs goes back farther than just the Beats. The drug lineage in America traces its origins (omitting, in this context, native American religions) to William James, Havelock Ellis, and others. James's *The Varieties of Religious Experience*, Aldous Huxley's *The Doors of Perception*, and Alan Watts's *The Joyous Cosmology: Adventures in the Chemistry of Consciousness* all became counter-culture bibles before Richard Alpert was transformed into Baba Ram Dass and Timothy Leary became "High Priest." The "cosmic connection," however, antedates all of this.

Leary rediscovered the themes of James and Huxley, and promoted the use of psychotropics as a religious activity. Some Oriental religious groups utilized the obvious association made by Leary and others in order to promote their own purposes. An example might be taken with regard to a large poster on the wall of a Hare Krishna temple in San Francisco that begins with the words "Stay High Forever" [7,10]. Buddhism never prompted such claims, constantly seeking to disavow any of its adherents' suspicions to the contrary. Nevertheless, not only was a drug background usual in the history of many 1960s Buddhists in America, but also present seemed to be the hope for the "organic trip," more powerful than the drug experience, but safer. Stressing not the exotic experiences to be attained through Buddhist meditational systems, the wisest of the Buddhist teachers in America constantly cited the "ordinariness" of Buddhist experience and the necessity of relating to the world "as it is," rather than as it can be adjusted.

It was in the language of the Human Potential Movement that Buddhism was to find a more impressive and useful (as well as unknowing) ally. The landmark work of Abraham Maslow, Fritz Perls, and others was to coalesce in the 1960s under the rubric cited above. Encompassing a wide variety of techniques and therapies, the Human Potential Movement was symbolized by Esalen Institute, where many of the superstars of the movement came to offer seminars and programs. The Human Potential Movement has often utilized techniques of "Eastern spiritual disciplines," and in this way a growing number of Americans became aware of Oriental religions. Buddhism in America in the 1960s (and 1970s) was also beginning to learn, however, that the converse might be true, and that appropriation of the terminology of the movement (and to a lesser extent, techniques) might enable Buddhism to attract some of the several million Americans who had (by mid-1970s) associated with the Human Potential Movement. Consequently, it was not unusual to hear words like "growth," and "openness" in newly emergent Buddhist centers. "Peak experience" was a frequent synonym for nirvāna, and often one would hear a discussion of Charlotte Selver or "Rolfing" in place of the expected discussion of D. T. Suzuki or satipaṭṭhāna. The Human Potential Movement gave Buddhists a new language for expressing human problems.

Unlike the 1950s, in which Buddhists sought to either retrench and ignore their association with America altogether, reject America and its culture and replace it with a perverted Zen culture (as the Beats did), or popularize Zen in a less than effective or accurate fashion (as Alan Watts did), in the 1960s, Buddhists in America became much more aware of their potential American identity, and even took the first small steps towards achieving it. Of course, this does not dismiss those who were attracted to Buddhism precisely because of its "otherness." For many, the newness, supposed rootlessness, and hoped-for ecstasy made Buddhism attractive in quite the same fashion as other counter-culture expressions of antiformalism and pursuits of a seemingly elusive wholeness. Consequently, we find the somewhat paradoxical situation of Buddhism gaining adherents in some circles because of the sameness with American ideals and in other circles because of its separateness. In spite of the above, Buddhism in the 1960s was still searching for a lifestyle consonant with its pursuits in America. In the first place, there was virtually no monastic samgha present, and almost no Buddhist monks or nuns in residence. Nevertheless, Buddhist community meant *lay* community, and, to a large extent, *city* community.

Buddhist communities, however, faced problems that have proved difficult. First, as Rosabeth Kanter suggests, "Successful communities provided not only guide for work but also free time and recreation in line with the group's ideals" [11]. Buddhist groups were notably remiss in providing such guidelines. Consequently, not only did a transcendence facilitating tradition not develop, but community members (many of whom were "dropouts" of some kind) found it too easy to fall back into their old patterns, or to transfer their Sunday morning Protestantism into Sunday morning Buddhism. In many cases, Buddhist communities defined themselves in terms of what they rejected rather than what they affirmed, allowing a severe sense of ambiguity to persist. In other words, Buddhist communities sought legitimation with no greater success than their Western counterparts. And since the sectarian distinction among Buddhist groups in America was now becoming more apparent, American Buddhists were finding themselves in the midst of their own identity crisis, one not alleviated by their community life.

With an increasing emphasis on the laity, as a result of secularization and pluralism, Buddhist lay communities needed, more profoundly than in previous decades, to find a means by which they might participate in the sanctity inherent in the sacred center of their religion. As is the rule in post-primitive religion, the *actual* center itself remains at a distance (in this case, in Asia), but it is *transposed* into an American sacred center through its embodiment in American Buddhist temples and the ritual life enacted there. And this is critical, since the sacred center is the place of creation and renewal, the realm of absolute reality, the place where chaos becomes cosmos. Unfortunately, in the 1960s, the Buddhist temples in America were for the most part not only Asian in design (obviously manifest in their architecture), but also in *ritual function*. Thus, robbed of sacred American centers, American Buddhists—even the large number of non-Asians that had become part of the Buddhist movement—found themselves expressing a religious ideal and creativity more appropriate for Asia than America. Buddhist community life in America was consequently handicapped by its lack of mythic meaning, relegating its activities almost exclusively to the profane rather than sacred realm [12].

As noted above, the Buddhist movement in America, and specifically Buddhist community life, has been a city movement. Nevertheless, in the 1960s a large number of Buddhists deserted the city and sought to practice their religion in a wilderness setting. Of course, some of these practitioners simply rejected the evils of city life. Others seemed to be motivated by a concern for the preservation of a sane ecological environment, and a goodly number were simply naïvely pursuing a "back to nature" style of life. Many American Buddhists had been blindly seduced by the rural, country settings of monastic institutions in Asia or the rustic settings of Japanese landscape painting, or some other suspicion that Buddhism could *only* be practiced in the pristine wilds. In any case, these Buddhist practitioners searched for a peaceful spot in which, they were certain, it would be much easier to "actualize themselves." Most have now returned to the city, but they do not seem to know why.

Wilderness has a long history as a major symbol in American religious life. Filled with trials and tribulations, it was a place for faith to be tested, but with mastery, it was also a locus of creativity in which the (recreation of the) Garden motif was predominant. The key issue is mastery, not a mastery that is dependent on the destruction of the environment, but a consonance and resonance with it. And as the wilderness is mastered, so is the individual mastered, and sacredness restored. American Buddhists had no intention of mastering the wilds. It was simply a physical depository for their cumbersome bodies, enabling them to pursue their "spiritual" quest in an ideal environment, free from the responsibilities of city life. Apparently they did not realize that the wilderness imposed its own responsibilities, and it took little time to discover that they were no better prepared to master themselves isolated from the urban life they had grown used to, than they were in the city. Buddhism has always maintained that the best place to practice Buddhism is precisely *where you are*, and that the environment that needs tending is the *interior* environment. Of course this does not mean abandonment of concern for the ecological balance. It just means that one needs to be painfully honest about what one is pursuing in the first place. An old Buddhist saying remarks, "When the cart does not go, which do you whip, the cart or the horse?" Buddhists would have been more consonant with the actual situation of their American quest if they had identified with the city as the new American wilderness. Just as the biblical wilderness was inhabited by monsters, the city-wilderness had its own monsters in crime, racism, drug addiction, and other demons. Just as the biblical wilderness represented uncultivated lands, the city-wilderness had its own uncultivated lands in the inner city and ghetto. Thus the city symbolizes the pre-Creation chaos which highlights the negative aspects of the wilderness, but it also symbolizes, in positive fashion, its potential for taming and creativity.[1] Consequently, settlement or establishment in the city is a mythic act of creation, and like all acts of beginning, it would have afforded Buddhism the truly American basis that it avowedly sought. Buddhism now finds itself, somewhat unawares, creating its first true acculturation in the wilderness of the American city.

While it is clear that the Buddhist movement in America

gained a broad-based support in the youth culture during this decade, it was not the youth culture alone that swelled its ranks. To some degree, although it is difficult to estimate accurately, the problem of acculturation was exacerbated in the late 1960s by a kind of "Dharma hopping" [14], that is, moving from one spiritual scene to another, inhibiting a sense of commitment to one specific group. Still, more than ever before, the American Buddhist is now American rather than Asian, of any age, of any career, of any degree of seriousness. Equally, the sexes are about evenly split, and the educational level of American Buddhists is higher than ever before.

III

As inflation persists and values erode, many Americans are faced with a pervasive loss of wholeness. The average American is no longer the "rugged individualist" or "organization man," but rather the "bifurcated searcher," struggling against polarizing forces in virtually every aspect of his life. And of course the complicating variables appear to be unending. In an age of mass media, data input systems, and intensified social fluidity, America flexes its collective muscles in the search for human completeness amidst Theodore Roszak's projected "Wasteland," and an overwhelming (and perhaps alarming) variety of alternatives appears in the social, cultural, and religious spheres: alternative marriage styles to combat an alarming (and constantly rising) divorce rate, electronic music and computerized art forms to tantalize the avant-garde, and esoteric cults promoted by self-styled gurus of the "pop" scene. It is no wonder that amidst the fallout of America's quest for wholeness, America makes itself more vulnerable than ever to the proliferation of techniques from outside its own boundaries.

Curiously enough, as the 1970s proceed, there is a distinct leveling off with regard to new Buddhist groups. Despite the stabilizing of new "imports," the numerical expansion of Buddhist practitioners abounds, yielding a rather peculiar paradox: in the age of supersonic transport, where boundaries between countries, continents, and cultures dissolve with no larger price to pay than "jet lag," the growth of Buddhism in America is no longer dependent on a continued focus on Asian developments. Indeed, with multinational corporations, SONY products, and advanced technology, even Japan hardly seems "Buddhist" to most Americans. As predominantly Buddhist cultures in Asia grudgingly modernize, they are rapidly learning that what Agehananda Bharati refers to as the "aloha-amigo" syndrome (which Bharati describes as "pathological eclecticism") may well be a product of the American mentality, but that it is highly contagious.

No one knows how far the numerical expansion of Buddhism in America has progressed to date, partly because it has become difficult to know what constitutes a Buddhist today. Holmes Welch [15] has made it clear that it is insufficient to simply ask, "Are you a Buddhist?" An affirmative response does not rule out the possibility that a similar response might be evoked, from the same person, to the question, "Are you a Taoist?" More appropriate questions might be, "Have you taken the Three Refuges?" Further, "Do you practice the five layman's vows?" If these questions were the standard for identifying Buddhists, we would be forced to estimate the number of Buddhists in America considerably downward, and in Asia as well. The issue is further complicated by the fact that various groups determine "members" in diverse ways. For example, some groups designate financial contributors as members, and thereby as Buddhists. Others identify members as those who frequently attend services or meditation sessions. The methods for determining membership, and Buddhist standing, are too numerous to cite here. The result, however, is that membership rolls are inflated, at least with respect to the traditional criteria for determining Buddhist affiliation. And the above discussion of membership determination ignores a consideration of the *quality* of membership and *commitment* to the tradition. Consequently, we must consider whether new modes of standardization (and new criteria) are more appropriate today, and whether it is possible or valuable to maintain multivalent allegiances in such matters. Thus, while Buddhism grew in numbers in the 1960s, it was unable to consolidate these gains due to its untimely association with a counter-culture that, in large part, rejected American culture and values. American Buddhism of the 1970s, on the other hand, is beginning to more fully implement its identification with American culture, and in the process, has been able to achieve a greater and more enduring growth.

In the 1960s, Buddhists' infant community life in America was more seriously disrupted than were those of more established communities in the mainstream of American culture. Consequently, through its association with the counter-culture, Buddhist community life was, to some extent a hotbed of current or defunct radicals, practicing everything from do-it-yourself macrobiotics to various forms of multilateral marriage. In reaction to these elements in Buddhism, some Buddhist teachers in the 1970s have returned to the traditional mode of instruction for laymen, i.e., emphasis on non-harming, abstention from theft, false speech, intoxicants and drugs of any kind, and illicit sexual behavior. In so doing, these teachers began to realize that the traditional mode was generally outdated (and consequently, rendered ineffective and unbelievable) or ill-suited to modern America. These problems are certainly not distinct to Buddhists. Nevertheless, in confronting them directly, Buddhists squarely face not only the immediate problems in the ethical domain, but the greater problem of American identity. For struggling as Americans with critical issues in American life, Buddhists in this country are able to emphasize their sameness rather than their separateness. Further, in beginning to alter the traditional patterns of Buddhist ethics, they are for the first time creatively dealing with their plight in the modern world.

In the 1970s, with its monumental advances in all aspects of technology, this problem becomes a strategic concern for American Buddhists. Theoretically, at least, "Future Shock" has never been a frightening issue for Buddhists in that it is the logical, modern application of the Buddhist theory of impermanence and its development into the doctrine of momentariness. In simple language, each presently existing moment manifests a latent (but now inexistent) past and a potential (but not yet existent) future. In the hands of the most adept Buddhist scholastics, namely the Sarvāstivādin school, it was propounded that the past, present, and future all exist simultaneously. Although this school eventually died out in India, it left its heritage by shaping much of the Buddhism that was to follow it. It also provides a tool which, when applied to the seemingly premature arrival of the future in the present, identifies this phenomenon as congruent with the "normal" state of affairs. Just as the ongoing explication of the theory of momentariness (in the Abhidharma period) demonstrated Buddhists' willingness and capability in addressing scientific matters, this attitude would be helpful in the 1970s. Not only does the lack of confrontation inhibit their acculturation, but it also cannot be expected that modern American Buddhists will accept overly simplistic or naïvely undemonstrable tenets for much longer. While American Buddhists vainly chase the simplicity that they *think* Buddhism represents, they fail to recognize that the *context* has changed. Thus, as Americans consider the potential abandonment of their dream of the "innocent Adam," American Buddhists must abandon their dream of the "innocent Buddha." Although the innocent Buddha may be transmuted into a cybernetic version of the HAL computer in Arthur C. Clarke's *2001: A Space Odyssey,* Buddhists in America must end their silence on the relationship between Buddhism and Science (or end their *simplistic* approach to the relationship), and in the process, assert their sameness with the American mission rather than their separateness.

IV

There have always been two distinct lines of development for Buddhism in America. One form of Buddhism places primary emphasis on sound, basic doctrines, shared by all Buddhists, and on solid, religious practice (which may reflect sectarian doctrinal peculiarities). These groups are slow to develop, conservative in nature, and remarkably *stable* in growth, activity, and teaching. The other line of development includes those groups which seem to emerge shortly after radical social movements (such as the Beat generation or the drug culture). They tend to garner the "fallout" of social upheaval. Stressing less the basic doctrine and painstaking practice, they usually base their attraction on the promise of something new, frequently centered in the personal charisma of a flamboyant leader. In other words, they replace the old social order, now in decay or disfavor, with a new one, replete with the same sort of trappings, but transmuted into what is thought to be a more profoundly "relevant" religious foundation. By nature flashy, opaquely exotic, and "hip," these movements gain much attention in the press, but are inherently unstable. Some of these groups do endure, but only after the pandemonium has passed and they have adopted a more solid working basis. It is usually only these flashy groups that generate significant public interest and are noticed in the press. Yet because of their chaotic nature, they are perceived with ambivalence at best, and more often than not, are regarded as clearly undesirable. Thus, *all* of Buddhism—even the "quiet" and honest Buddhism—is misunderstood or rejected outright in the curious public's eye. The misunderstanding filters its way down to scholars, leading to their inappropriately facile dismissal of a religious tradition with several hundred thousand adherents in America. Since there have always been no fewer than two Buddhisms on the American scene, we must learn to discriminate more clearly between the various forms and their validity.

NOTE

[1] The images are Eliade's [13], the application mine.

REFERENCES

1. Agehananda Bharati. *The Light at the Center*, p. 127. Ross-Erickson, Santa Barbara, 1976.

2. Harvey Cox. *The Seduction of the Spirit*, p. 284. Simon and Schuster, 1973.

3. Frederick Streng. *Understanding Religious Life*, p. 95. Dickerson, Encino, California, 1976.

4. Joseph Kitagawa and Frank Reynolds. "Theravada Buddhism in the Twentieth Century." In *Buddhism in the Modern World*, p. 48. Edited by Heinrich Dumoulin and John Maraldo. Collier, 1976.

5. Bruce Cook. *The Beat Generation*, p. 89. Scribner, 1971.

6. Peter L. Berger. *The Sacred Canopy: Elements of a Sociological Theory of Religion*, p. 134. Doubleday, 1966.

7. Ibid., pp. 140–147.

8. Gregory Johnson. "The Hare Krishna in San Francisco." In *The New Religious Consciousness*, pp. 36–39. Edited by Charles Glock and Robert Bellah. Univeristy of California Press, 1976.

9. Theodore Roszak. *The Making of a Counter Culture*, p. 163. Anchor, 1969.

10. Harvey Cox. *Turning East: The Promise and Peril of the New Orientalism*, p. 32. Simon and Schuster, 1977.

11. Rosabeth Kanter. *Commitment and Community*, p. 121. Harvard University Press, 1972.

12. Mircea Eliade. *Cosmos and History*, p. 28. Harper Torchbooks ed., 1959.

13. Ibid., p. 9.

14. Emma McCloy Layman. *Buddhism in America*, p. 203. Nelson-Hall, Chicago, 1976.

15. Holmes Welch. *The Practice of Chinese Buddhism, 1900–1950*, p. 357. Harvard University Press, 1973.

CHARISMA AND RITUAL IN NEW RELIGIOUS MOVEMENTS
Frederick Bird

A CHARACTERISTIC feature of new religious movements is an emphasis upon praxis rather than upon abstract theory, upon the participation in certain intrinsically valued, stylized activities rather than upon philosophical or dogmatic discussion.[1] To be sure, a number of practitioners of these movements declare they are anti- or a-religious, and many more criticize the given liturgies of the major Christian and Jewish denominations (and usually, as well, ignore the most elaborated Hindu and Buddhist rituals). Still, almost universally, the adherents of these movements are practicing certain stereotyped, repeated, collectively and authoritatively designated, and intrinsically valued activities, which are best termed "rituals." Moreover, in spite of the extremely wide variety of rituals practiced by these groups, these movements tend in common to assign particular prominence to certain cultic rites—such as those for initiation, meditation, healing—and little prominence to other more sectarian or ecclesiastic rites—such as those for the stages of life or seasons of year or for confession and penance.

Why do participants in these movements emphasize the importance of these ritual practices? Their aim seems to be to find some means, by practicing certain exercises or rituals, to protect their sense of self-worth from the exigencies of various external and internal threats and to enhance their personal experience of power and worth. These ritual practices serve adherents like armor, to protect and strengthen them, rather than like strategies for battle, or armaments for struggle, or ground rules for jousts. The purpose of these ritual practices seems not to be the development of techniques for more effective socializing but the fostering of certain self-authenticating experiences for practitioners. The experiences are not as players of roles (members of families, occupiers of careers, etc.) but as human beings continuously concerned with what Goffman refers to as "face," namely "the positive social value a person effectively claims for himself" [2]. I suggest that the appeal of these varied religious movements is that participants find their ritual practices provide them in variable ways with these kinds of self-validating experiences and this kind of self-protective armor.

This argument can be contrasted with one made several years ago by the anthropologist Max Gluckman to explain the greater prevalence of rituals in primitive rather than in industrialized societies. Gluckman argued that, in the absence of the structural differentiation of various roles and institutions, primitive rituals served to identify the passage from one role and function to another. The rituals marked those transitions which were not structurally identified and invested persons with authority needed for their new roles. Gluckman notes the parallel between modern etiquette and convention and primitive ritual, but argued that the latter was far more elaborated, and the former were more secular and were simply instrumental [3]. In contrast, ritual in these movements does not function as etiquette, conventions, or primitive ceremonies do. There, ritual establishes and orders social relations; here, ritual serves to arm practitioners with a sense of self-worth. So armed, adherents in varying degrees feel prepared for the dramas of life.

BASIC TERMS: NEW RELIGIONS AND RITUAL

Most of what we would designate as "new" religious movements have been established during the past two decades, even though some movements, such as Theosophy, the Spiritualists, or the Self-Realization Fellowship, are considerably older. Many movements bear a striking resemblance to what Ahlstrom has referred to as the Harmonial religious tradition in America [4,5]. All groups utilize ritual practices which have in the past been part of recognized religious traditions. The new groups are led by core members, for whom participation in these movements has become almost a way of life. The aim of the movements is to foster the realization of self-transcending, self-authenticating experiences. Many of these groups do not require an exclusive affiliation of adherents, so practitioners may participate in them while still affiliating with other equivalent religious or secular groups. In most of these movements, there is a spectrum of involvement, from passing interest to deep commitment.

The term "ritual" has often been used disparagingly as a label for empty routines or meaningless, habituated behavior. This paper assumes a different perspective. Generally defined, "rituals" are a family of stereotyped, stylized, repeated, authoritatively designated, and intrinsically valued activities.[2] In keeping with this relatively broad, yet still restricted, definition, the enactment of various liturgies, ceremonies, therapeutic techniques, games, etiquettes, social conventions, and even exercises, may all varyingly be identified as ritual activities. Hence, numbers of observers have noted the parallels between religious ritual and, for example, ceremonies and games [2,7,10,11,12,13], between religious rituals and therapeutic techniques [14,15], as well as between religious rituals and etiquette and social convention [2,16]. This spectrum of stylized, often repeated activities shares several additional characteristics. In all cases, attention is focused on conformation to an already stereotyped, objectively given form of acting, rather than on the consequences of that acting. Moreover, ritual activities constitute not only a kind of performance, but also a form of communication. All ritual actors use highly restricted linguistic codes which make use of redundancy, regularity, and multiple or fused meanings, in order to make certain images or realities present to both their active and subliminal minds [17,18,34]. Furthermore, in all its various forms, ritual action is dramatic, either because actors are consciously re-enacting traditional or trans-historical dramas, or because they feel they are in the process of acting and being acted upon [19,20].

Functionally analyzed, these various rituals provide the means of acting in situations which are frequently emotionally troubling, anomalous, or critical. For example, ritual activities, and especially religious rituals, have developed around critical transitions within the life cycle; around critical transitions during the seasons of the year (at times of planting, harvest, and the beginning of winter); around encounters with relatives and strangers, ambivalent as they are; and around the passages from night to day, and from work to play. In these situations, ritual provides a point of reference, a means for making critical and confusing situations thinkable [21]. Ritual actions guide persons through such situations in part because they function further to protect what may be sacred—ultimate values, revered institutions, gods—from being profaned by uncontrolled exposure or trivial considerations. Correspondingly, if what persons in contemporary society value ultimately is their sense of dignity, and their "face" as an expression of that dignity, then one would expect contemporaries to find particular appeal in those kinds of rituals which seem best designed to guard this sacred reality from trivial, uncontrolled exposure and threat.

Often, but not without parallel with other ritualized activities, participants of religious rituals expect the ritual re-enactment will bring about some kind of self-transcending, self-transforming experience. To an extent, participants in therapeutic techniques share this same outlook: that in some fundamental way they may become different, transformed beings by ritual re-enactment. In both instances, the ritualized forms become dead if they only serve to aid participants to re-collect past events, rather than to put themselves in a context for this transformation, this becoming.

Ritual forms may be alive, that is, expressing and activating the actors' feelings, or they may be dead. Today, both within and outside some of the major religious denominations of North America, many persons feel that the inherited ritual forms, as ordinarily practiced, have become empty, arbitrary conventions. The liturgical renewal movements among Christians, and the Chassidic and *havurah* movements in Judaism, have grown in response to these feelings. These movements have tried to revivify some ritual practices, often relatively successfully. Especially successful have been small group practices, in homes or elsewhere, or else large gatherings apart from the regular congregational services.[3] Participants in religious movements seem also to reflect the conviction that the inherited rituals for social intercourse, as well as for religious worship, have become sterile conventions, unattuned to the pace and crises of present society.

RITUAL PATTERNS IN MOVEMENTS

In general, the rituals practiced in new religious movements are not designed to give order to social relations, or to celebrate the seasons of the year, or to mark the passage of life. Moreover, in their ritual activities, these groups do not provide the kind of liturgical setting in which practitioners can reinterpret their on-going life activities in relation to a given, paradigmatic drama, such as the death and resurrection of Jesus, or the Exodus and conquest of Israel. This central feature of congregational wor-ship services is missing from the ritual repertoire of these groups. Rather, insofar as these groups do sponsor congrega-tional rituals, the liturgical model to which they refer involves characteristic sequences such as "I was asleep, then I woke up," or "I was weak, and then I received power." They make no reference to a universal, human drama, of conflict (death, slavery) and resolution (life. freedom).[4]

In addition, with the exception of the Charismatic and Jesus groups, these movements have established no rituals for confes-sion, penance, or atonement. The testimonies given by adherents within several groups do not take this form. The absence of the rituals for confession is significant because of the central role which confession plays in Christianity and Judaism as a means of reinforcing commitment to particular moral standards.[5] This absence, however, is not surprising. It seems reasonable, in our utilitarian, somewhat anomic milieu, that persons subjected to its relative standards, who yet hold high career and personal expectations, might develop aggravated feelings of inadequacy and guilt. Where forgiveness was authoritatively and objectively bestowed, confession might ease these feelings, as happens, for example, in some of the more evangelical movements; but where forgiveness is vague, platitudinous, or empty, it would not. In general, one would expect rites for confession to be absent from these new religious movements, because most North Americans, and most of the adherents of these movements, would rather not be reminded of the gap between their achievements and their ideals. This gap is made less bearable by the absence of any lively belief in an authoritatively pronounced grace, or else in a utopian belief in the prospects for a new society.[6]

Having identified these ritual practices, which generally are not emphasized by new religious movements, we can better as-sess the significance of the ritual practices to which they seem to give especial attention. Three kinds of rituals enjoy prominence in most of these movements: (1) various therapeutic rituals for healing or purification; (2) a range of meditation rites, which may be practiced both alone and within a group setting; and (3) rites

of initiation, which may be performed either on a single occasion
or as a series of occasions.

I

Most of these new religious movements have rites for either
healing or purification. Specially designated healing rites exist in
Silva Mind Control, Charismatic Renewal groups, the Self-
Realization Fellowship, and the Spiritualist groups. Silva Mind
Control, for example, trains initiates to become functioning psy-
chics capable of transmitting healing vibrations to others through
mental manipulations. Self-Realization Fellowship meetings end
with a ritual designed to disperse healing energies to loved ones
and friends. Interest in healing in these groups parallels a widespread interest in non-medical and faith healing. While they have
no explicit rites for healing, several other new religious
movements, such as the Institut de Yoga Sivananda, Integral
Yoga Institute, and Tai Chi Chu'an, do claim that the practice of
their central ritualized activities will have an immediate and
beneficial influence on practitioners' physical and psychic well-
being. Almost universally, respondents to a questionnaire distributed to participants of the local Integral Yoga classes indicated that their primary reason for practicing Yoga was to
achieve physical and mental well-being. In a recent survey of new
religious movements, "complete physical and mental health"
was assigned higher value by more groups than any other goal
[25].

In a way which complements this focus on healing and health,
a number of new religious movements assign special importance
to rites which are designed to purge or purify practitioners from
various pollutants, such as noise, anxiety, or disorders. The
Latihan rite in Subud acts like a rite for exorcism, by creating a
setting where persons in altered states of consciousness can release all manners of tensions and give voice to the daemons they
feel possess them. In a more typical manner, many groups encourage breathing exercises by which impurities in the lungs can
be removed, dietary regulations for avoiding toxic and adulter-
ated foods, and mantra meditations to purify the mind from wandering, anxious, "noisy" thoughts. TMers, in fact, describe
meditation as a rite which allows for "unstressing."

The concern with health and the preoccupation with disease

and dis-ease, which is well expressed by these new religious movements, may have arisen for several reasons. North Americans may feel more threatened by ill health because in this utilitarian, relativistic, and anomic milieu, they may in fact have less tolerance for dis-order and dis-ease. Mary Douglas argues that "dirt" is matter out of place. Dirt is whatever violates the ordered boundaries established to regulate social relations. In the contemporary milieu, where many persons feel that the boundaries protecting their own egos are elusive because of changing roles and expectations, it is understandable that many persons would become increasingly concerned about pollution. Furthermore, because of the atomistic individualism which the larger social milieu fosters, many persons may feel especially bothered by disease and dis-ease because, both proximately and ultimately (in death), the lack of health cuts people off from others [26].

II

These new religious movements have developed and given prominence to a variety of meditation rites. Meyer and Kitch found that rites for meditation were practiced by 80 percent of the groups responding to their survey, a much higher rate of response than for any other activity [25]. Meditation rituals may take several forms: chanting, the silent repetition of a sound or word, stylized exercises for breathing, bodily postures, or bodily movements. The aim in all these activities is non-cognitively to attune one's mind and being to certain realities, which are ordinarily unacknowledged by most persons, but which are felt to be sources of peace and power. None of these meditation rites are designed to encourage persons to reflect or ponder about particular ideas, as often happens in prayers, or to formulate and communicate discrete information (even to one's self), or even consciously to organize one's thoughts (as in psychotherapy).

The language used in meditation rituals of these groups often makes little or no appeal to cognitive understanding. Even while reciting an English translation of the *Heart Sutra*, practitioners at the Montreal Zendo are instructed to recite these words without thinking about them. Unlike other contemporary movements in Catholic and Protestant Christianity, these movements seem to want to minimize the use of the vernacular in meditation and to use instead either foreign or ancient languages (Hare Krishna, Nichiren Shoshu, Sri Chinmoy, Zendo), or glossolalia (Charismatic and Subud), or non-verbal body language (Tai Chi, Gurdjieff, Yoga), or avant-garde science fiction language (Scientology, Shakti).

Several variations in meditation rites can be noted. Often, when the higher reality to which one seeks to attune one's mind is felt to transcend individual persons, as is the case with Hare Krishna, the Divine Light Mission, and Charismatics, then greater emphasis is placed upon group meditation. Whereas in movements in which this higher reality is believed primarily to be within one, as in Transcendental Meditation, Dharmadhatu, or Nichiren Shoshu, then individual meditation is felt to be of greater importance. In this instance, social relations mirror and channel ontological assumptions. A further set of distinctions can be made. Some groups have meditation rites which foster a still, quiet state of mind as an end in itself developed by a discipline, such as Zendo, Integral Yoga, or Transcendental Meditation. Others, like Subud and perhaps Divine Light, have developed meditation techniques for realizing a more trance-like state of mind as an end in itself. Finally, there are movements, like Silva Mind Control and Arica, in which meditation is not an end in itself, but a means to achieve other ends.[7]

In all these instances, meditation rites set adherents' consciousness in two complementary motions. There is a conscious tuning out of troubling and stressful thoughts, a censoring of the everyday distractions and automatism which drive the mind hither and thither [28]. Chanting, mantra meditation, and stylized exercises immediately serve to turn the attention of practitioners away from two interrelated states of mind: (1) wandering, anxious, distracted states of mind, occasioned perhaps by the anomic absence of compelling norms for personal interactions or the personal bewilderment about the relative importance of one's round of activities; and (2) tragic, guilt-ridden states of mind, occasioned perhaps by the sense of inadequacy or failure. In keeping with this theme, Arica, for example, counsels those who attend its sessions not to identify themselves with all the conditioned responses cluttering their minds. The implicit message is that one's real self is not one's anxious ego, and is not the *me* shaped by the roles one assumes. Gurdjieff followers proceed further, arguing that one's real self is not one's personality, which simply identifies this *"me"* [12,29]. By means of these varied meditation rites, practitioners seek to attune their minds to hidden but powerful realities. Except for the International Society for Krishna Consciousness, which argues that Krishna is ultimate reality, these movements do not necessarily assign ultimacy or exclusive preeminence to these otherwise unacknowledged realities. Rather, they view these realities as powerful, life-enhancing but neglected dimensions of self and world. For example, Charismatics seek to make participants aware of and responsive to the presence of God's Spirit. Transcendental Meditation hopes to bring persons into touch with their own inner, but otherwise hidden sources of creative intelligence. Tai Chi seeks to orient persons by means of their stylized exercises in relation to otherwise ignored and often abused ways of nature within themselves and with others. Some groups simply strive to make persons aware of and responsive to the feelings and intuitions related to the often neglected and stifled right hemisphere of their brain. These movements in general do not propose clear alternatives to the dominant spectrum of cultural values, which honor personal success and happiness. Rather, they propose that by meditation, adherents will come into contact with neglected dimensions of reality which may well enhance their chances, if not for success, then certainly for happiness.[8]

As a result of this two-fold shift in consciousness, those practicing these assorted meditation rituals in varying degrees realize and reinforce a sense of selfhood connected not with particular roles, with particular personality traits, with their status or lifestyle, but with their intrinsic dignity as anonymous human beings [30,31]. In a world where one is always passing back and forth through various roles, institutions, and faces, the meditation rites of these new religious movements help to establish a kind of transitional milieu, where one can identify oneself not as a collection of roles but as a soul. Pre- and post-liminal statuses and claims are set aside as attention and energy are caught up by the chant or recitation or exercise. The result is that practitioners often experience a kind of immediate, self-forgetting, yet self-validating, and often personally energizing, experience.

III

Of the variety of rites of passage, only initiation rituals are widely practiced by these new movements. Some groups, like Scientology, or the Integral Yoga Institute, or Dharmadhatu, have established a series of initiation rites to mark the spiritual progress of adherents. In other groups, adherents may be involved in classes or meditation for considerable time without formal ritual introduction. In many groups, like TM or the Divine Light Mission, there is one clearly demarcated initiation. These initiation rites, which have a certain prominence in all groups, have several common characteristics. For example, with the exception of Jesus groups, the symbolic metaphors accompanying these rites refer to awakening from sleep or gaining sight after blindness, rather than being born again. Participants in these movements often further assume that an authentic, enlarged vision of one's self and world cannot be communicated through discursive arguments or empirical demonstrations. Rather, in a fundamental sense, this vision can only be imparted through a special kind of relationship. Much as psychoanalysts argue that their insights can only effectively be communicated through a relationship with transference, these movements appear to maintain that these new visions can only be imparted through a tutelary relationship in which the instructor who imparts the vision is viewed as having some kind of achieved yet bestowed charisma. Consequently, almost universally, the initiation rites of these movements do not so much indicate a shift in social status from non-member to member, as they enact a shift in personal status such that adherents become devotees, disciples, or apprentices of some honored lord, teacher, or discipline. In summary, the initiation process, which may be more or less formally stylized, introduces potential practitioners to the central ritual activities, assigns adherents to a special, personal, yet private status, and licenses them to re-enact these rites in the appropriate fashion [22].

THREE TYPICAL PATTERNS TO RITUAL PRACTICES

The adherents of these new religious movements may be classified as: (1) devotees of a spiritual leader or Truth; (2) disciples of spiritual discipline; and (3) apprentices of some sorcerer or magic/science. The setting and pattern of ritual practices vary with these different relationships.

Devotees say that they ultimately seek to become one with their revered Lord or Truth, to surrender themselves to this Holy Being, and to be receptive to his or its influence. Identified by these terms, one can perceive devotees especially in the Charismatic groups, the Divine Light Mission, the International Society for Krishna Consciousness, the Nichiren Shoshu Academy, and among the followers of Sri Chinmoy. Because they believe their Holy Being is inaccessible to no one, devotees feel that relating to this Being is not something which they must achieve or for which they must qualify. Rather, they are invited to submit and devote themselves. They believe that through this relationship they can become new or renewed persons. Several characteristics are associated with this general orientation. Thus, in the process of devoting oneself to this Holy Being, they are also called upon to devote themselves to a group of fellow devotees. The relationship to this Holy Being and to the group of devotees tend to be exclusive, but not rigidly so. Devotees are asked or encouraged to renounce competing loyalties. Meditation ordinarily takes place within the group, although adherents may also, as in the Nichiren group, be instructed to perform the meditation ritual at home. Devotees become members of these groups through a clearly designated initiation rite, which involves a single step. The group itself becomes, for devotees, an important point of reference. Congregational activities play a central role for devotees, who are ordinarily encouraged to support the group through donations and pledges rather than fees. All such groups of devotees assign some importance to the interrelated activities of giving testimonials within the group and witnessing to others outside the group. Although discursive speech is used in both cases, the actual process of giving testimonials is highly stylized in relation to the symbolic phrases used, the types of stories told, the forms of the stories, and even the lexical ordering of the sentences. Testimonial-giving provides occasions for adherents to exhibit their skill in adopting the hermeneutic of the group. From the perspective of devotees, the primary purpose of such witnessing is not to gain converts, even though this aim is not unimportant, but to express one's faith and devotion as one may well have done earlier in the group through a testimonial [32]. Overall, devotees do not orient themselves to these varied rites for meditation or testimonial simply as the revered means for achieving certain ends which are yet to be realized fully, but as a pattern of revered activities which re-enact the fundamental, given, heretofore unacknowledged, but now celebrated relation between devotees and their Holy Being.

Disciples claim ultimately to seek a mystical, enlightened consciousness by following a prescribed discipline of meditation. Ultimately they seek to transform their consciousness, not only momentarily, but in some abiding fashion. They believe that the highest clarified state of mind requires much effort to achieve. In the meantime, disciples expect to realize more peaceful, more energizing states of mind than before adopting this discipline. They seek to realize an enstatic rather than ecstatic state of mind. So characterized, disciples in varying degrees may be found in groups like Zendo, Dharmadhatu, the Integral Yoga Institute, Shakti, and the Gurdjieff fellowship. Several features are characteristic of the ritual patterns of groups which foster this kind of discipleship. The group meetings are important, but primarily as the context for meditation and discipline. Disciples frequently express great reverence for the leaders of their groups, people like Philip Kapleau, Chögyam Trungpa, Swami Satchidananda, and Gurdjieff, who are believed to exemplify the state of mind and being which disciples eventually hope to realize. Usually, disciples consider themselves to be not so much members of these groups as students of their discipline, which they variously support by donations, pledges, as well as prescribed fees. Disciples pass through not one, but a series of initiation rites, which may be more or less formalized. Disciples must qualify in appropriate manner for both initial as well as subsequent initiations. Only on some occasions are testimonials given in such groups. In the Integral Yoga Institute, they were given at a special retreat, but only by recognized and ordained leaders whose testimonials all honored Swami Satchidananda.

Apprentices ultimately seek to realize greater power or well-being. Rather than seeking to conform their minds to an existing higher Truth, they seek to utilize and domesticate higher powers or spirits for immediate, often secularly defined, ends. They want to become warriors or men/women of power, by learning and becoming skilled at the particular techniques and/or exercises which they believe can strengthen and empower them. For apprentices, meditation becomes a means to realize desired ends, variously identified as greater success in one's career or personal relations. So characterized, apprentices in varying degrees tend to be found in groups like Transcendental Meditation, Scientology, Silva Mind Control, Arica, and Subud. The pattern of ritual practices of groups which foster this kind of apprenticeship orientation have several common features. In the first place, the group in which one learns these valued techniques or exercises is viewed simply as a class. Apprentices honor their leaders as charismatic authorities, but do not revere them as models of the ends which they are seeking to realize. Apprentices support their groups almost exclusively with fees. There is in all these groups a relatively stylized rite of initiation, which serves to introduce apprentices to the special ritualized techniques and exercises. Applicants for apprenticeship qualify for this initiation relatively easily by donating in prescribed manner certain money, time, or other gifts. There are in these groups also specially designated ordination rites for those who become teacher/leaders; for these rites apprentices must both qualify by demonstrating their achievement in using the group's special techniques and be designated by the charismatic leaders of the movement. Testimonials are sometimes used in these groups, but in very selective ways: either experienced apprentices are asked to present testimonials to interested applicants, thereby offering verification that ritual techniques once learned and regularly re-enacted can produce the results promised, or, in the process of learning the ritualized techniques, apprentices are asked to testify in order to give evidence that they understand and are attempting to follow directions. The orientation of apprentices to their ritualized activities is the least religious of the three types.

Through the ritual practices, devotees are able to relativize other claims upon their lives by attuning themselves to their revered Being. With the exception of followers of a monastic group like the Krishna Consciousness Society, devotees do not embrace a totally new ethic or philosophy. By participating in these groups and their rituals, devotees are able to achieve occasional self-validating experiences and to put at greater distance the secular expectations for success and achievement. There is an interesting affinity between the orientation of devotees to these secular dramas and orientation of young adults in some counter-cultural movements. To be sure, many of the latter expressed bitter disenchantment with the hypocrisies of major economic, political, familial, and even religious institutions, from which they attempted, but had not always succeeded in gaining, a psychic distance. Most of the devotees of these new religious movements no longer express this kind of disenchantment; in part, no doubt, because by participating in these movements, by devoting themselves to their Holy Being, and by faithfully enacting their round of ritual practices, they have gained psychic distance.

Disciples of these new religious movements likewise gain a kind of psychic distance from secular role expectations through the practice of their discipline. This discipline does not so much result in a shifting of loyalties, but in a new sense of self. Even initially, the rites for meditation force one to tune out numerous everyday concerns, anxieties, and role expectations. Perfecting these various disciplines requires much work, with the consequence that many disciples appear to choose to remain at relatively elementary levels in relation to their ultimate goals. In practicing their ritualized activities, apprentices, too, seek to turn their attention away from everyday concerns—such certainly is the goal of Transcendental Meditation at one level. However, apprentices try to become skillful with their ritualized exercises and techniques, so that they ultimately become more effective in their social relations. Apprentices most closely resemble adherents of the New Thought movement: they share the same self-conscious concern for health and success. However, unlike the positive thinkers, apprentices do not seek to gain their successes in careers or personal relations by strengthening their power-to-will nor by developing marketable characters, but by regularly practicing certain ritualized techniques and exercises. Moreover, apprentices feel that these practices not only provide self-validating experience but also often, with results that have been scientifically verified, enhance their personal effectiveness and energy.

CONCLUSION

With several exceptions, these new religious groups are not compensatory movements. The decision to become involved rarely seems to result from material deprivation or even relative social status deprivation. With some exceptions, most groups and their followers do not militantly oppose the dominant utilitarian values of North American society. In fact, often while pointing to certain hypocrisies in society, they indirectly honor these values which they see being ignored. In varied ways, adherents of these movements seem to seek sucess in their personal relations and careers, but often by reducing their expectations and by relativizing various demands upon their lives. What stands out about the adherents of these groups is that they seek to achieve personal well-being in society not by drawing upon given traditions (social conventions, religious groups, or systems of etiquette), not by embracing some rational program (an ideology, a plan of action or an ethic), but by faithfully practicing some ritualized forms, which are not only authorized by a charismatic authority, but are felt to bestow a kind of secret, hidden charisma on practitioners themselves.

NOTES

[1] This paper is based upon the findings of a group research project on new religious movements in the Montreal area, funded in part by the Quebec Ministry of Education. The criteria used to identify these movements were developed in an earlier paper [1]. This paper is based upon field research and interviews with core members of the following groups: Protestant and Catholic Charismatics, francophone and anglophone Spiritualist groups, the International Society for Krishna Consciousness, Nichiren Shoshu Academy, Divine Light Mission, Sri Chinmoy followers, Montreal Zendo, Montreal Dharmadhatu, the Integral Yoga Institute, the Institut de Yoga Sivananda, Transcendental Meditation, Subud, Tai Chi, Silva Mind Control, the Self Realization Fellowship, Scientology, and Arica.

[2] The definition of "ritual" proposed here is more specific than several others: Bocock [6] defines rituals as "bodily actions in relation to symbols." Harrison [7] defines rituals as "a re-presentation or presentation, a re-doing or pre-doing, a copy or imitation of life." Benedict [8] defines rituals as "a form of prescribed and elaborated behavior . . . for occasions not given to technological routines." Wallace [9] simply describes rituals as "religion in action."

[3] Our survey data indicate that there has been a decline in congregational religious practices from parents to children, but little or no decline in the frequency of religious practices that take place at home [22,33].

[4] In the prayer meetings of the four groups of Charismatics that we have studied, little reference is made to the central Christian drama; however, this drama plays a central symbolic role in the eucharist services that follow.

[5] Whether this absence reflects the monism to which Anthony and Robbins refer [23] is not simple to determine. There are a number of ways of defining philosophical monism and even ethical monism. Traditionally, as Weber has noted [24], the most radical forms of philosophic monism in India were inextricably intertwined with the most radical forms of philosophical dualism. There may, in opposition to Anthony and Robbins, be a basis for arguing that

these groups express a gnostic dualism, which views everyday existence as being predetermined by fate and/or chance and encourages an enlightened detachment, a Gurdjieffian mindfulness, about everyday exigencies.

⁶ Many persons are already tyrannized by their super-egos in this permissive, anomic milieu, perhaps even more so than in previous ages of commitment. In the absence of any clear standards of accomplishment, it is possible that many will feel more threatened by the sense of inadequacy, since there are always some who appear to accomplish so much. Moreover, in a permissive milieu, it is likely that many persons will feel even more accountable for how they act and what they do—and more vulnerable to feeling they have not measured up—than in a milieu where they could assign such responsibility to given role expectations, established institutional norms, and the claims of tradition.

⁷ These distinctions correspond to those proposed by Douglas [27] and Eliade [20], who make the distinction between the enstatic yogin and ecstatic shaman.

⁸ Meditation may be favorably compared to psychoanalysis. The latter argues that persons can live more harmoniously by acknowledging their own unconscious feelings and impulses as otherwise ignored, but influential, dimensions of personal reality. Health and freedom are promoted as persons establish some kind of balance between the conscious and unconscious dimensions of themselves.

REFERENCES

1. Frederick Bird and Bill Reimer. "A Sociological Analysis of New Religions and Para-Religious Movements in the Montreal Area." In *Canadian Religion*. Edited by Stewart Crysdale. Macmillan, 1976.

2. Erving Goffman. *Interaction Ritual: Essays in Face to Face Behavior*, pp. 5, 35, 47, 1. Anchor, 1967.

3. Max Gluckman. "Les rites de passage." In *Essays on the Rituals of Social Relations*. Manchester University Press, 1962.

4. Sydney Ahlstrom. *A Religious History of the American People*, ch. 48, 60, 61. Yale University Press, 1972.

5. Stillson Judah. *The History and Philosophy of the Metaphysical Movements in America*. Westminster, 1967.

6. Robert Bocock. *Ritual in Industrial Society: A Sociological Analysis of Rituals in Modern England*, p. 36. George Allen and Unwin, 1974.

7. Jane Ellen Harrison. *Ancient Art and Ritual*, p. 90. Oxford, 1913.

8. Ruth Benedict. "Ritual." In *Encyclopedia of the Social Sciences*, XIII and XIV, 396–397. Edited by E. R. A. Seligman. Macmillan, 1953.

9. Anthony F. C. Wallace. *Religion: An Anthropological View*, p. 102. Random House, 1966.

10. Herbert Fingarette. *Confucius: The Secular as Sacred*, p. 11. Harper & Row, 1972.

11. Johan Huizinga. *Homo Ludens: A Study of the Play Element in Culture*, ch. 1. Beacon, 1950.

12. Adam Smith. *Power of Mind*, ch. 4, pp. 159–168. Ballantine, 1975.

13. Victor Turner. "Betwixt and Between: The Liminal Period in 'Rites de Passage'." In *Reader in Comparative Religion*, p. 339. Edited by William A. Lessa and Evon Z. Vogt. 3rd. ed., Harper & Row, 1972.

14. Kurt W. Back. *Beyond Words: The Story of Sensitivity Training and the Encounter Movement,* p. 126. Penguin, 1972.

15. Jerome Frank. *Persuasion and Healing: A Comparative Study of Psychotherapy,* ch. 3 and 4. Rev. ed., Schocken, 1974.

16. A. M. Hocart, "Etiquette." In *Encyclopedia of the Social Sciences,* IV and V, 615. Edited by E. R. A. Seligman. Macmillan, 1953.

17. Basil Bernstein. *Class, Codes, and Control: Theoretical Studies Towards a Sociology of Knowledge.* Routledge and Kegan Paul, 1971.

18. Edmund Leech. "Ritualization in Man in Relation to Conceptual and Social Development." In *Reader in Comparative Religion,* p. 334. Edited by William A. Lessa and Evon Z. Vogt. 3rd ed. Harper & Row, 1972.

19. Emile Durkheim. *The Elementary Forms of the Religious Life,* p. 464. Translated by Joseph Ward Swain. Collier ed., 1961.

20. Mircea Eliade. *The Myth of the Eternal Return,* ch. 1. Translated by Willard Trask. Harper & Row, 1959.

21. Mary Douglas. *Purity and Danger: An Analysis of the Concepts of Pollution and Taboo,* ch. 4. Routledge and Kegan Paul, 1966.

22. Frederick Bird. "Initiation Rites and the Pursuit of Innocence: A Comparative Analysis of the Relation Between Initiation Rites and Feelings of Moral Accountability in New Religious Movements." *Journal of Social Issues,* in press.

23. Dick Anthony and Tom Robbins. "A Typology of Non-Traditional Religious Movements in Modern America." In preparation, 1976.

24. Max Weber. *The Religion of India: The Sociology of Hinduism and Buddhism.* Free Press ed., 1958.

25. Egon Meyer and Laura W. Kitch. "The Path Seekers Follow: Ideology and Ritual in the New Religious Groups." In preparation, 1976.

26. Frances Westley. "Faceless Bodies: A Study of Pollution Beliefs and Healing Rituals in New Religious Movements." In preparation, 1977.

27. Mary Douglas. *Nature Symbols: Explorations in Cosmology,* pp. 105–108. Barrie and Jenkins, London, 1970.

28. Mircea Eliade. *Yoga: Immortality and Freedom,* p. 45. Translated by Willard Trask. Princeton University Press, 1969.

29. Darrell Leavitt. "A Study of the Transformation of a Gurdjieff Group." Master's thesis, Concordia University, 1976.

30. Peter Berger, Brigitte Berger, and Hansfried Kellner. *The Homeless Mind: Modernization and Consciousness,* p. 89. Random House, 1974.

31. Donald Stone. "The Human Potential Movement." In *The New Religious Consciousness,* p. 111. Edited by Charles Glock and Robert Bellah. University of California Press, 1976.

32. Paul Schwartz. "The Testimonial as Religious Discourse." In preparation, 1977.

33. Susan Bernstein. "Transcendental Meditation: Consumer Product or Spiritual Philosophy." In preparation, 1975.

34. Edmund Leech. "Ritual." In *International Encyclopedia of the Social Sciences,* XIII, p. 411. Macmillan and Free Press, 1968.

RADHASOAMI AS A
TRANS-NATIONAL MOVEMENT
Mark Juergensmeyer

IN BERKELEY, there is a local chapter of Radhasoami, a guru movement from North India which has had a formative influence on such popular movements as Eckankar, Divine Light, and the Ruhani Satsang, and which has a growing following of its own in the United States. In some fundamental respects, the movement I have observed in Berkeley is the same as the parent movement that I have observed in Beas, in India. And therein lies a puzzle. When Americans join the Radhasoami movement, are they joining an Indian movement, an American movement with an Indian name, or something which is neither Indian nor American? The way one answers that question will indicate whether one regards Radhasoami, and other religious movements like it, as an example of Hindu expansionism, a vestige of the American counter-culture of the sixties, or as something quite different.

Superficially, American participation in Radhasoami appears to be a cultural anomaly—an outpost of Hinduism in an alien American culture, or an exotic Hindu identity for Americans who were already marginal in some way, even before they joined the movement. These observations are popular explanations for the appeal of movements such as Radhasoami. There are problems, however, with these explanations; they contradict one another, and they do not quite fit the facts. Hinduism is not the sort of religious tradition which sends out missionaries and establishes outposts; it is not organized for that sort of thing. Radhasoami and the other "Hindu" religious movements are regarded even within India as unusual, for religious *movements* occupy a special separate place within Hindu tradition. And the American adherents of Radhasoami come from a mixed section of the population; their "marginality" is the *result* of their participation in Radhasoami as much as it is the *cause* of it. Thus, if participation in Radhasoami may appear to be a cultural anomaly, it may be not because Radhasoami is an Indian movement out of place, but rather because it is culturally distinct from both the Indian and the American contexts.

This has not always been the case for Radhasoami, however. When this movement began in the 1860s, it was reminiscent of the *bhakti* movements of medieval India. The first guru in the lineage of teachers, Shiv Dayal Singh, came from a Punjabi family who were familiar with the medieval *bhakti* teachings enshrined in the Sikh tradition, and who also followed forms of Vaisnava *bhakti*. The earliest teachings of Radhasoami, then, had a mixture of various forms of *bhakti* devotion and spiritual techniques; but if the mixture was unusual, it was not exotic. At first Radhasoami's teachings were exclusively Indian, and so was its following.

INTERNATIONALISM OF RADHASOAMI

Over the years, new ingredients have entered into Radhasoami's ideas, and new followers have entered into the movement; both have been foreign. The foreign ideas have been those of science, managerial organization, and developmental progress. The foreign persons have been British civil servants, American theosophists, and young religious seekers.

The international dimension to Radhasoami apparently came with the second guru, Rai Saligram, who became, in 1881, the first Indian to be appointed Postmaster General of the United Provinces. It was through Saligram's influence that foreigners began to be involved in Radhasoami, including British colleagues of Saligram in the civil service. Max Müller had known Saligram, holding him in high regard [1]; and the foreign admirers also included "a German theosophist and an American lady" [2].

When the Radhasoami movement split into several factions around the turn of the century, the branches of the movement retained their interest in foreigners. The diary of Anand Sarup, the guru of Dayalbagh from 1913 to 1937, hardly mentions his Indian followers, but he seems fascinated with the foreigners, especially Miss Bruce, who "adopted Satsang ways . . . squats on the ground . . . and must have been a Hindu in her past life" [3], and Mr. Hurst, who was interested in Theosophy and Meher Baba, and who gave Anand Sarup some practical advice about managing the movement. The Dayalbagh branch of Radhasoami continues to have foreign followers, through a Radhasoami Association of Europe and a Radhasoami Association of North America; but the numbers are not large, and the main emphasis of the Dayalbagh branch since 1937 has been the development of a huge industrial center of some fourteen factories, which produce everything from fountain pens to underwear. The Beas branch of Radhasoami, in the Punjab, has developed quite differently. Jaimal Singh, the founder of the Beas branch, established a *dera,* a sacred center, on the banks of the Beas River, near Amritsar in the Punjab; and Beas's second guru, Sawan Singh, who had been a member of the military engineering corps of the Indian Army, built the dera into a model city.

Two Americans have been important in the development of the community at Beas, and its international outlook. Dr. Julian Johnson, a medical doctor from California, who earlier had been a Baptist missionary to India, wandered through Theosophy and occult writings in search of a great spiritual teacher before finding Sawan Singh, in 1932. He remained the resident American attendant at the court of the guru for nine years. The other influential American was Dr. Randolph Stone, an osteopath from Chicago, who discovered in Radhasoami teachings a meta-science that was useful for healing purposes. Dr. Stone's "polarity therapy" was established at a clinic at the Beas *dera* and it now enjoys wide usage outside of Radhasoami circles.

In their spiritual writings, the gurus of the Beas branch became eclectic, pointing out the similarity of the eternal sound current in *Surat Shabd Yoga* to the logos in gnostic philosophy, and similar notions in Taoism. The present Master of Beas, Charan Singh, contends that the "word" of St. John is *shabd,* the sacred word in Radhasoami teachings [4]. According to the Great Master of Beas, Sawan Singh, "spirituality is . . . not reserved for any particular country or nationality" [5].

The Radhasoami movement's spirituality is expressed in English. The English language is used as the medium for most of the Radhasoami publications and the conduct of organizational affairs. This seems to have been a deliberate choice, probably as early as the second guru; and this decision has been important in making Radhasoami teachings available throughout India, and throughout the world.

The Beas Radhasoami is, in fact, a vast international organization, by virtue of 120 local centers in some forty different countries. The number of foreign initiates is probably about twenty thousand; the largest numbers are in the United Kingdom, South Africa, and the United States. The organizational control of the network is carefully maintained by the headquarters in Beas; for example, a local group in Northern California waited patiently for the guru's approval before moving its meeting from someone's living room to the Menlo Park Recreation Hall. The foreigners are treated well, however. At the sacred dera of the Beas branch of Radhasoami, there is a modern guest house especially for foreigners; and at the Satsang meetings, they are seated in a reserved space at the front. The Annual Reports list, by name, every foreign Satsangi to have visited the dera in that year, lists which number many hundreds. Within the past ten years the foreign membership has expanded considerably; and the amount of foreign income has increased even more [6]. But the non-Indian participation has assumed a symbolic importance beyond that which their mere numbers might warrant. It is, I suppose, a matter of some prestige to reverse the direction of missionary conquest. Perhaps more important, the Westerners provide Radhasoami with the *bona fides* for the notion that Radhasoami transcends the cultural limitations of Indian soil and Indian tradition.

RADHASOAMI IN AMERICA

At the same time that foreigners were coming to India to receive initiation from the Radhasoami gurus at Dayalbagh and Beas, other foreigners were hearing about Radhasoami without even leaving home. The first foreigners to be involved abroad were in America, when the faith was transported to the Pacific Northwest by a Punjabi immigrant, Ker Singh Sasmus, in 1910. When Dr. Brock, a Port Angeles, Washington dentist, asked for initiation for himself and Mrs. Brock, Sasmus was given the power to initiate them by proxy; and the American expansion began. The guru and his secretary in Beas screened the proxy applications by mail; but even so, the increase in numbers was remarkable. The concept of initiation by proxy, along with the use of the English language, were perhaps the most critical developments in the internationalization of Radhasoami.

The concept of proxy initiation also enhances the status of local leaders, since the channel of spiritual authority flows through them. In the United States, there are five representatives of the guru with the power of proxy initiation; they administer five geographical regions, and fifty local centers. The representatives have not always worked well together, and personal visits of the gurus to America has included the adjudication of organizational differences. A merger finally took place in 1972 when two of the United States leaders, H. F. Weekley of Washington, D.C., and E. R. Berg, a retired air force colonel from Minneapolis, Minnesota, acknowledged the primacy of Roland G. de Vries of Riverside, California, who became the General Secretary of the American Sangat (Association) of Radhasoami, Beas branch.

Roland G. de Vries has the demeanor of an elderly pastor; and he was, in fact, formerly a Presbyterian minister. His style is devotional; he admonishes the Satsangis to eschew the "whispering voices of pleasure," in anticipation that "heaven-sent joy will wing its way out of eternity into our hearts." But more frequently, he talks about his visit with the Master, what to say in writing to him, advice about not being possessive about tape recordings of the Master's voice, or demanding his *darshan* (presence) like a *"darshan* hog" [7]. Mr. de Vries is characteristic of a good many of the older American members of the movement, many of whom, like Dr. Randolph Stone, are capable of quoting Madame Blavatsky [8], and might easily have been Theosophists or even Rosicrucians, had Radhasoami not been available. The largest percentage of new American initiates are young seekers after religious truth; many, but not all, have been through an assortment of drugs and meditation experiences.

The fact that many of the American members of Radhasoami are somewhat unusual, by America's cultural norms, should not be exaggerated. It is one of those facts which appears to explain more than it in fact explains. For even if one could prove that the American members of Radhasoami are culturally more unusual than, say, Episcopalian clergy or a university faculty, one would still have to explain why those persons, unusual or not, find a movement such as Radhasoami so appealing. Thus, we might find it more fruitful to look at the cultural characteristics of the movement, rather than the social characteristics of its members.

THE TRANS-NATIONAL APPEAL OF RADHASOAMI

There appears to be little interest in Indian culture, as such, among the present American members of Radhasoami. In the earlier years, some of the first American members of the movement, such as Mrs. Bruce, were attracted to Eastern culture, and through that to Radhasoami; and there are some younger members of the movement today for whom that was their initial interest. Yet after joining the movement, interest in India as such seems to wane. Foreign visitors to the dera in Beas usually arrive by the shortest route and leave the same way, with little attention to the rest of India.

There are several reasons for this lack of interest in Indian culture. The most obvious reason is the one which the members themselves give: their primary interest in the movement is in the spiritual techniques and teachings, which are largely personal. This motivation among the members is so palpable as to be undeniable. Yet the facts remain that they have sought out a movement based in India, and one which has created its own cities and separate societies; that is to say, Radhasoami appears to have a social appeal as well as a spiritual one. And since the foreigners in Radhasoami do not appear to have an interest in Indian culture, the social appeal of Radhasoami for them must be located in the movement itself.

Radhasoami seems to have a special appeal to Indians for precisely the same reason—its distinctiveness within traditional Indian society. The international and trans-national characteristics of the movement are emphasized in the ways described earlier—special treatment for foreign visitors, publications aimed at a worldwide audience, and global tours of the gurus. More important, however, are those cultural elements which are distinctive features of the movement, and which appeal to its Indian and American members alike. The following are some of these elements.

Separate tradition. Radhasoami religious teachings are an interesting blend of various sources, including devotion to a personal guru and devotion to a concept of the sacred without attri-

butes and forms (*nirguna bhakti*). In the Punjab, where the Beas
branch of Radhasoami is located, the movement appears in some
instances to be a modern replication of the Sikh tradition, and a
competition with it. But to some Sikhs, Radhasoami is both an
anomaly and an affront: Radhasoamis insist on the authority of
living masters, rather than on the authority of historical gurus;
they include Hindus and foreigners into the faith; and they have
evolved teachings which appear to rely as much on Christianity
and Western science as they do upon the traditions of India.

Moreover, Radhasoami has established a *parampara,* a lineage
of gurus, which is distinctly its own. The birth celebrations and
death anniversaries of these masters are the great festival days
of the year. Their pictures and books of their writings are central
to Radhasoami households; and the memories and stories of
their lives are the *kerygma* of the faith, the core of their tradition.

Science as a model for spiritual knowledge. There are two
sources of authority in Radhasoami teachings: the guru, and
one's own experience. The latter validates the former; but there
is also the notion that one's own experiences comprise a laboratory for spiritual experiments. The claim is made that
Radhasoami "extends the scientific method into the areas of
moral and spiritual relationships" [9]. The third guru of the Beas
branch, Jagat Singh, was a professor of chemistry at Punjab
Agricultural College, Lyallpur, and his collected writings are
entitled *The Science of the Soul* [10].

Scientific religion has had its witnesses in the West, in the
forms of Christian Science, Theosophy, Scientology, and in Protestant liberal theology. In India, scientific thought in the
late-nineteenth century made a significant impact on reform
religious movements such as the Arya Samaj. Radhasoami appeals to the same people who found these other movements
engaging in both India and the West. Radhasoami blends two
disparate aspects of the modern self: science and religious consciousness. Thus, in both India and the United States, those
people impressed with science and challenged by it, are able to
control it through the spiritual science of Radhasoami.

The spiritual character of the body. In Radhasoami thought, as
in other areas of Indian thought, the soul (or consciousness)
permeates the body, but longs to leave the body; the mind traps
the soul and enslaves it to sensual experience. The primary techniques of Radhasoami—*simran* (chanting the holy names) and

bhajan (meditating, listening to the higher sounds)—are intended to liberate the soul by linking it with the "audible life stream," the primordial and eternal energy force, which exists in the form of a sound current. This yoga of Radhasoami is called *Surat Shabd Yoga,* the yoga of linking the soul (*surat*) with the eternal sound (*shabd*).

Since the body is quite literally the battleground of spiritual warfare, purity of body has special emphasis—including abstention from meat, drugs, alcohol, and extramarital sex. These strictures are especially difficult for the American followers, and help to set them apart. This way of looking at the body, however, is not unusual in India. What is peculiar in India is Dr. Randolph Stone's "polarity therapy," the meta-science which utilizes Radhasoami concepts of the body in healing techniques.

A spiritual family. Members call each other "brother" and "sister" and feel a paternal affection for the guru, to whom they write their most intimate problems. The dera in Beas has the character of a family home, and for some members the dera is a retirement home. The brotherhood of followers of a guru is common in India, where there is a term, *gur-bhai,* for this special relationship, which parallels the relationships of the joint family. Moreover, for urban professionals in India who are alienated from their traditional joint families, the Radhasoami family replaces the old ties. Perhaps the alienated Western followers of Radhasoami find in the movement a similar attraction; so, for both Indian and Western followers, the movement provides the character of home.

Social service. The concept of *sewa,* or service, traditionally refers to money, gifts, and work to support a guru's activities. The Radhasoami notion of *sewa* is considerably broader, for it encompasses not just the guru, but the whole of the Radhasoami organization. Furthermore, the concept is stretched to apply to any good deed which is done in the name of the guru. For example, the American representative of the Beas branch said that in seeing several old ladies in need, he felt that "Master had provided a *sewa* for me" [7]. The concept of social service in Radhasoami is thereby derived as an extension of religious teachings, and provides the basis of a Radhasoami social ethic.

Spiritual socialism. The guru has administrative as well as spiritual authority over the Satsangis. The organizational lines of that authority comprise a separate realm in which the guru is fictive king. In that way, Radhasoami and movements similar to it recreate the princely states which were once dominant throughout the sub-continent. Yet, there is also a strong egalitarian strain in Radhasoami, and the communities established by Radhasoami have an almost socialist quality: all property is owned by the organization, tasks are assigned in teams according to ability, wages are regulated accordingly, and meals are taken in common. These two administrative styles—paternalistic authority and communitarian equality—may appear to be contradictory, yet they are in part modelled on the politics of a family. These two styles are able to co-exist only when religion, or some other harmonious ideology, provides fusion for the two in the sacral family of a religious community such as Radhasoami [11,12,13].

TRANS-NATIONAL RELIGION

These elements which I have singled out as being distinctive within Radhasoami are probably not unique to the movement. The *Sant Mat* tradition of northern India, of which Radhasoami is a modern manifestation, shares many of these characteristics. Other movements based in India have labored more openly at the creation of a trans-national culture; the experiment at Auroville, near Pondicherry, immediately comes to mind.

This trans-national dimension is frequently found within religious societies, but the trait is more prominent in some than in others. Between Islamic Morocco and Islamic Indonesia there are massive differences; and only a continuity of faith makes them both identifiably Muslim. In other cases, a central organizational authority, that of the Vatican, for example, gives force to a trans-national unity. The medieval centuries of Christendom were those of a trans-national culture without peer. Protestant Christianity has the reputation of being more closely identified with national interests, but the post-missionary attitudes—the acceptance of Christian-native syncretism and indigenous forms of faith—seem to be changing that image as well. H. Richard Niebuhr has well summarized the options for the church's cultural identity in his book, *Christ and Culture*.

Hinduism has less claim to universality, since it has been confined to the Indian sub-continent for most of its history, with the single exception of the medieval expansion of Hindu cultural influence into Southeast Asia. One might argue that Hinduism is not a religion at all, but a name given to India's religious culture. When Buddhism, a heterodox offshoot from Brahmanical Hinduism, became a tradition accessible to all of Asia, it disappeared within India. India did not seem to need or want a transnational culture then; but perhaps this attitude has changed. With the appearance of the Moghuls, and especially with the presence of the British, currents have developed within Hinduism which seem similar to Islam and Christianity in their international appeals. Swami Vivekananda's famous speech at the World's Parliament of Religions in Chicago in 1893 was a dramatic indication of these currents; and the Vedanta Society is a further illustration.

One might argue that the trans-national appeal of Radhasoami verifies a view of Hinduism as a "world religion" in the manner of Buddhism, Christianity, and Islam. On the other hand, one might argue that the trans-national elements of the Radhasoami movement ultimately reflect only on that movement and not on the character of Hinduism as a whole. In either event, Radhasoami as a trans-national entity provides for Indian and American followers alike a neutral territory for those who wish, for the moment, to shed the limitations of their national identities and transcend the parochial claims of traditional cultures.

REFERENCES

1. Max Müller. *Ramakrishna: Life and Sayings*. Oxford, 1898.
2. Agam Prasad Mathur. *Radhasoami Faith: A Historical Study*. Vikas, Delhi, 1974.
3. Anand Sarup (Sahabji Maharaj). *Diary of Sahabji Maharaj (1930–31)*. Radhasoami Satsang Sabha, Dayalbagh, 1973.
4. Charan Singh. *St. John, The Great Mystic*. Radhasoami Satsang, Beas, 1970.
5. Kirpal Singh. *A Brief Life-Sketch of Hazur Baba Sawan Singhji Maharaj*. Ruhani Satsang, Delhi, 1949.
6. *Annual Reports*. Radhasoami Satsang, Beas, 1962–1973.
7. Roland G. de Vries, General Secretary of the Radhasoami Satsang, Beas, United States. Public address at the Northern California Satsang, Menlo Park Recreation Center, November 10, 1974.
8. Randolph Stone. The Satguru's message during his visit to Chicago. In *R. S. Greetings*, June 1970.
9. Sawan Singh (Huzur Maharaj Sawan Singh Ji). *Philosophy of the Masters*. Radhasoami Satsang, Beas, 1973. Abridgment of the first edition of 1943.

10. Jagat Singh (Maharaj Sardar Bahadur Jagat Singh Ji). *The Science of the Soul*. Radhasoami Satsang, Beas, 1972.

11. Julian P. Johnson. *With a Great Master in India*. Radhasoami Satsang, Beas, 1933, 1973.

12. Swami Dayal Singh. *Sar Bachan*. Radhasoami Satsang, Beas, 1955.

13. *Souvenir in Commemoration of the First Centenary of the Radhasoami Satsang (1861–1961): A Brief Account of the progress of the Rhadhasoami Satsang*. Radhasoami Satsang Sabha, Dayalbagh, 1962.

NEW RELIGIONS AND
RELIGIOUS LIBERTY
J. Stillson Judah

THE PRACTICE that has come to be called deprogramming has created for society a serious problem of religious liberty and for scholarship a serious problem of interpretation. Deprogramming as a societal problem is complicated by the
fact that deprogrammers have not only deprogrammed members
of the new religions, but have also turned their attention to persons belonging to well-established churches. The appearance of
anti-cult bills in state legislatures is evidence of successful lobby-
ing on the part of new organizations, such as the Freedom of
Thought Foundation and the Volunteer Parents of America,
which have been formed to serve as deprogramming agencies
and public information centers.

My involvement with the problem of scholarly interpretation
stems from my own research on American religious movements,
and at present depends particularly upon studies of both the
Hare Krishna movement and the Unification Church, two of the
most controversial new religions. I began my research on the
latter with the intention of producing a study similar to my *Hare
Krishna and the Counterculture* (1975). I started with a similar,
very detailed questionnaire which would provide data concerning the total environment of the typical member. The questionnaire pointed to the changes that had taken place in the life of
the person after he or she had joined the church. I was particularly interested in changes related to personal goals, and attitudes toward family, politics, and society. Because of the
known frailties of the questionnaire method, I combined direct
questions, often of multiple-choice kind, with essay questions.
The use of essay questions furnished data that could be studied
by techniques of content analysis. In this way I hoped to answer
broad questions, such as these: What has participation in the

Unification Church meant to the respondent? How has the respondent's life been changed? How does the respondent regard his or her presently-held religious beliefs in relation to beliefs previously held?

I made my first survey of the Unification Church in 1976. It involved a nation-wide study of sixteen centers, and it consisted of an initial random sample of two hundred persons who answered the questionnaire, in addition to many hours of taped interviews. Because the results of this survey produced data conflicting with reports of deprogrammers and parents, and because of the importance of the research project in relation to the societal problem of religious freedom, I decided to widen the scope of my research.

I

The problem of interpretation with regard to what has been called mind control is not as simple as the reports of deprogrammers would lead one to suspect. The scholarly solution to this problem will require that the members of these movements and the movements themselves be viewed holistically as a *gestalt*. The phenomena under study must include the total environment during a period of change in culture and values. The study must be a complete *Sitz im Leben*. The scholar must draw upon the disciplines and discoveries of philosophers, sociologists, clinical and social psychologists, and even the historians. My own research on these new religions has led me to some conclusions; but because of the complexity of the problem, they must be regarded as tentative.

One of the first observations made is that, contrary to what many critics say, a weekend workshop does not mean that a person is likely to be converted in the two days. Although further investigation needs to be made, only a small percentage of those attending even appear to remain for a longer period. Of those surveyed who are at present Unification Church members, only ten percent were converted within a two-day period.

There are great differences in the needs of individuals which determine their susceptibility to conversion. I have talked with a number who have been extremely critical of their weekend experience; more, however, were sympathetic to what they believed the purposes of the Church to be, even though they felt that the Unification Church was not for them. Others were able to find great meaning in the teachings and fellowship of the Church.

The statistics for those who were converted to the Unification Church indicate that sixty-five percent believed that religious experience was important and that the incapacity of receiving this in their parents' religions was one reason for changing to another faith. Seventy-six percent of the Hare Krishna devotees gave the same answer. Thus, in both movements, conversions with attendant religious experience have seemed to be the case.

As a testimony to their conversion, nearly all were able to speak concerning a meaningful transformation in their lives. This was expressed in various ways: always changes in attitudes, although not uniformly the same; the adoption of a new style of life, often quite different from one formerly associated with varying degrees of drug abuse; sometimes, for at least sixteen percent, a transformation from their involvement with crime that had probably been associated with drug abuse. Their most common testimony was concerning the lack of purpose and direction in their lives they had experienced before their conversion, and how their conversion gave new meaning to life.

By and large, they represented youthful idealists who seemed confused by the accelerated cultural changes, particularly in value systems, and by the direction in which their country seemed to be moving. They were not generally those who were using religion as an escape from their problems, nor to validate a different culture when dissatisfied with their own, as was the case with those who have found their needs satisfied in the Hare Krishna movements. On the contrary, they have been those, who unlike most devotees of Krishna, have represented a high percentage of former demonstrators who strove to effect changes in our own cultural system. They appeared to have suffered in varying degrees from cultural alienation or anomie, and consequently from a lack of identification with the symbols of their culture and of its religions which their parents have espoused. As members of the Unification Church, they adhere rigidly to ethical precepts that are similar to, but generally more embracive than, those of many conservative Christian churches. This has been aided in validation by their religious experience and close fellowship with others of similar mind and needs within the

Church. Therefore, they are no longer confused by the present ambivalence in value systems. Their testimonies lead one to believe that, at this particular time, most have had definite and strong commitments to their faith, and that in accord with their needs a truly religious conversion has taken place.

The foregoing reveals part of the problem requiring further investigation. Are these young adults who have joined one of these new religions the subjects of coercive mind control, as deprogrammers, some parents, and psychologists claim? Are they under some type of hypnotic spell from which they should be freed? Or are these truly religious conversions which have occurred in answer to definite needs of these young people?

At this point of the investigation I submit that there is a degree of mind control, not only in conversions to new religions, but to any religion. We are generally Christians, Moslems, Buddhists, or of whatever faith, because of our particular culture, heritage, and education. The fact that most of the people of Burma or Thailand are Buddhists, those in Egypt are Moslems, and most in Spain are Roman Catholics cannot be ascribed to their absolutely free choice of a religion. It is indeed not without similar reason, though too early to be called "coercive mind control," that Nehru, when first gaining power in India, banned missionaries from propagating the Gospel among unconverted Hindus. Indeed Christian schools and hospitals in foreign lands have been important sources for Christian conversions. Also, I fail to find a great difference between the conversion of a youth attending a Unification Church weekend workshop and one converting to a mainline Christian church after spending a weekend with a Young Life group or after attending a denominational summer camp. Indeed there was probably a higher percentage of conversions during the historic revivals of the two Great Awakenings, and even at present-day revivals in conservative or fundamentalist Christian churches. Where does one draw the line? And what about weekday church schools some Protestant churches foster, and Roman Catholic parochial schools? Or Buddhist or Christian monasteries? Therefore, at this point in the investigation I feel that although one may express disapproval concerning some of the proselytizing practices of some of the new religions, as long as they perform no overt illegal acts, to censure them by new laws would be a severe blow to religious freedom of all Americans.

Because there is just this possibility of infringing upon the religious liberty of all Americans, there is need of an objective investigation of both sides of this complex problem. For example, in spite of the criticism of many parents reported by the media, less publicized is the fact that there are also parents of those who are members of these new religions who do neither object to their children's choice of faith, nor note any harmful personality changes, nor do they feel that their children have been alienated from them.

Moreover, there are also psychologists who dispute the claims of others that the new religions have had such a deleterious effect upon its members. They have examined subjects who were to be deprogrammed and have produced affidavits testifying to their mental health in confutation of those psychologists who were hired by the deprogrammers. In fact, the tragedy for many who have been abducted without any due process of law has been that deprogramming has been done without any psychological examination, but often on the assumption that conversion to one of the new religions or to even one of the established churches signified the effects of coercive mind control.

Although it appears there are varying degrees of mind control, one of the most extreme would involve well-known Oriental techniques that employ *physical* restraint and sometimes severe coercion. While the so-called "cults" certainly cannot be accused of this, it has been reported as applicable sometimes to the techniques of the deprogrammers. There are two major differences, however. In the Orient, the process consisted in first breaking down one's beliefs and getting the subject to confess his wrong ideas and actions. This was followed by "educating" or programming him into a new viewpoint. In this country, unfortunately, only the subject's faith is usually broken, and invariably each subject is programmed to believe he or she was coercively mind controlled whether this was true or not. These young adults are not given a substitute belief, but only a negative viewpoint. Therefore, evidence at this point that is valid at least for some, though still insufficient as a general conclusion, points to the apparent fact that many of our youth who had been converted to a new faith meeting their needs have been left in a state of limbo. One young man who had been deprogrammed confessed that he had not returned to his parents' faith, but had presently found a charismatic cult more meaningful. He explained he still had some doubts about Christianity, however, but would probably join another cult before the end of the year.

Another Unification Church member who had been deprogrammed testified that he believed he had been mind controlled, and therefore was not returning to the movement. Further questioning, however, revealed that his relationship with his family was not at all amicable, because he apparently still believed most of the *Divine Principle* of the Unification Church, and his defense of its tenets was causing difficulties with his parents.

Therefore, research must include not only an investigation of persons within the movements, as has been done, but also persons who have been deprogrammed. Questions need to be answered, such as: What has taken the place of the faith that appeared to be very meaningful up to the time the deprogramming occurred? Have they now suddenly found meaning hitherto undiscovered in their parents' faith? Or is another so-called "cult" the answer? Are they now leading productive lives, or are they now apathetic, in contrast to the previous period in which life seemed to have so great a meaning? Why do some former devotees become deprogrammers, while others return to their former life of alcoholism or drug abuse, as it is in at least some cases?

The same questions should be asked of persons who have dropped out of one of these new religions on their own accord. Indeed statistics from the survey of the Unification Church indicate a fair rate of dropout, since fifty-five percent of those surveyed had been in the Church for a maximum of one year or less. Therefore, we shall also want to study more extensively the reason for this change.

One member of the Unification Church, who otherwise had found great meaning and satisfaction in the Church, reported that he was leaving because of critical articles against the Rev. Sun Myung Moon that he had been reading in *The New York Times*. At the same time, such criticisms, which can be part of a deprogramming process for some, seem to strengthen the faith of others, even as the persecution of early Christians led in many cases to martyrdom.

Notwithstanding the strong faith of some, one of the frequently observed characteristics of many persons who join these new religions is that they often change faiths, going from one movement to another. The majority of those surveyed in both the Hare Krishna movement and the Unification Church indicate that they had been following other spiritual paths than those of their parents before they joined either of these movements. There is also evidence from some who were deprogrammed that they had already become dissatisfied and would have soon dropped out of the movement anyway.

Cultural differences in non-indigenous religions that observe a strict discipline and have a communal life have also been a pitfall for others. For example, some former women members of the Hare Krishna movement have left it because of the great contrast observed between an American culture that is increasingly recognizing full equality of the sexes and the traditional Hindu culture giving dominance to the male. In the even more controversial Unification Church, these differences in culture have also taken their toll. The Church emphasizes the daily expression of a sacrificial sharing in loving fellowship—being "love bombed," as dropouts and those deprogrammed have often declared concerning its techniques of conversion. Add to this the close living and working relationships of young men and women thrown together day after day, and then instruct them that there is to be no physical expression of sex, nor of falling in love, and the typical American may experience difficulties. The Rev. Moon not only demands at least three years of celibacy in the Church before marriage, but then arranges the marriages, deciding the partners himself in the traditional Oriental fashion as the "true parent." Consequently one young lady gave as a reason for leaving the Church the fact that she had fallen in love with one of her coworkers, who not only rebuked her for it, but then became married to a Korean girl who had been selected for him. Although there are reports that such mixed marriages have caused difficulties for some, this has not apparently been true for others, and the divorce rate among members of the Unification Church is far lower than among those in the United States who marry for love.

Among the communal movements, discipline, which seems to be so important to many persons to deepen the faith to which they have converted, has also been to others an obstacle. Even the communal life itself after a period of time has had its drawbacks for some. A demand for obedience in an authoritarian system may prevent the fulfillment of an ambition, such as writing or art, as reported by some in the Hare Krishna movement. Still, it would be entirely untrue to press this argument too far. Contrary to the criticisms of some psychologists, who cite the lack of creativity as a sign of mind control, the Hare Krishna movement has made a place for many creative artists and craftsmen whose works both here and in India are outstanding. Likewise, the Unification Church has allowed one of its many talented musicians to work almost full-time on composing music.

Since the parents themselves of members of new religious movements differ so widely in their feelings concerning their children both before and after conversion, they, too, should be included as part of the investigation. Do their religious, social, political, and economic views have any bearing on their children's religious decisions? What has been their own social and economic status, education, ambitions for their children, theories and practices of raising their families, the amount and kind of attention given to them, etc.? Finally, are there any appreciable differences to be observed between those who oppose or do not oppose their children's choice of religion?

Since differences of opinion exist among psychologists concerning the effect of being a member of one of these new religions, it seems fitting to include in the project appropriate psychological examinations to test the mental health of members, and to determine whether such reported adverse personality changes are a general characteristic. Therefore, it is planned that a random sample of present Unification Church members, those who have been deprogrammed, and those who have dropped out, together with a control group, be given the same tests, and that a blind evaluation be made by a psychologist who does not know the status of any of the respondents. The results should be computerized to make the correlations, and all data inspected by a committee of appropriate representatives of the fields of religious studies, of sociology, and of clinical psychology. This committee could also act in an advisory way during the course of the project and call upon other researchers in these areas not only for further suggestions, but for their own contributions as well. However it turns out, such an objective study must be made in order to contribute toward the solution of a very important and complex problem.

BLACK REFLECTIONS ON THE STUDY OF NEW RELIGIOUS CONSCIOUSNESS

Archie Smith, Jr.

THERE IS a growing awareness among many scholars that we stand in witness of a great transition in Western culture, and the dawning of a new religious era. Jacob Needleman has written that

Significant though it is, the revolution that is striking the established religious institutions of the West is only part of a spiritual phenomenon that promises to transform everything modern man has thought about God and human possibility. The contemporary disillusionment with religion has revealed itself to be a 'religious' disillusionment [1].

Something new and liberating is stirring in the depths of Western religious consciousness which promises to be the source of a new vision for a new society. The religious focus is shifting and new interpretations of religion, conscience, God, and the role of the person in social life are emerging. The new religious consciousness is a symptom of a complex process of revolutionary changes going on in traditional roles and Western institutions. True, the current trend in universities by students seems to be more and more toward materialism. Many want to become doctors and lawyers for the money and prestige. Yet hundreds of thousands of Americans are turning East and towards the mystical core of all religion.

The new religious consciousness suggests that new themes of ultimate significance are emerging, further contributing towards a crisis in a materialistic culture premised upon modern capitalism, secularism, technology, and individualism. White scholars have been drawn to this movement, assessing its meanings and sharing their insights. It is too early to tell what will emerge from this new religious ferment. But while we stand in the presence of something new that promises liberation, we also stand in the presence of something old and enduring—which has made its impact in American society and the world.

W. E. B. DuBois, around the turn of the century, argued that the problem of the twentieth century is the problem of the color line:

. . . we must remember that living as the blacks do in close contact with a great modern nation, and sharing, although imperfectly, the soul-life of that nation, they must necessarily be affected more or less directly by all the religious and ethical forces that are today moving the United States. These questions and movements are, however, over-shadowed and dwarfed by the (to them) all-important question of their civil, political, and economic status. They must perpetually discuss the "Negro Problem,"—must live, move, and have their being in it, and interpret all else in its light or darkness [2].

DuBois' point may be more relevant today than it was then. The problem of color is rooted in an even greater problem of economic oppression—supported by apathy and antipathy of the affluent towards their disinherited compatriots. The twin problems of racism and poverty conspire to form the basis of black victimization.[1] With the growing backlash of such hate groups as the American Nazi party, the increased interest and growth of the Ku Klux Klan, and other hate groups, one must ask: Can the new religious consciousness generate a new spirit of social commitments and a vision of society profound and heroic enough to effectively counter economic oppression, racism, and its subsequent effects?

I

With few exceptions, white scholars of the "New Religious Consciousness" have failed, so far, to perceive racism as a significant factor worthy of their attention in the study of the new religious movements. Yet racism has been endemic to white religion in America; and a reality in determining the real priorities in the everyday activities of this society. Racism, born of capitalism, continues to be a dominant form of oppression as well as a source of meaning in America. Yet it was ignored or trivialized when the white scholars who met at Berkeley assessed the meaning of the "new religious consciousness."

The relationship of race and racism to the new religious consciousness did not occupy a significant place in their deliberations. Indeed, the new religious consciousness was discussed without significant reference to "the problem of the color," and discussed as if the new forms of religious consciousness were of universal significance in an otherwise pluralistic society. I suspect that if a group of Black or ethnic scholars had met to discuss the new religious consciousness and its significance, racism and its effects upon social and religious life would be of central importance. Why, at this point in history, is racism not more central in the hierarchy of concerns of first-world scholars who study new, predominantly white, religious movements? Is it that racism and color oppression are completely absent from the "new consciousness" and therefore, simply "not there" to be investigated?

The search for "truth" in the new religious consciousness may be seriously compromised when those who study it trivialize or ignore the fact that racism is endemic to American intellectual and religious life. While sex and age, alienation and anomic conditions, conformity and dissent, truth, guilt, salvation, and the search for meaning were discussed, everyday realities of racism and social and economic oppression were left largely untreated.

The problem is one of relevance. Relevance is concerned with the investigator's interest, particular angle of observation and selective mapping of experienced reality. The interest of the investigator is critical. Interest selects what is an important area of study and what is to be ignored as unimportant. It plays a central role in the development of our stock of knowledge about the new religious movements and those who study them. The relevant task of social theory and scholarship is not only to codify data, but interpret social reality and help give society expressions that are truly creative and life-enhancing.

The problem of relevance in studies of the new religious consciousness cannot be settled by simply adjusting Afro-American concerns within the current scope of scholarship. Our understanding will be enhanced when non-white scholars and women make significant contributions from their perspectives and experiences, and when white Western scholarship is brought into dialogue and challenged beyond its traditional perspective.

The new religious consciousness was largely treated at the Berkeley conference as a universal affecting young people in general, i.e., W.A.S.P., rather than youth from certain ethnic backgrounds and particular social strata. Recruits to the new religious movements tend to be urban white youth, well-educated and from middle- and upper-class families. Their disaffection is with the inability of established white religious traditions and materialistic strivings of family life to yield depth of meaning in living.

II

The literature on the "new religious consciousness" is growing, and suggests that the "new religious consciousness" is indeed a complex phenomenon. The new religious consciousness has arisen both within and outside of main-line religious traditions; some have taken more of a political emphasis, while others have emphasized individual salvation. The reasons for joining and methods of recruitment vary considerably. Initiates themselves are drawn to the new movements for reasons that range from sheer curiosity to a profoundly personal or spiritual quest for acceptance and growth towards wholeness. Many recruits lacked little in the way of material possessions in their family of origin. They are, after all, products of a powerful and wealthy economy and have been among its chief benefactors. They have been exposed to the best our society affords in terms of health care, education, homes equipped with the latest in modern technology, travel, and sophisticated psychotherapies. Many were participants in the antiwar movement of the 1960s and early 70s, and maintain their commitment to radical political action for a just society. Yet some perceive through disillusionment, that politics alone cannot achieve justice in society, or bring about the necessary social transformation apart from religion. Politics alone cannot satisfy the deeper strivings of the human spirit, or meet the moral requirements for justice. Neither can the requirements for social and spiritual justice be met by domesticated pietism, which abdicates risk and responsible self-conscious participation in the construction of a new society. The relational and prophetic dimensions in religious commitment can help pave the way to a more human social order.

Other recruits were among the uncommitted youth of the 1960s who participated in the hippie, dropout and psychedelic drug cultures. Still others are from homes where real intimacy and emotional gratification were overshadowed by materialistic pursuits and search for security. They have not found fulfillment in the religious traditions in which they have been raised and are turning to non-traditional, often non-Western, forms of spirituality.

The personal forces that drive the youth to the new movements are a sense of alienation from main-line Protestant, Catholic, and Jewish traditions which some perceive to be decadent, and a search for an identity that has its roots in the conscious and unconscious strivings of the human soul. Some do not perceive that such a spiritual quest can be meaningfully fulfilled in the established religious traditions of the parent generation. Many come to the new movements as a part of an inner search for happiness, for friendship, communal living, authority, a personal sense of integration and intimate contact with a higher power. The new religious movements promise to be, for many, an alternative way of life, a more acceptable way of living in this society—where inner happiness and friendship can develop in community through sacrifice, purification rites, and where contact can be achieved with the sacred—a living reality more personal and powerful than any combination of people.

Individualism or personal transformation is a pervasive theme in the new modern religious movements. In some groups there is an emphasis upon diet and nutrition; forms of mysticism, trance behavior or altered states of consciousness, other forms of meditation; a stress upon separation from non-devotees; and a search for new social roles as ways to transform society. There is also a strong political element in the new religious consciousness among those who continue to be committed to (root) economic, political, and social structural transformation in America. What is new in this complex religious phenomenon is an unparalleled turn from the values of utilitarian individualism and established white religious traditions towards new forms of religion by white, urban, well-educated, and affluent youth from middle-class American families.

The Graduate Theological Union conferees did not address themselves to the question of "Black Religion,"[2] its impact upon social reality in America, and its implications for their own life and work. Religious movements such as the Black Muslims, Black Holiness and Pentecostals, Black sects and cults, the Ras Tafari movement, development within Black Christian theologies of liberation, and their impact upon Black main-line church persons and denominations. Black Jehovah's Witnesses and Seventh-Day Adventists—were not addressed at the conference, or recognized as significant aspects of the new religious consciousness in America. Perhaps these white scholars felt unprepared to address these topics. But if this were the case, then their own studies of the new religious consciousness should be qualified—as studies of a particular aspect of the new phenomena, especially if the groups studied are predominantly white. We argue that the Black experience is also part of the new religious phenomenon in America. But there is a difference for why Blacks are not turning to the same new forms of religion as whites.

While Black Americans experience more or less the same forces that contribute to disillusionment with the American dream, their experiences are nevertheless profoundly different because they are *Black* in America. Black Americans share a common culture with all other Americans, but due to African origins, the heritage of slavery, long-standing and complex patterns of oppression, Black Americans have evolved a different perspective, and set of norms and values that have enabled them to survive in a hostile environment. Black people in America have been victimized because they are Black, and Blacks continue to be the nation's largest impoverished group of urban Americans. Forty-point-four percent unemployment (August 1977) among young urban Blacks is one indication of structural impoverishment; the subeducation received by many inner-city youth in large metropolitan areas is another indication; the increasing welfare roles, and imprisonment among inner-city Blacks is yet another indication of structural oppression with its subsequent permanent effects.

The Black experience in America is epitomized in the Black struggle for survival in a hostile white society. Their sole struggle centers in survival, and what they have to defend is their life. Historically, it has been out of conditions of brutal oppression and cultural alienation, not affluence, that has been the creative ground of Black religious consciousness and radicalism. Sometimes out of necessity that consciousness found radical expressions in the culture of the street as well as in the Black Church. Sometimes it turned to cynicism, resignation, and despair or rage. But always the underlying theme in Black religious consciousness has been liberation from oppression in white America [3,4,5,6,7,8].

When white scholars ignore racism, they legitimize covert violence in a racist society and contribute to problems of interpretation in the study of predominantly white new religious movements. The challenge for them is to show how the new religious consciousness can overcome the problems of racism so deeply embedded in white established religious traditions. Scholars are in a unique position not only to identify and interpret various forms of innovative folk religions, but also to provide the new movements with a reflexive, self-critical perspective regarding their own claims to be beyond racism, as well as a perspective for authentic liberation in society. The sign of authentic liberation in America is when the oppressed are set at liberty and the blind can see. No group is free as long as their compatriots are humiliated and oppressed . . . and so the struggle goes on.

Harvey Cox, reflecting upon the new religious consciousness, wrote:

The spiritual crisis of the West will not be resolved by spiritual importations or individual salvation. It is the crisis of a whole civilization, and one of its major symptoms is the belief that the answer must come from elsewhere. The crisis can be met only when the West sets aside myths of the Orient, and returns to its own primal roots [9].

Those roots extend deep into the history of Black oppression. Scholarship cannot adequately address the issue of salvation and release from guilt in the new religious consciousness by ignoring the strivings in the souls of Black folk, and the corresponding search for meaning in the souls of white folk. When scholarship ignores the problem of the old in the search for the new, I suspect that we compound rather than shed meaningful light upon our destiny and common spiritual pilgrimage in this country.

III

I have been arguing that "the problem of the color line" has been ignored by white scholars in the study of the new religious consciousness, while it continues to be a pervasive theme in American life and in the everyday reality for Black Americans. By ignoring the problem of color, the experiences of young educated white and middle-class Americans tend to function as the norm for what is going on in the new religious movements. This has permitted a partial vision of religious experience to function as a universal in a pluralistic society. The problem of the color line, echoed by the eminent sociologist W. E. B. DuBois, needs to be reaffirmed as "a problem" to be addressed by white scholars.

The problem of the color line in the study of the new religious consciousness is broadened beyond traditional boundaries of Black, native, and white Americans with the emergence of Asian and Chicano presence, especially on the West Coast. The problem of the color line has implications for the conscious and unconscious strivings of white North Americans in general, and the souls of white scholars in particular.

The problem is not who is studied, but the integrity or quality of the dialogue among scholars from different ethnic backgrounds and perspectives. All are needed to assess the meaning of the new religious consciousness in North America, and to move us beyond partial frames of reference towards new concepts which will release our reality from a narrow point of view generated by a small minority of white scholars.

Racism was cited in the 1968 Kerner Commission Report as a pervasive American problem, and referred to by the late Reverend Dr. Martin Luther King, Jr., as "the corrosive force that may well bring down the curtain of Western civilization." Racism was the force that brought his own life and the lives of countless other Black Americans and Jews in Europe to an end. Black Americans have perceived the problem of racism and oppression to be far more deepseated and fatal to American life than has been generally appreciated by white Americans. Racism is a reality deeply rooted in American social history, intellectual life, and consciousness. It can no longer continue to be ignored or trivialized by white scholars in their study of the "New Religious Consciousness." If the new religious consciousness is "new," and if it is able to adequately counter the disruptive effects of racism and imperialism, then this is important data. Ought not this data be an object of investigation for white scholars in their pursuit of truth? Perhaps, the "new religious consciousness'' is a reaction or response to the failure of the older religious orientations to give meaning, to establish justice, and to live out the great covenant of this nation—as one nation in diversity, under God with authentic liberty and justice for everyone—especially the oppressed.

The new quest in America is but the ancient quest of the human spirit for wholeness and Truth, personal and social integration and transformation. These are manifestations of a genuine spiritual-moral quest. To be whole is, in part, a quest for union with the primal source which lies in the depths of our own nature. The journey inward must lead outward and affirm life comprehensively, intentionally, and for everyone. The mark of maturity in religious commitment is vulnerability manifest in faith and action within specific social processes. Spiritual-moral resignation or political activism alone lack the moral depth, breadth, and vision to liberate the Self or a social order from an exploitative, self-serving system of capitalism. Political apathy or activism alone cannot liberate persons from oppressive exterior pressures and interior psychic forces. The real transforming energy in the new religious movements will need to transcend (not deny) self- and class-interest, and will move towards the full realization of social and economic justice as a manifestation of liberation and authentic Selfhood. The new spiritual quest in America may be a sign of new and creative possibilities on the horizon, but such a quest will not be authenticated by ignoring personal and systemic sources of color, sex, and class oppression.

NOTES

[1] Definitions of "racism" abound. Some readers may argue that "racism" is now an over-used term and has little heuristic value to warrant further use. Many may take exception to the author's angle of vision and use of the term "racism" and wish to replace it with some other, less volatile term, such as "ethnocentrism" or "cultural differences." This author, however, maintains that racism is the more accurate term to use. Mine is the viewpoint of a minority group member whose perception of reality has been shaped within a society without fundamental acceptance of Blacks. Hence, this essay is not written from a dispassionate, scientifically objective perspective. The author is involved and writes from a point of interest within this society. Consequently, my experience and perception as a racial minority group member will vary significantly from the dispassionate observer and from that of dominant group members. Unlike racism, ethnocentrism is a universal phenomenon. It is the

tendency of human groups with similar characteristics to think of their cultural and social heritage as superior to others. Ethnocentrism is a sense of group pride and a source of self-esteem. However, in encounters with other groups, ethnocentric justifications of superiority are subject to modification in the process of intergroup interaction. Ethnocentrism may lead to racism when human groups fail to give up their claim to superiority and seek to impose their institutionalized definitions of reality upon those who are racially and culturally different. Black skin color is not the only criterion for invidious distinctions between groups in a racially heterogeneous society. But Blackness is as significant a criterion for exclusion as is sex and class and age. Black is a highly visible color in white America, and endowed with pejorative attributes. Blacks continue to be singled out for differential and unequal treatment both as individuals and as a group. Unequal and differential treatment of Black people in America has decisively shaped American social and religious history. Although Blacks are not the only ethnic group to be singled out for special treatment in America, they are the largest racial minority group which has had a difficult time coming out of poverty and overcoming institutionalized discrimination— as a group. "Cultural differences," as a more acceptable explanation, fails to address the fact that those few Black Americans who participate in white institutionalized structures often do so at the price of denying their Blackness and African heritage. Blackness and African traditions are more often perceived as pathogenic deviations from acceptable white norms, or perceived as impediments to success within white institutional arrangements. Even when Blacks become culturally similar to whites, they are still Black and vulnerable to unequal and differential treatment. Many Black Americans, especially since the turbulent 1960s and Alex Haley's *Roots*, have had to face the fact that Black self-consciousness must be redefined in terms of its African heritage. Many Black Americans are responding to white racism by affirming their Blackness, their African heritage and cultural uniqueness. These responses are essential themes in the burgeoning religious consciousness among younger Black Americans. This essay is written with these ideas in mind.

[2] Scholars are not agreed upon the precise meaning of the term "Black Religion" or whether it exists apart from white religion in America. This paper argues that there is a difference. Although the ultimate or primal source that underlies Religion is One, the experiences of a people who confess it (religion) are located within the framework of a particular social history and culture which gives shape to their experiences and ways of apprehending the fundamental nature of Reality. Suffering from racial oppression in America, experience of a God who can make a way out of no way, and the continuation of African cultural residuals in Black experience have been distinctive sources of Black Religion in America.

REFERENCES

1. Jacob Needleman. *The New Religions*, preface. Doubleday, 1970.
2. W. E. B. DuBois. *The Souls of Black Folk,* p. 148. Fawcett ed., 1961.
3. C. Eric Lincoln, editor. *The Black Experience in Religion*. Doubleday, 1974.
4. Joseph R. Washington, Jr. *Black Sects and Cults*. Doubleday, 1972.
5. James H. Cone. *God of the Oppressed*. Seabury, 1975.

6. Albert B. Cleage, Jr. *Black Christian Nationalism*. William Morrow, 1972.

7. Gayraud S. Wilmore. *Black Religion and Black Radicalism*. Doubleday, 1973.

8. Clifton H. Johnson, editor. *God Struck Me Dead*. Pilgrim Press, Boston, 1969.

9. Harvey Cox. "Eastern Cults and Western Culture: Why Young Americans Are Buying Oriental Religions." *Psychology Today*, July 1977, p. 42.

THE SPIRITUAL MOVEMENT OF RADICAL FEMINIST CONSCIOUSNESS

Emily Culpepper

AN INCREASING development in the women's movement community is the explosion of interest in and expression of the spiritual dimensions of radical feminist consciousness. This phenomenon has many facets and is a source of diverse opinions among women as to the relevance, significance, and forms of this direction. In this paper, I intend to describe/assess/evoke these developments through surveying representative examples of this activity. Let me first be clear about several important aspects of the perspective from which I write. First, I am not including here the considerable work for *reform* of traditional religions in which many feminist and nonfeminist women are involved. Certainly such "equal rights" movements within patriarchal religious structures do involve a partial critique of these traditions which has then become for some women the starting point or initial impetus toward a different, woman-identified spiritual quest. Nevertheless, remaining with this concern for reform is not my own perspective, nor is it that of the women I will be considering here.

Second, most contemporary "new" religious movements (for example, Baba Lovers, Hare Krishnas, Maharaj Ji followers, independent charismatic Christian groups—to name a few) offer only a pseudo-newness for women. The roles for women within such movements are heavily traditional, patriarchal ones—usually urging a norm of heterosexist, reproductive, nuclear family goals. The theology is frequently explicitly or implicitly woman-hating. Often membership in such groups may present an outward appearance of difference from various conventional feminine roles, or a woman's individual personal history. However, this very semblance of difference functions to obscure the basic fact that, for the female membership, what is offered is in reality a new/old religious reinforcement of the conventional oppressive female roles which are so up for criticism and reevaluation in contemporary society. Other more individualistic "new" movements (such as TM, Subud, and varieties of zen and yoga) often offer women a method of personal calming and adjustment within a largely unchallenged patriarchal status quo. Many cults offer only yet another male guru/deity/leader whose insights and directions women are once again supposed to trust and follow. For these reasons, radical feminists regard such "new" religious movements as a stopping place or side track for the energies of questioning women who are unsettled and uncertain about the deeply different directions facing women today.

Third, my subject matter, the movement of radical feminist consciousness, and my own perspective as a radical feminist place me quite firmly "on the boundary" (as Mary Daly has described it) of this discussion of new religious movements. Some of the women's activities I will describe are considered by the women involved to be not a new religion at all, but the resurgence of an old, in fact ancient, pre-patriarchal religion. Others (and I include myself here) most emphatically do not see ourselves concerned with developing a religion or a spiritual sense; rather, we are exploring a philosophy of feminist consciousness that has inherent spiritual dimensions. Furthermore, none of these distinctions are particularly mutually exclusive. All participate in a similar mode of consciousness about the implications of radical feminism and we all inform/inspire/influence each other.

Finally, I must in all honesty say that my reason for presenting this survey is not to urge any conventional "study" of these developments. My concern is to spread the word among women and to propose that these movements should be heard, pondered, and responded to as evidence of a felt need for a deep and necessary transformation of our consciousness and existence.

That there is emerging a feminist interest in spiritual expression really should come as no surprise, since it is essentially inherent in the initial feminist insight that "consciousness raising" is what we are about. As Mary Daly [1] expressed it in 1973 (already light-years ago), the women's revolution, insofar as it is true to its own essential dynamics, is an ontological spiritual revolution, pointing beyond the idolatries of sexist society and sparking creative action in and toward transcendence.

As the processes of female becoming are taking shape and form, more and more women are taking "the qualitative leap beyond patriarchal religion" and embarking on what Daly has later called an Otherworld journey in feminist time/space [3]. At present I see three main streams in the development of this creative flow of "Gynergy."[1] For the purposes of these reflections, I have called them: (I) Feminist Witchcraft and Worship of the Goddess, (II) Woman-Identified Culture; and (III) Woman-Identified Chronicles, Philosophy, and Theory.

FEMINIST WITCHCRAFT AND WORSHIP OF THE GODDESS

Witchcraft is a religion. It is the Worship, not of the Christian Satan, but of the Great Mother, the Supreme Creatrix, the Primum Mobile. It is the celebration of the Goddess [5].

These are the words of Morgan McFarland, High Priestess of the Covenstead of Morrigana. She is one of the leaders of an organized religion that has a tradition running back through lines of inheritance and inspiration to the witches and midwife healers of the middle ages and further back through the many ancient religions and rituals that focused on the worship of a Goddess who was a Divine Mother. It is perhaps the most conventionally organized (in the sense of having initiation procedures and a hierarchical membership) form of feminist spiritual interest. The Craft has clearly identified rituals and special days (sabbats), although even within the Craft there is great diversity as to how much emphasis is put on standard practices and on how much any group or individual might choose to improvise and invent for what best suits these times. Most practitioners of the Craft worship a three-aspected Goddess, often described as Nymph, Maiden, and Crone. Sometimes these aspects are understood to represent different stages in a woman's life (girlhood, maturity, old age) and sometimes to represent different roles within the coven or different modes of being. When possible, women form groves or covens, which sometimes include men. A common thread among most practitioners of the Craft is the belief in matriarchal forms of social organization, both as the original history of the human race and as the form to which we should turn once again for a life that would be in harmony with nature and each other.

I can only briefly sketch here the complexity and diversity of the Craft. Essentially, witchcraft is learned in person from one witch to others. McFarland has in the past edited a magazine about Wicca called the *New Broom*. Another and somewhat different source is the Susan B. Anthony Coven Number One and its priestess, Z. Budapest, who has been harassed through arrest for fortune telling. This group has published *The Feminist Book of Lights and Shadows* (1976), which contains articles about witchcraft history and theory as well as information about the eight sabbats, various specific rituals and spells, and herbal lore. Sources frequently mentioned within the Craft for information and theory include: *Myth, Religion, and Mother Right* (1967), by J. J. Bachofen [1815–87]; *The Golden Bough* (1911–15), by James Frazer [1854–1941]; *White Goddess* (1948), by Robert Graves *Women's Mysteries* (1955), by Esther Harding; *God of the Witches* (1933) and *Witch-Cult in Western Europe* (1921) by Margaret Murray, and *The Great Mother* (1963), by Erich Neumann. There are also the recently published *Moon, Moon* (1976), by Anne Kent Rush and *When God Was a Woman* (1976), by Merlin Stone. These sources are also of interest to many women other than those who officially or formally practice the Craft as a religion.

McFarland [6] believes that "women together remember their old ascendency, their art, their magick, their roots." This is a vital point for women in the Craft, since much of "The Old Religion" has been destroyed and distorted through persecution. This same theme is echoed by Z. Budapest [7]: "We believe that Feminist witches are wimmin[2] who search within themselves for the female principle of the universe and who relate as daughters to the Creatrix." At precisely this juncture, we can see where the practitioners of the Craft share much with other feminists who do not, however, place themselves within the framework of a religion worshipping a goddess. A deep and radical new acceptance of one's self as female and a trust in women's thought and living for clues as to how to get out from under the reigning androcratic social order are key realizations of feminism. This search for knowledge through female self-awareness/reflecting/remembering is occurring not only in the specific direction the Craft has chosen, but also throughout a rapidly spreading feminist culture.

WOMAN-IDENTIFIED CULTURE

More widespread than the formal religion of the Craft is a vast array of ways in which feminists are exploring forms of thought and behavior that are inspired and informed by ancient female imagery and by modern invention/intuition/intellection about women. Multitudes of women are involved in expressing feminist insights about the spiritual dimensions of be-ing—in art, poetry, music, fiction, political analysis, philosophy, health care, sexuality, lifestyles, and on and on . . . the list is literally endless. There are references to many goddesses from diverse religions and to mythic and legendary females as symbols and metaphors of meaning and power. Particularly prevalent are references to amazon imagery, which I explored in an article [4] on "Female History/Myth Making." Mentioned often are: Anath, Artemis, Fairies, Furies, Tiamāt, Kali, Crones, Kybele, Rhea, Metis, Minerva, Harpies, Hathor, Hags, Spider Woman, Gorgon, Demeter, Sappho, Isis. Where imagery of goddesses and/or mythic females is not explicitly present, the language with which women are communicating ourselves to each other is replete with phrases and tones and imagery of profound, urgent, and energizing self-transformation.

The feminist insight that "the personal is political" has become "the personal is political is spiritual." A great many interests and themes mingle together here, overlapping and informing each other, with each woman finding her own best combination of approaches for survival/enjoyment/struggle. One fascinating example is Sister Heathen Spinster's "Lunar Calendar," with its drawings and its passages on women's history, healing, science, poetry, astrology, wicca lore and lunar-month names and cycle charts. It proclaims: "Remember and affirm that one of the first political acts of radical transition is to change the calendar. Reclaim Woman Time" [8]. One sort of mystical direction is found in the pamphlet by Diane Mariechild, "Womancraft: The Consciousness Development of Psychic Skills We All Possess." In 1974, Susan Rennie and Kirsten Grimstead traveled across the country and reported finding, among women's communities,

a widespread and surging interest in what we can, for the moment, loosely call the spiritual aspects of life. . . . In acknowledging this side of our being, women are in effect striving for a total integration and wholeness. Accepting the wholeness that includes psychic awareness and exploration takes feminist consciousness into an entirely new dimension—it amounts to redefinition of reality [9].

The fountain for this explosion of spiritual/political phenomena is the primal level of change that is necessary to leave behind gynocidal patriarchy. I have space here only to discuss three representative examples (a magazine, a conference, and an art) from the scope of these developments. Taken together, these are all manifestations of a contemporary women's culture that is one visible sign of the free woman space within which we come to know and to create who we are.

WomanSpirit Magazine. This journal, which has been published every solstice since fall 1974, is one excellent source of articles, poems, songs, and drawings from many different women recording/expressing what I will call the tribal/ritual aspects of woman-identified spirituality. Many articles recount women's experiments and techniques for meditation and spiritual energy and support. Often such accounts are excerpts from women's personal journals. (I find these records of thought in process especially fascinating and powerful reading—very raw and real—whether or not I feel/think in sympathy with what is specifically being articulated.) *WomanSpirit* reflects a great deal of current feminist interest in simple, close to the land, vegetarian, communal living. Women's reinterpretations of astrology and tarot; the significance and effect of plant, animal, and cosmic rhythms; herbal and dietary healing; dream exploration and interpretation; esp and astral travel; story-telling and myth making all figure prominently in these pages. A major element is the creation of individual and group rituals for women. These focus on significant experiences and life stages (such as menstruation, birth, aging, death, personal commitments, partings, etc.) and on the summoning of female power and energy through chanting, dancing, meditating, and celebrating. Often, native American

Indian lore is a source of information and inspiration. Many of the sources important to the Craft are also relied on here and references to "The Goddess" and especially to "the Goddess within each woman" abound. Also there are frequent practical articles about various skills involved in changing into a self-sufficient, country, communal, agrarian lifestyle.

Spirituality Conference. In April 1976, the Pomegranate Grove sponsored a three-day conference on women and spirituality, attended by more than two thousand women, called "Through the Looking Glass: A Gynergenetic Experience."[3] More than any other single event so far, this conference exemplified the myriad directions of feminist spiritual revolutionary change. "Through the Looking Glass was offered as a meeting place—a crossroad. . . . This cross-coastal gathering was for all self-loving women in process" [10].

There were three major addresses. Theorist Sally Gearhart spoke on "WomanPower: Energy Re-Sourcement." Philosopher/Theologian Mary Daly spoke on "Procession, Professions, Possessions: The Breakthrough from Phallocracy to Feminist Time/Space." Poet Barbara Starrett spoke on her recent theoretical work, "I Dream in Female: The Metaphors of Power." The concerns at this conference ranged from intellectual analysis and theory through four dozen different workshops and presentations to enactment of rituals. My own two workshops—one on "Menstruation: Body and Spirit" and the other on "Martial Art Meditation"—reflect some of the plurality of interests that converged here. Perhaps especially clear at this gathering was the fact that many of these developments are not completely in harmony with each other. Most women seem now to recognize the value of an attitude of creative anarchy. Women are following many different leads and needs in the search for spiritual development and generally encourage each woman to find her own contributions to add to the process. Concern was clearly evident at the conference that even more insights are needed for the feminist movement to continue to grow and that feminists be alert to the dangers of any spirituality that is merely a comfortable retreat. The conference was significant not only as a "cross-roads" for the exchange of so much information, but further as a forceful catalyst for the critical reflection on and continuing exploration of the spiritual dimension of feminism.

Women's Music. In addition to the activities in women's movement culture that are specifically designated as spiritual or religious, there is a profusion of other women's cultural/political activities that resonate with spiritual import and energy for those involved. Outstanding among these is the amazing growth in the last few years of a specifically "women's music." At least three of the more widely known recording artists explicitly identify their music as having a spiritual-feminist dynamic. Composer/conductor/flautist Kay Gardner considers her album "Moon Circles" to be expressing not only feminist lyrical content, but also to embody specifically female sound patterns. Cris Williamson, on "The Changer and the Changed," and Casse Culver, on "Three Gypsies," both describe themselves as being especially concerned with a music of women's spirituality. In my own experiences attending festivals and concerts in several states and in producing women's music events in Boston as part of Artemis Productions, I have seen these and other feminist musicians (such as Willie Tyson, Meg Christian, Hazel Dickens, Alice Gerrard, and Holly Near) perform and participate in the context of a vivid energy flow between themselves and their audiences. Such music events are one public manifestation of the radical ontological processes set in motion by women Naming our Selves and our own reality and purpose. The liberating force of this musical validation of women's strength, diversity, courage, hope and struggle brings into existence a qualitatively different time/space.

Following the paths of this musical outpouring is one good means of touching on the multi-faceted women's cultural/political network that makes up the growing fabric of this new spirit. We can follow the sounds of this music from the concerts and festivals to the new independent women's recording companies (Olivia and Urana) and production groups; through countless women's bookstores and shops where the records are sold; to an increasing number of women's restaurants and coffeehouses and bars where we hear it playing; to the music collectives encouraging emerging local performers and informal community music making events; to the health centers, refuges for battered women, and numerous political action groups contributed to by benefit concerts; to women's prisons; and to the homes of thousands of very different women, especially those who are isolated and for whom this music is one dramatic sustaining link with like-minded sisters [11,12]. In short, what I am tracing here are the developing social structures of what is essentially the sense and the spirit of a new reality for increasing numbers of women. Of course, I have only depicted some of the more clearly visible signs of this woman-identified creative impulse in order to indicate the breadth and depth of what is already happening and the potential that is stirring.

WOMAN-IDENTIFIED CHRONICLES, PHILOSOPHY, AND THEORY

The third major current of the spiritual dimensions of radical feminism is the rich continuing development of philosophy and theory. Women are doing a lot of clear-minded, original work to explore and express the knowledge and analysis of women's situation and the nature of female be-ing. Mary Daly figures especially prominently here, due not only to the character and quality of her work, but also to the enthusiasm with which she acknowledges and explores her own radical, dynamic processes of change. Already in 1973, in her pivotal book, *Beyond God the Father: Toward a Philosophy of Women's Liberation,* Mary Daly knew herself to be on the boundary of both theology and philosophy. She is a rigorous thinker. Her work stands as a primary source of insight, exciting and inciting women on the path of self-discovery and self-actualization. Daly says,

I suspect that what is required is *ludic cerebration,* the free play of intuition in our own space, giving rise to thinking that is vigorous, informed, multi-dimensional, independent, creative, tough. *Ludic cerebration* is thinking out of experience . . . the experience of be-ing. Be-ing is the verb that says the dimensions of the depth in all verbs, such as intuiting, reasoning, loving, imagining, making, acting, as well as the couraging, hoping, and playing that are always there when one is really living [2].

Here she is expressing what I consider to be the essential spiritual dynamic of radical feminist thought. Basically, it is *all* modes of this ludic cerebration by woman-identified women that constitute the current flow of philosophy and theory. This is, at the heart and soul of it, a new form of communication—of women's hearing and speaking and seeing and understanding with each other—the wisdom of women. This knowledge and learning crop forth in a profusion of forms. Indeed, the very use and nature of language is being of necessity questioned, challenged, analysed, and changed. Women's own words have only begun to be discovered—and it is this experiment and discovery that is at the core a primal hearing, an ontological speech. Linguist Julia Stanley has described the prevailing conditions quite well {13]:

Women have been systematically excluded from the English language, split off from the sounds, words, and syntax that should be our most powerful means of expressing our feelings, thoughts, and desires. We have been disposed of our tongue as we have been separated from our experiences of motherhood, sisterhood, self-knowledge, and the other complex relationships that define our dwelling in the world. Our separation from language defines and maintains our separation from our experience.

Women are increasingly succeeding in creating woman-identified speech. The response from those to whom this is too threatening is the continued and intensified use of language as androcratic weapon. Stanley has called this "The Rhetoric of Denial: Delusion, Distortion and Deception," in her recent article with that title which brilliantly unmasks this process.

In this light, it is obvious why the "conventional" distinctions about what is or is not "philosophical" or "theological" or "spiritual" writings are not appropriate. Indeed, women are abandoning them as we emerge from our long, painful Absence to each other and become increasingly truly Present to our Selves and with each other. This is not to say that expression becomes blurry, undisciplined nonsense. The fact is that we are finally finding our own Sense—our own forms for the radically Whole, Self-Affirming Spirit of woman-identified women. What follows is a collage of instances of different forms of this intellection/intuition/imagination by women intended to indicate/invoke the communicating/collaborating that is the only collage concerned with knowing women. Let me stress with a scarlet accent that these writings be seen as some of what has so far crystallized in the context of the current in current thinking. They are both shells and seeds, the tip of the iceberg, the first extrusions of lava, the mirror and prism of our acknowledgement among ourselves. So much is being said, so much is not yet said.

Point: There are the controversial true-fiction, mind-journey journals probing the regions of the self. Here is the risky work of Millett leaving her straight thesis style in *Sexual Politics* (1970) and moving on to *Flying* (1974). In their two-woman journal, *Womanfriends: A Soap Opera,* Shirley Walton and Esther Newton record/report/reproduce the dialogue of two women demanding of themselves that they dare to defy the differences dividing them as feminists. Such writing is rooted in the long suppressed and unrespected form of women's diary keeping, now being reclaimed as a means of recalling and reflecting upon our reality [14,15].

Counterpoint: There is the searching, searing analysis on scores of subjects by women remolding traditional training into tools for building our own scholarship and theory. Andrea Dworkin's disturbing book, *Woman Hating* (1974), documents the deep denial and degradation of women that exists transculturally. Phyllis Chesler's *Women and Madness* (1972), with its trans-disciplinary method, has sparked many women's insights concerning the connections in our lives among mythic, religious, and psychological images of women. Susan Brownmiller, in *Against Our Will* (1975), thoroughly researches the enormous extent of rape and analyzes the deeply entrenched attitudes that perpetuate its existence and its function as an ever-present threat. Ethicist Janice Raymond's forthcoming book on what she has called "the transsexual empire" pushes past the sensational popular attention focused only on the transsexuals themselves. She probes and exposes the vested interests of the patriarchal support systems involved in reducing these "potential critics of sex role subjugation" to surgically and hormonally reconstructed, readjusted "persons" [16,17]. Mary Daly's next book on the *Meta-ethics of Radical Feminism* (1978) unveils the sadorituals of androcentric atrocity against women and moves into the mode and means with which women spin into our fiercely free, a-mazing, ecstatic journey.

Undertone: There are the articles, position papers, pamphlets, manuals, and statements by women who are beginning a host of new enterprises and endeavors in which they chart and assess and reflect on what we are all doing—seeking the principles and clues that can be discerned, distilled, and passed on. There are the countless unpublished papers by women at work within and without universities on feminist studies which women circulate among ourselves. This is a network of thought, the range and extent of which is only beginning to be felt.

Chord: There are an increasing number of journals to provide forums for the exchange, criticism, and development of this knowledge. The names themselves of the journals are telling: *Amazon Quarterly, Second Wave, Quest, Sinister Wisdom, Conditions, Chrysalis.* A recent issue of *Sinister Wisdom* contains an article by Susan Leigh Star called "The Politics of Wholeness: Feminism and the New Spirituality," with a clear critical analysis of how these new religious movements "function to short-circuit woman-identification" [18].

Scale: There is the work of filling out our own sense of history. Masses of material orchestrated into a new overview appear in Helen Diner's *Mothers and Amazons* (1973) and Elizabeth Gould Davis' *The First Sex* (1971). Then there is the rediscovery of the echoes of this gynergy in the work of newly seen foresisters— Woolf, Dickenson, Stein, Gage—the lists grow longer as we return to work by women and turn it over again in our minds with a different ear, catching notes we now recognize.

Lyrics: The poetic expression that is overflowing staggers and sustains the imagination. Impossible not to mention is the practical, matter-of-fact lyricism with which Robin Morgan writes in her two books, *Monster* (1972) and *Lady of the Beasts* (1976). The sure subtle skill of Adrienne Rich's incomparable verse expresses an ecstasy and an endurance that aid us in our determination to survive. The common note in all this poetry is its force as an artistic expression that is radically enabling, deeply validating, and affirming. These are the women whose incantations of their own visions amaze us by their exquisite shaping. Judy Grahn, Audre Lorde, Susan Griffin . . . I realize that I wish I could sing a list of names, syllable after syllable in a great round chant in an attempt to invoke them.

Tones: Making and creating a new female frame of reference occurs in a very particular form in the fantasy writing that feminists are composing. In *Les Guerilleres,* Monique Wittig [19] has produced a social/science fiction conjuring a world in which women are just on the verge of being truly free. Her characters speak with the knowledge of how they have come this far, to urge each other (and each reader) on,

There was a time when you were not a slave, remember that. You walked alone, full of laughter, you bathed bare-bellied. You say you have lost all recollection of it, remember. . . . You say there are no words to describe this time, you say it does not exist. But remember. Or, failing that, invent.

This is the writing that takes the space gained by saying one is weaving dreams about the future or the ancient past and uses it to find the messages needed for the present. In her science fiction book, *The Female Man* (1975), Joanna Russ interweaves the lives of women time-traveling from four different ages to open up the free play of thought about our female possibilities. Deena Metzger, in *The Book of Hags* (1977), winds together the voices of archetypal women writing survival notes to each other to stay alive and to search for the "blue tone" that will awaken the sisters who do not know their rage and are in a deep, isolated sleep. I want to conclude with her words,

And one of us, I, the writer, could no longer bear being with people without that feeling, which perhaps I shall call simply . . . a blue tone. . . . After a while we forgot how to speak without the tone. The lack of it made me sad or angry. . . . There were places with the blue tones, . . . though they were all almost without exception women's places. I found that women who had been out in the world a long time and had rubbed shoulders with men too long had had the blue rubbed out of them and sometimes they couldn't remember the tone. . . . So I came away to garner the tone. . . . I wanted to send out a blue signal to penetrate your heart . . . and it is a long process. And the gulf between us and the others who hate the tone increases and we struggle against that also. To this part of the story there is no ending. It is probably a middle point. It is the point the writer has come to at this moment [20].

Final Note: I have had space to mention only a few of the brave spokeswomen of this rising tide of the spirit of women. Feminists know that we must be about transforming the course of life on the planet—within ourselves, our ways of living, and our social forms. It is important to note that not all the women included in the phenomenon I am describing would self-identify with the designation or label of "spiritual." Indeed, many women (myself among them) who still do choose to use the word sometimes have a distinct unease about it. The term "spiritual" has a heavy load of dualistic, anti-body associations behind it which feminists recognize as ultimately being a key component of the androcentric oppressive dichotomy between female and male. Frankly, we are not too concerned with getting bogged down in reclaiming this word or urging its use on sisters who are justifiably suspicious. However, as women seek to articulate the wholistic, primal level of change that radical feminism means in their lives, reference is increasingly made to spiritual depths of truth and knowledge. I think this is because we recognize a mood, a spirit in the root sense of an animating principle, that is alive and afoot. Here is the very coming into existence of the world that is *not* patriarchal. Whatever the choice of word, feminists agree that we are about ultimate things—change in the very nature of what has been the female condition. This metamorphosis is simultaneously spiritual/psychic/social/political/mental/physical. Today the "spiritual movement" of woman-identified women is not finally a "religion"—with its root etymology of "binding"—but is rather the set-loose power/process/perception of radical feminist consciousness.

NOTES

[1] I coined the term "gynergy" to refer to the female energy "which both comprehends and creates who we are. It is woman-identified be-ing" [4].

[2] "Wimmin" is a new, feminist spelling of "women." Singular forms are "womon" and "womoon."

[3] A report on the conference may be found in *WomanSpirit* (June 1976).

REFERENCES

1. Mary Daly. *Beyond God the Father: Toward a Philosophy of Women's Liberation*, p. 6. Beacon, 1973.

2. Ibid., p. 28.

3. Mary Daly. "The Qualitative Leap Beyond Patriarchal Religion." *Quest* 1 (1975):20.

4. Emily Culpepper. "Female History/Myth Making." *Second Wave* 4 (1975):14–17.

5. Morgan McFarland. "Witchcraft: The Art of Remembering." *Quest* 1 (1975):41.

6. Ibid., p. 47.

7. Z. Budapest. *Feminist Book of Lights and Shadows*, p. 1. Luna Publications, 442 Lincoln Blvd., Venice, Ca., 1976.

8. Sister HeathenSpinster. *Lunar Calendar*. Luna Press, Box 511, Kenmore Station, Boston, Ma., 1977. Published Annually.

9. Susan Rennie and Kirsten Grimstead. "Spiritual Exploration Cross Country." *Quest* 1 (1975):49.

10. Pomegranate Grove. "A Right of Passage." *WomanSpirit* 2 (1976):4.

11. *Ladyslipper Music: 1978 Catalog of Records and Tapes by Women.* Box 3124, Durham, N.C. 27705.

12. *We Shall Go Forth: Resources in Women's Music.* 12751 Park Place, #H-1, Crestwood, Il. 60445.

13. Julia Stanley. "The Rhetoric of Denial: Delusion, Distortion, Deception." *Sinister Wisdom* 3 (1977):82.

14. *Matrices: A Lesbian/Feminist Research Newsletter.* Department of English, Andrews Hall 202, University of Nebraska, Lincoln, Nebraska 68588.

15. *Women in Distribution Catalog.* P.O. Box 8858, Washington, D.C. 20003.

16. Janice Raymond. *The Trans-sexual Empire: The Making of the She-Male.* Beacon, forthcoming.

17. Janice Raymond. "Transsexualism: The Ultimate Homage to Sex Role Power." *Chrysalis* 3 (1977):11–23.

18. Susan Leigh Star. "The Politics of Wholeness: Feminism and the New Spirituality." *Sinister Wisdom* 3 (1977):36–44.

19. Monique Wittig. *Les Guerilleres,* p. 89. Bard Books, Avon, N.Y., 1969.

20. Deena Metzger. "The Blue Tone." *Chrysalis* 1 (1977):95–99 (an excerpt from *The Book of Hags,* in preparation).

RESEARCHING A FUNDAMENTALIST COMMUNE[1]

James T. Richardson
Mary W. Stewart
Robert B. Simmonds

WE HAVE been involved for almost seven years with research on a large youth, communal, evangelical, fundamentalist organization that originated in the late 1960s as a part of the so-called Jesus Movement (JM).[2] This research, which has resulted in some of the first published reports on the Jesus Movement [2,3], continues even now, and has furnished considerable information to scholars involved in studies of such movements and groups.[3] During the course of the study a number of different methods have been used to gather data, including survey questionnaires, personality assessment instruments, content analysis of organization documents and publications, structured and unstructured interviews with selected members and leaders, participant observation of many different activities of group members, and considerable interpersonal contact with key informants.

One question that arises quite often when we present results of our research to professional and lay groups concerns how we have managed to maintain rapport with the group for such a long period of time, and gain the sorts of information that we have. This question often derives from simple curiosity about how research is "really done." However, the question is fair and important, especially in light of a rather general feeling that long-term research on evangelical groups is difficult to accomplish unless one converts or does covert research (neither of which was done in the present case). This general belief in the difficulty of researching evangelical groups has gained support through the reporting in the scholarly literature of the apparently problematic research experience involving another JM groups. Robbins, Anthony, and Curtis reported considerable difficulty in accomplishing their research objectives in a study of the Christian World Liberation Front (CWLF), a fairly well-known and active group in the San Francisco Bay area [24].

The fact that our own experiences differed so from that reported in the paper of Robbins, Anthony, and Curtis caused us to consider the points of difference in the two research experiences. It seemed obvious to us that the report of the Robbins team could not be generalized to even all Jesus Movement groups, and that the more general belief that long-term research on evangelical groups was especially difficult was simply not correct under certain conditions.[4] Our consideration of the issues involved has led us to certain conclusions about research tactics and ethics, and has also contributed to understanding the group and movement being studied. Thus, we have an example of the interaction of substantive and methodological questions, an interaction that has, we think, been fruitful from both points of view.

In what follows we will briefly discuss our approach to the research and characterize our research experience. Then we will specifically compare the reported experience of the researcher from the Robbins team with that of our own. A major thrust of our presentation will be a discussion of group practices and beliefs that contributed positively to our research project. This discussion will contrast with treatments which discuss features of group culture that deter research efforts.

I

The study of evangelical groups presents a difficult problem that affects both the method of investigation and the content of interpretations. The problem that concerns us here is the proselytizing behavior of members of the evangelical group that is directed toward members of the research team. Pressure to convert, which has taken both overt and covert forms, has been brought to bear on us throughout our study, although such pressure, which was also reported by Robbins, Anthony, and Curtis [24], has lessened somewhat in recent years. In many ways, the overt pressure was easiest to handle. In nearly every interview, early in the research, attempts were made to convert the interviewer. We warned interviewers about this, but even so, some were rather unprepared for the intensity of proselytization attempts. All of us were asked repeatedly what we believed and why we did not "believe in Christ." Open disdain was shown by a few members for the value of what we were doing. They simply defined our presence there as being sent to them by God for conversion. The "subject" often tried to reverse the usual respondent/interviewer relationship, making the interviewer the "subject" of an intense witnessing and conversion effort. Most interviewers were successful in handling such attempts, but problems arose as a result of this overt pressure. Some interviewers got caught up in the situation and wanted to argue with some particularly forceful respondents. We continually counseled against argument *per se,* but it was a problem, particularly for some of the more politically conscious and articulate of the interviewers, some of whom had very strong negative feelings about the apparent "dropout" type of existence being lived by members of the group. A few other interviewers had a different type of problem. They were influenced by the situation to consider converting, and staying in the group. One person in the 1972 interview team, in particular, was hard-pressed when it came time to decide whether or not to return home after interviewing was complete.

The last comment illustrates the more subtle pressures of such research situations. We, being somewhat aware of the possible problems, had chosen carefully among selected mature undergraduates for our interview teams. We talked with them about what to expect and tried to prepare them mentally for the interviewing. The fact that one considered staying with the group, and that a few others found themselves responding so strongly in a negative way only illustrates the problems caused by dropping people literally into a "new and different world."

This "new world" was one where life "outside" was viewed as worthless. The fundamentalist-oriented world view had everything defined and ordered in a way considerably different from the experience of most interviewers. The most compelling aspect of this new world was its total permeation with genuine peace and love. It was obvious to all of us that the people being studied enjoyed being where they were, and that they loved one another. *And,* they "loved" us as well, and treated us as "prodigal sons and daughters.'' We were welcomed with open arms (not with-standing some concern by a few group leaders), fed, and furnished with a place to sleep. They constantly expressed great concern that we should come to share their "peace that passeth understanding.'' One has to be hard-hearted indeed not to be moved when his or her name is mentioned in earnest prayer before meals and during Bible studies. This loving and caring atmosphere was hard to ignore, and different people responded differently to it. Lofland has also reported the use of "love" by a new religious group [15].

As a group, we made serious and systematic attempts to maintain what Berger called the "thin thread of conversation" [16], so that our view of reality would be reinforced. In the June 1972 visit, the research team of seven met every evening and during breaks during the day in a large pickup camper, which was brought to serve as a "headquarters," and which was generally off limits to members of the group being researched (except by special invitation). In these essential meetings in the camper, we talked about the experiences of the day (and also drank a little wine and smoked a little, just for good measure). If we had not had the camper along, we would have been forced to seek refuge by withdrawing, and going to a nearby town, as the smaller interview team of summer, 1971, did. As it was, we had a "retreat" at the research site which allowed us to withdraw quickly if desired, but, at the same time, we were continually around to observe activities and record information.

Our basic approach to research such as this is to be open about our objectives. This does not mean that we explain every detail of our research plans, but it does indicate a basic posture of lack of deception. This contrasts sharply with the work of some past and present researchers who have seen fit to use overtly deceptive tactics [17,18,19]. We think that generally such deception is unnecessary, impractical, and unethical. A more open approach *appears* (and may well be) more humane, more ethical, and it certainly is a demonstration that the researcher *probably* takes the beliefs of the other seriously. From a practical point of view, such an approach seems more honest, and will usually bear the "fruits of honesty" in human interaction.[5] Also, much information may be directly gained in such discussions. In our own research, we discouraged interviewers from engaging in serious discussions (because we feared what Robbins, Anthony, and Curtis had feared, namely, that such might terminate the research project), but we did *not* totally rule them out. Some interviewers and all three of the authors took part in such exchanges on occasion, especially with some group leaders. It was obvious that we did not fear being questioned and entering into serious discussions, and this openness was appreciated by those on whom we were doing research. Thus, instead of being seriously hindered by group beliefs and practices, we think we actually gained considerable information from the willingness of respondents to share their beliefs.

We are aware that this apparently more honest approach is subject to misuse, which raises potential ethical problems. Someone could be "planted," because of his or her personal beliefs, in a group more open to such a person. This is neither what we suggest nor what we did. No member of the interview teams we have used was a "believer" in the tenets of the group studied, although the background of some of us made it easier to understand the jargon of the group and its practices. We simply felt that we wanted to be as open as possible in our research, and that it was possible to do sound research of this type under such conditions. This decision was made mainly out of respect for the people being studied, and it was implemented with some qualms. We were a bit surprised at the "success" of the decision when it became translated into a strategy of research. We found out through personal experience that, at least with the group being studied, a decision to be more open was a "tactical success," although this was not the reason for deciding to operate as we did.

Because of our experience (along with other successful, more open research experiences, such as that of Liebow [20]), we are now convinced that being open with certain kinds of groups is an extremely successful research tactic. And, although we do not recommend it, if one is willing to carefully select interviewers to "match" the characteristics of the group being studied, then researchers of "deviant groups" truly do have a "secret weapon" against which many such will have little defense. Thus, certain groups, such as sectarian religious organizations that have heretofore been studied "successfully" using deceptive practices [17,18,19], may now be studied easier and "better" using "true converts" (or reasonable facsimiles). The question is whether or not to use this technique, and the reason the question is asked derives from ethical considerations, *not* tactical ones. From a tactical point of view, such an approach may be actually easier, and possibly promises more "inside information."

We have suggested several times that group beliefs and practices actually aided (rather than hindered) our research. The following section will discuss this idea more systematically.

A usually unnoticed, or at least uncredited, item, sometimes of great importance to a research project, involves the openness of the "culture" of a group (or the "personality" of a specific subject) to the research and the researcher. It is obvious that normal rules of courtesy generally aid any researcher who asks permission to interview a potential subject. Chances are usually quite good that the potential subject will treat the researcher with courtesy, unless there is some special problem (such as using non-Black interviewers with Black respondents in a time of racial confrontation). This "rule of common courtesy" plainly gives an initial advantage to any researcher willing to intrude her or himself into another's life. Further, Milgram's research on obedience to authority [21] (and Mixon's simulation replication [22]) has demonstrated that many people will obey some requests that go far beyond the realm of normal courtesy, if such requests are couched in certain terms. Also, it is just as obvious that sometimes research is allowed because it is thought to be advantageous by the one (or the group or group leaders) being researched. Research on such captive populations as members of the armed service fits this latter category, as does much research in industry (the Hawthorne studies) and in sociology of religion (or religious sociology).[6]

However, when we talk of the value of group culture and/or personal attributes to our research, we mean something more overt—but in some ways more subtle—than the kinds of things just mentioned (all of which admittedly have operated in our favor). The group studied has an authoritarian structure of organization, a factor that may be based on necessity, but which is usually justified by the group reference to ideology through the medium of quoting certain Bible verses that support such an approach to group life. Because of this definite authority-structure, we were not faced with having to justify our existence to every subject, in an attempt to convince them to grant us an interview. Instead, we had only to persuade the leaders (and only a few of them) that our project was worthy, and that it should be done. When they decided that our work was acceptable, they told the members to allow us to interview them. We had very high response rates (95–100 percent) because of this, and it is worth admitting that the response rate would probably have been virtually zero if we had not cleared the project with those in charge. This is plainly a place where some knowledge of the group ideology (gained through previous experience of one author and through the initial contacts with the group) helped a great deal. If we had not known or found out that the group was authoritarian in nature, we might have just tried to start interviewing selected subjects, a tactic that would have virtually guaranteed the failure of the project, since members would not have cooperated without the express permission of their leaders. So, in a sense, the group was easier to study than a group in which each individual could decide whether or not to be interviewed. This latter situation is, of course, analogous to just about any survey research where interviewers go from house to house, trying to interview as many members of a sample as possible. And the low response rates of some such studies evidences our point.

The actual interview situation and the situations of the administration of personality assessment instruments was also helped considerably because of group beliefs and practices. Because the subjects really believed that their past life had been "washed clean" by virtue of their conversion, they were very willing to talk about their personal histories. It seemed as if this past life could no longer harm them in any way, and they could treat it in a very objective fashion (the problem of sometimes making it sound worse than it really was notwithstanding).[7] Also, their new beliefs contained a strong emphasis on honesty in personal relations, and, especially since we were "approved" by the leaders of the group, the respondents were quite open to us, a fact that we even had to take into account in comparing some of the results of personality inventories with "normal" populations, which are assumed *not* to be so honest [7,11].

It is interesting to examine in more depth the decision of group leaders that we were to be welcomed, and to look at group beliefs in an effort to understand how and why the decision to be open to us was made. We, of course, do not have secret tape recordings of deliberations of the group leaders as they were trying to decide what to do with us. However, we do have enough knowledge of how the group functions *and* of its belief system to construct fairly well, we think, key elements of the probable scenario. And, here especially, we see the importance of group beliefs to be the success of our research.

Jesus Movement groups, including the one we are researching, generally adopted the traditional dualism of fundamentalist Christianity (Robbins, Anthony, and Curtis contrast this perspective to that of Eastern monism [14].) This system of thought is one of few categories, and can be described as simplistic in nature [24]. Things are good or bad, black or white, the "work of Satan" or the "work of the Lord." We think that this lack of differentiation served us very well, especially when taken *in conjunction with* some other important group beliefs and practices.

The group is very evangelical, and defines as a (possibly *the*) major goal, the conversion of "sinners" (which, simply defined, means those who do not accept the basic tenets of the group). Also, the ideology of the group is very "God-centered" in that they believe that their God is omniscient and omnipotent, and takes an active role in the affairs of the world, including their personal and group life. According to group beliefs, God *at least* "permits" *all* that happens. These elements of belief combine to force an interpretation of every contact with a "nonbeliever" (including us) as being an opportunity, even responsibility, sent by God to them, so that the nonbeliever might be witnessed to by members of the group.

The dualism of fundamentalist Christianity does, of course, include the concept of an "anti-God" (Satan) who also can move in human history, but we were fortunate enough not to be categorized as being a part of this evil contingent. Instead, partially because of our real and honest interest in what was taking place in the group, and because the group members were sincerely concerned about us, we got classified in just about the only other possible category in this simplistic system of thought, with its inherent lack of differentiation. We were classified as potential converts—converts who obviously were to be "won to

Christ" by members of this group. This situation was similar to that reported by Robbins, Anthony, and Curtis [24]; there were, however, important differences.[8] Members and leaders of the group were led by their own beliefs to assume that God had sent or directed us (potentially even against our own wills and without our knowledge) to this group. The least they thought was that God had *permitted* us to come there, and had thereby given us over to this group as a part of their Christian responsibility. It is possible, of course, that we could have been considered a "test" sent from God in a manner akin to the boils visited upon Job, but if some seriously entertained this thought we were unaware of it. And even if some had this thought, *that interpretation would still have probably resulted in our getting to stay with the group,* simply because we desired to do this and intended to stay until asked to leave.

In short, the beliefs of the group rendered members somewhat *passive* in the face of a concerted effort to study them. We, the active agents in all this, were apparently assumed somehow to be tied up with the will of God. Which group member or leader was going to try to thwart that? At least partially because of such ideological considerations, we were welcomed with sincere concern, even relish, and feted (to the extent that group resources allowed). Their usual practices of making potential converts welcome (at least for a time) seemed to be carried to the extreme.

It seemed that there was an implicit contest going on among group members to see who could convert one of us first. As stated, for the first few years of our research, nearly every interview was a contest of wills (and patience—on both sides). We regularly heard our names mentioned in prayers in their public gatherings, and some members made continual efforts to "win us to Christ." The importance of this issue to the group members was graphically illustrated when rumors of the impending conversion of a member of the June 1972 interview team swept the camp. There was much premature rejoicing among group members, who plainly assumed that the only "real purpose" of our being there was to "get converted."[9] Apparently what had happened was that an interviewer had expressed to a respondent an interest in finding out more about the group ideas, and he had started to read the Bible during his spare time. Just the sight of him reading the Bible seemed to be enough to set the rumor mill in motion. In some of our later visits, people still asked about the interviewer, desiring to know if he finally decided to convert. The tenacity of such ideas demonstrates their importance to the group (just as the continued interest of this interviewer in the group evidences the effect the research experience had on him).

II

As has been stated, we are continuing our research, and have been studying the group since early 1971. That is a long time for the group to labor without converting us, and this suggests that there has been some redefining, by the group members, of us and our role *vis-à-vis* the group. We agree that such has occurred, but would suggest that the new definition, while being more elaborate, still is congruent with the basic beliefs of the group. First, we believe that we are still looked at as potential converts and may even be potential converts of special "worth," since we are people of relatively high status *vis-à-vis* the group members. But the days of the "hard sell" seem to be over, and now the approach is much more subtle. We are being witnessed to "by example" instead of using forceful argumentation. Second, the worldview of the group members appears to have gotten more complex in that the basic two-category world (saved and unsaved) has become more differentiated. Perhaps our presence has even hastened the predictable differentiation process. Whatever the cause, there now seem to be several categories of nonmembers, some of whom are viewed much more positively than others. For instance, some of the group view us as people with a special relationship to the group. They apparently think our being associated with the group has some "higher purpose," which will be revealed in due course. The fact that some converts have been gained through our publication of results serves to support such a view. It is entirely possible that the group is coming to think that we have been sent to chronicle their history for the larger public. Group leaders have indicated that they realize someone will eventually write their history, but so far they think it should be done by a member. However, their generally positive (even if somewhat unexpected) reaction to the first publication from our research [2] has caused us to think that perhaps they are reevaluating their view of us and their position on who will "write their history." Thus, our relationship with the group continues, but for reasons that we think are largely "out of control." We give a great deal of credit to the "positive" (from our point of view) features of group culture that have helped us continue our research. And we hope that our attending to these little-discussed features of group culture will balance the report of Robbins, Anthony, and Curtis [24], which chose to focus on the more problematic features. We will now contrast the experience of the Robbins team's research with our own experiences in more detail, as a way to illustrate some of the points just made.

COMPARISON OF TWO RESEARCH EXPERIENCES

Before comparing the two research experiences, some comment comparing the CWLF with the group we have been researching seems in order. First, the two evangelical groups studied are both a part of the Jesus Movement and have strong ideological boundaries. The group we have been studying is actually larger and more "organized" than the CWLF, with well over one thousand full-time members located in organizational outposts in about twenty-five states, and with capital-worth in buildings, land, equipment, and vehicles, accumulated in just seven years, of nearly two million dollars. They are, we think, more "conservative" both politically and theologically than the CWLF, which has the reputation of being the most "left-oriented" of all the Jesus Movement groups. This assessment of their general orientation suggests that we should have actually expected *more* difficulty in doing research on the group we chose to study. The fact that the experience of our research team differed so from that of Anthony (and seemed less problematic) prompted our attempt to re-examine the issues [24].

The report of Robbins, Anthony, and Curtis is a serious attempt to extend Bellah's "symbolic realism" [26] to the realm of the practical, a task that revealed problems with the Bellah approach [24]. Their effort was made out of a serious concern for not treating their subjects in a typical reductionistic fashion. Their concern notwithstanding, we think there are questions about some of the conclusions drawn from the research experience, especially since our own experiences were so different.

Robbins, Anthony, and Curtis report an experience that one of them (Anthony) had while doing research. The experience is described as traumatic for both the subject and the researcher [24]. The research apparently began amicably enough, with subjects actually asking to be interviewed. However, it deteriorated into shouting matches on occasions, after it became obvious that the researcher not only would not convert, but even refused to discuss his personal religious views with the subjects (a crucial tactical decision). Subjects lost their tempers at the researcher because of frustration caused by his apparent authentic acceptance of their reality as valid, but his simultaneous refusal to accept the beliefs personally. The researchers, after undergoing increased pressures, accompanied by guilt feelings, finally returned in kind, getting angry with subjects and taking an obviously (and admitted) negative view of the group and its members. Robbins, Anthony, and Curtis indicate that they think such research as theirs is a "limiting case" in terms of the use of symbolic realism, as they interpret it [24]. They imply that the stronger a set of beliefs is held by group members, the greater the difficulty in taking such an approach. In other words, the more well-defined the group ideological boundaries, the worse the problems of applying symbolic realism (as they implement it), a summarization that may be an extension and generalization of their view. They imply that the intensity with which the beliefs that define the group boundaries are held obliterates the distinction claimed by them and other social scientists between empathy and sympathy, and "forces" the researcher into a more reductionistic stance.

Robbins, Anthony, and Curtis interpret what happened by claiming that the refusal of the researcher to become a believer ". . . imperiled their sectarian ideology and threatened the subjects' total belief structure," causing "cognitive dissonance." We would suggest that such a claim is unsubstantiated in their research.[10] While it is possible some subjects felt personally threatened by the presence of the researcher, probably what was happening was that the people were *more upset at the refusal of the researcher to deal with them in what they defined as a fair and expected manner, reciprocating the treatment that they were giving the researcher.* (The situation may well have been aggravated by the interviewer's insistence on using a quasi-Rogerian "answer-back" technique, which added "irreality" to the interviewing.) Our conclusion is based in part on the discussion of the options they saw for the researcher when difficulties arose [24].

At this point the researcher had three options, all of which have obvious drawbacks: (1) he could have lied to the subjects and conducted "disguised observation" by feigning conversion, a strategy which he viewed as unethical; (2) he could have openly asserted his adherence to his own conflicting beliefs, which could have antagonized subjects and probably have terminated the study; (3) he could, as he did, refuse to discuss his own beliefs, *which seemed contrary to the spirit of the empathic stance,* and moreover simply led to increased tension between him and the subjects [emphasis ours].

We suggest that there are other options than those listed, and further, that options one and three are not as far apart, in view of the research subjects, as the authors seem to assume (but apparently question). It also seems plain that by choosing option three, the researcher may not have been implementing Bellah's idea of symbolic realism [26], as fully as he might have. Another option, different from that of Bellah already discussed, that seems very "live" to us (especially after our own research experience), would have been for the interviewer to openly discuss his beliefs, and, in special circumstances, even to enter into serious conversation about personal beliefs. Uneasiness was expressed with their chosen "option three," for they say that it "seemed contrary to the spirit of the empathic stance." Apparently, they were led to consider a more open approach, even if they did reject such an option.

Also the report of Robbins, Anthony, and Curtis was derived from a narrow data base, since the data of their paper are based on only a single "case study" (which did, however, last two years). The one person doing the interviewing obviously had some idiosyncratic features that might have been expected to cause problems in this type of research (the fact that he was a devotee of Meher Baba for instance [24]). This is not a major point, however, since it is obvious that the experience of one researcher is important and worthy of attention, and may have been more "intense" than our own, *especially* since he apparently had no fellow researchers to furnish personal support. Nevertheless, we would point out that our own discussion of problems associated with research on Jesus Movement groups is based on seven years of contact with a group, and on the experiences of ten different people, three of whom (the authors) have seen considerable intense contact with different group members.

III

Thus, it seems that the experiences of the two research teams (ours and that of Robbins) were somewhat similar but had important differences. We think our relative success at continuing our research (which still continues) is due to at least two major factors. One is the fact that, although two of us have made trips to the research site alone, the major data gathering efforts were done by *teams of researchers*, and this collective presence furnished us with some protections and was important in helping us maintain our "cool." The nightly (sometimes hourly) discussions held by the research team members allowed many tensions to be dissipated within our team and encouraged research team members, who found out that they were not alone in their difficulties of coping with the situation. A great deal of solidarity developed *within* the research teams, as we "fought" to maintain our "cognitive minority" status under such circumstances. A second major factor was the decision already mentioned that allowed a more open discussion of our own beliefs with some group members. This decision had the unexpected effect of defusing many tensions on the part of the subject group and its members (which is not to say that some leaders were not concerned about our presence there, for some were). Also, it helped us, for we were at least defending ourselves from the attempts to convert us.[11]

There are, of course, other reasons (some of which may not be known to us) why our research has been allowed to continue. Plainly, some members of the group like the attention we have paid to them, and they like the "anonymous fame" that our publications have brought to them. We have developed some rather strong affective ties with some members over the years of our research, and this means that there is more trust shared by all of us. And the mere passage of time has had another effect, in that the group as a whole may be growing more *tolerant* of outsiders as it gains strength and self-confidence. We have also *invested hard work to maintain contact and rapport* with the group and some key members. We have had our share of good luck, as well. And, one key thing has been the totally unexpected fact that the *group has actually gained some members as a result of our research*. Our first publication of material on the group [2] resulted in well over fifty letters being sent to us by people who wanted to join the group.[12] After some discussion, we sent these queries to the group, since we were bound by our pledge of anonymity and thus could not respond ourselves with the requested information. The next time we visited the group, there were a few people there who had first heard of the group through our publication! This situation demonstrates that no matter how hard one may try to avoid influencing a group being studied, it is virtually impossible to stop all influences. The gaining of a few members through our publication seemed to demonstrate to some group leaders that somehow we were "agents of God."

NOTES

[1] This is an expansion of part of a paper presented at the 1975 annual American Sociological Association meeting, which was derived from the research appendix of a forthcoming monograph, *Organized Miracles* (1978), by the same authors.

[2] The organization we have been studying is fully described in our forthcoming book, *Organized Miracles* [1]. The group described desires to remain anonymous, thus we cannot report their name or location, as per our original agreement with them when the research started.

[3] Our research is a relatively large study which has resulted in a dozen or so papers being read at professional meetings, along with numerous talks given by the three of us to other professional and lay groups, in the United States, Western Europe, and Scandinavia. Also, about ten papers have been published [2,3,4,5,6,7,8,9,10,11]. Two dissertations have resulted as well [12,13].

[4] We, of course, are not claiming that our own research experience is necessarily any more generalizable, but we think that discussing both experiences together may result in some general conclusions of value.

[5] We say "usually" because it is plain that certain kinds of research cannot be done without deception. The questions are whether or not such research should be done, and whether or not some professional body should perhaps be charged with allowing such endeavors (in a manner similar to the recent decision of some biologists to organize a review group, and, in the meantime, to refrain from certain kinds of research).

[6] We are all aware of the problems brought about by the desire of some to be "studied," with the resulting tendency to volunteer for studies, or the so-called "Hawthorne effect" that can cause workers to continue to put together complex devices in near darkness. Such tendencies "compensate" some for the features of a group or person that make most research "easier" than might first be thought, and must be taken into account in any research.

[7] This problem of "negative bragging sessions" seems a classic illustration of the "reconstruction of biography" mentioned by Berger [23]. While we do not think many subjects made deliberate attempts to mislead us, we were aware, because of previous knowledge of the fundamentalist subculture, of the tendency to claim a "more sinful" past than was really the case. In ways that are discussed at more length in the appendix to *Organized Miracles*, there seemed to be an assumption on the part of some respondents that the best Christians were the ones who had sinned the most in their "previous existence." Because of this possibility, we tried to double-check information that seemed especially prone to this "sinful reconstruction of biography."

[8] This definition of researchers as potential converts seems an ultimate example of the benefits of the "outsider role," as discussed by Trice [25]. The problem, of course, is to maintain this privileged status for a long enough time to do the research (and resolve ethical problems inherent in the situation).

[9] We should add that this incident led to much discussion among the interview team members so that none of us would do anything to encourage such interpretations of our activities.

[10] It is notoriously difficult to establish that a state of cognitive dissonance has been aroused in a person. Aside from that general comment, however, we suggest that support for our interpretation of what was taking place in Anthony's experience is found in the report of Robbins, Anthony, and Curtis [14]. Their view, however, *may be correct;* for there is obviously a "self-validating" element in most evangelical attempts.

[11] A third possible factor involved our own personal philosophies and beliefs. Robbins and Anthony, after reading a variation of this paper, point out that Anthony's acceptance of Meher Baba placed him much further ideologically from the CWLF than we were from the group we studied, and that this difference significantly distinguishes the two research experiences. This point may be valid, but we note that several of us and our interviewers were strongly committed to left-oriented ideas and to "women's liberation," beliefs which were in sharp contrast to the individualistic and sexist beliefs of the group studied.

[12] Our first publication was in *Psychology Today* [2], which, we understand, printed 450,000 copies of that issue. Perhaps we should have expected such a reaction from some in such a large readership, but nonetheless we were a bit taken aback by what happened, and had to make a decision about what to do with the letters. Some will disagree with what we did, but we are still satisfied with the decision.

REFERENCES

1. James T. Richardson, Mary White Stewart, and Robert B. Simmonds. *Organized Miracles.* Transaction Books, forcoming.

2. Mary White Harder, James T. Richardson, and Robert B. Simmonds. "Jesus People." *Psychology Today,* 6 December 1972, pp. 45–50, 110–113.

3. James T. Richardson, Robert B. Simmonds, and Mary White Harder, "Thought Reform and the Jesus Movement." *Youth and Society* 4 (1972):185–200.

4. Mary White Harder. "Sex Roles in the Jesus Movement." *Social Compass* 21 (1974):345–353.

5. Mary White Harder, James T. Richardson, and Robert B. Simmonds. "Life Style: Sex Roles, Courtship, Marriage, and Family in a Changing Jesus Movement Organization." *International Review of Modern Sociology* 6 (1975):155–172.

6. James T. Richardson. "The Jesus Movement: An Assessment." *Listening: Journal of Religion and Culture* 9 (1974):20–42.

7. James T. Richardson and Robert Simmonds. "Personality Assessment in New Religious Groups: Problems of Interpretation." In preparation, 1977.

8. James T. Richardson, Robert B. Simmonds, and Mary White Harder. "Evolving Structures of a Jesus Movement Organization." *Journal of Voluntary Social Action Research,* in press.

9. James T. Richardson and Mary White Stewart. "Conversion Process Models and the Jesus Movement." *American Behavioral Scientist* 20 (1977):819–838.

10. Robert B. Simmonds, James T. Richardson, and Mary White Harder. "Organization and Structure of a Jesus Movement Community." *Social Compass* 21 (1974):269–281.

11. Robert B. Simmonds, James T. Richardson, and Mary White Harder. "A Jesus Movement Group: An Adjective Check List Assessment." *Journal for the Scientific Study of Religion* 15 (1976):323–337.

12. Mary White Harder. *The Children of Christ Commune: A Study of a Fundamentalist Communal Sect.* Ph.D. thesis, University of Nevada, Reno, 1972.

13. Robert B. Simmonds. *The People of the Jesus Movement: A Personality Assessment of a Fundamentalist Religious Community.* Ph.D. thesis, University of Nevada, Reno, 1977.

14. Thomas Robbins, Dick Anthony, and Thomas E. Curtis. "Youth Culture Religious Ferment and the Confusion of Moral Meaning." In preparation, 1974.

15. John Lofland. "Becoming a World-Saver Revisited." *American Behavioral Scientist* 20 (1977):805–818.

16. Peter Berger. *The Sacred Canopy.* Doubleday, 1967.

17. Leon Festinger, H. W. Reicker, and Stanley Schachter. *When Prophecy Fails.* University of Minnesota Press, 1956.

18. John Lofland. *Doomsday Cult.* Prentice Hall, 1965.

19. Hiley Ward. *The Far-Out Saints of the Jesus Communes.* Association Press, N.Y. 1972.

20. Elliot Liebow. *Tally's Corner.* Little, Brown, 1967.

21. Stanley Milgram. *Obedience to Authority.* Harper & Row, 1973.

22. Don Mixon. *Further Conditions of Obedience and Disobedience of Authority.* Ph.D. thesis, University of Nevada, Reno, 1971.

23. Peter Berger. *Invitation to Sociology.* Doubleday, 1963.

24. Thomas Robbins, Dick Anthony, and Thomas E. Curtis. "The Limits of Symbolic Realism: Problems of Empathetic Field Observation in a Sectarian Context." *Journal for the Scientific Study of Religion* 12 (1973):259–272.

25. H. M. Trice. "The 'Outsiders' ' Role in Field Study." In *Qualitative Methodology,* pp. 77–82. Edited by W. J. Filstead. Markham, Chicago, 1970.

26. Robert N. Bellah. "Christianity and Symbolic Realism." *Journal for the Scientific Study of Religion* 9 (1970):89–96.

WHAT IS NEXT IN THE STUDY OF NEW RELIGIONS?

Charles Y. Glock

THE UNEXPECTED privilege has been extended to me in this report to reveal the contents of the will of the late Gilda Poundollar. Those who knew and loved her anticipated that her eccentricities in life would be reflected in her will. But no one, I suspect, will be prepared for her decision to have all of her extensive fortune devoted to the support of research on the study of new religions. Her will calls for the establishment of a foundation to be known as the Gilda Poundollar Endowment for the Study of "New" Religions, to oversee the distribution of the largesse. One will recall, I am sure, Miss Poundollar's profound commitment to the belief that "Nothing is new in life; it has always been experienced in different guises before." Consequently it will not surprise anyone to learn that the word new in the Endowment's title is in quotes.

Until reading her will, I had not known about Miss Poundollar's passionate interest in the phenomena of new religions. It was a passion which she pursued in virtual secrecy. Her companion, Alice Lostak, knew about it because of the many times she had gone to bookstores and to libraries on Miss Poundollar's behalf. But, otherwise, Miss Poundollar never talked about her interest to any in her circle of friends, among whom were very many who are actively engaged in the study of new religions.

Her diary reveals the reasons for her reticence. Judging from her diary, she was both an avid and well-informed student of new religions. Yet, her assessment of the state of our field was, to put it kindly, considerably less than euphoric. In life, for reasons which she has taken with her to her grave, Miss Poundollar was unable to confront her friends with her reservations about their work. In death, her reticence was overcome, for her diary, which her will authorizes now be made public, affords ample documentation of her disquietude.

Space limitations do not allow me to present all of the relevant portions of the diary, but a few quotations will afford a sense of the reasons for her disaffection. I should note, before beginning, that no one need anticipate being embarrassed by Miss Poundollar's revelations. Always the soul of discretion, she was consistent in her diary always to use pseudonyms when referring to people who were the subject of her sometimes biting tongue. In an entry dated August 17, 1976, she writes:

What troubles me most about present-day studies of new religion is that there is no confrontation by different investigators of the profound differences in epistemological assumptions which inform their work. It isn't that I expect everyone to agree on epistemology. But wouldn't it help if, for example, those who are accused of being reductionists and their accusers talkea with rather than constantly past each other? Spencer and Pearson, judging from their new book, collaborated with each other for three years. I see no evidence that they ever really sat down and seriously tried to sort out their different assumptions about how the world works.

Here is an entry dated October 7, 1976:

I was pleased to have a copy of Harbison's new book on the new religious movements spawned by the sixties. He writes well and I read it with interest, but the man has no sense of history. It is as if the world began when he was born in 1948. He isn't either an exception. Many contemporary students of new religions assume that what we are witnessing today is happening for the very first time. Even a comparison of the religious movements of the thirties with those of the sixties would be refreshing.

This entry is from December 8, 1976. She writes:

Johnson's must be the seventy-sixth article I've read on glossolalia. I still don't understand it. The phenomenon appears to escape rational description, much less explanation. Is glossolalia destined always to remain a mystery? If a phenomenon so fundamental to religion cannot be explained, I despair really for scientific inquiry into religion.

Another entry reads:

It was exciting today to read about the new discoveries in DNA research. Why is it the natural sciences seem to have a monopoly on discovery?

Among more recent comments, here is one from February 9, 1977:

I recall someone, I forget who it was, saying in the mid-sixties that the problem with the scientific study of religion is that it equated religion with institutionalized religion and never attended to anything but. Today the opposite might be said. Everything but institutionalized religion is being studied. Why the schizophrenia? Isn't it about time that attention was paid again to studying religion in all of its great variety? I, for one, would be especially interested in a satisfactory account of what appears to me a tremendous resurgence in evangelical religion.

And, the entry for April 7, 1977, the day before she died, reads:

I see that Holmes and Watson have come up with another theory of what leads youth into new religion. How many theories are we going to have before anyone goes about trying to test them?

I could continue, but I am sure students of new religions are more interested in learning about the will's provisions for the foundation, than in being further subjected to Miss Poundollar's disenchantment with endeavors thus far. One may perhaps be wondering, given her disaffection, why she chose to give her money to this cause. As will shortly be seen, Miss Poundollar was a reformer at heart. While she did not like especially what work has been done, she saw some good in the efforts and conceived that, tempted by the resources of the foundation, students might be persuaded to mend their deviant ways.

Miss Poundollar's aspirations for the foundation, and for students, are set forth early in the will. I quote the relevant paragraphs:

At the root of my concern about the state of research on the new religions is their failure to achieve anything which is widely acknowledged as a discovery. It may be that genuine advances to new knowledge are being made, but if they are, they are not acknowledged. I attribute this to the failure of students of the new religions to be agreed upon the questions which the field ought to try to answer. I also suspect that if they could agree on the questions, they would be in disagreement about what constitutes satisfactory answers.

She goes on to say,

I harbor no illusions that the study of new religions can be transformed wholly into a science. This is really not my aspiration for it, since I do not believe that a scientific perspective is the only one from which religious phenomena can be understood. I do aspire, however, for the field to experience, as the natural sciences now often do, the thrill of discovery, the acknowledgement that progress has been made, and the recognition that there are new worlds to conquer. I wish for the study of new religions that the knowledge gained be cumulative and that in this respect, the present be clearly distinguished from the past. I should like, in effect, that the study of new religions be clearly and unreservedly beyond the classics that spawned them rather than, as now seems so much to be the case, still in the midst of them.

To these ends, the will sets forth the following provisions for the operation of the new Endowment:

I should like for the endowment to assume as its first task a stocktaking of where we stand in the study of new religions. This impresses me as a needed first step to setting forth an agenda for future study in the field which, as my prefatory observations make clear, I feel ought to be decided more collectively than in the past. I don't propose to dictate how the foundation is to set about this stocktaking task. It is my hope, however, that among the questions it seeks to provide answers to would be the following:

—At a macro level, what do we know, with any authority, about the social conditions which have given rise to new religious movements throughout history? Are there generalizations which can be made across the board, or are the conditions specific to particular times and places?

—What can be said about the impact which new religions have had on social change? Have they generally fostered social change and if so how and under what conditions? Or, have new religious movements been more often derailers of social change and, if this has been their major influence, what are the underlying processes? Or, further still, have new religions had no influence on social change at all, but merely been epiphenomena making no significant impact on the course of history? What do we know in these regards?

—What also do we know with any authority about the etiology of new religious movements—about what determines whether they flower briefly, only to die, or flourish over an extended period of time in their original form, or are transformed over time into quite different movements from where they started?

—What do we know, really, about the nature of such phenomena as mystical experiences, speaking in tongues, faith healing, and other phenomena which historically and contemporarily have been associated with the rise of religious movements?

—What do we know, at the social-psychological level, about the sources of recruitment to new religions, about the processes of conversion to religious perspectives, deviant or otherwise, and about the more long-term transformations which such conversions make in people's lives?

Such stocktaking, if it is pursued effectively, ought to help in setting priorities on where the foundation invests it resources in the future.

In addition to taking stock, the will goes on to say,

I should like the Endowment to explore ways to bring together scholars with different assumptions about what religion is phenomenologically and about what they would accept as evidence for explanations of religious phenomena. I don't know what form such confrontation should take. Perhaps the Endowment could arrange to lock divergent scholars in a hotel suite until they are ready to emerge with something they can agree upon. Whatever the means adopted, however, I prescribe, as a primary task of the Endowment, raising to the level of manifest discourse the divergent viewpoints which now characterize the study of religion.

As to research, I want the Endowment to be generous in its support of research, but to exercise its generosity in ways which especially will do the following things:

—encourage scholars whose theoretical and methodological orientations diverge, to work together on common problems;

—encourage research of a longitudinal nature which will allow for theories about new religions and social change to be tested more effectively;

—discourage parochialism in research, especially the penchant of American students of religion to confine their inquiries to the American scene;

—encourage the interplay of quantitative and qualitative research on new religions.

I should also like the Endowment to establish a fund for "firehouse" research, a fund which will make resources quickly available to scholars so that they may study events of importance to our understanding of "new" religions as the events are unfolding.

I should like the Endowment, finally, to indulge me by supporting a project which promises, once and for all, to illuminate the processes through which individuals are converted from one perspective—religious or otherwise—to another.

I wish that I could conclude by wishing all students well in completing the research proposals that have begun to formulate in their minds, and to encourage their prompt submission to the Endowment. Alas, there has appeared a cat in the ointment. Mister Yen, Miss Poundollar's beloved feline, has brought suit to overturn the will, charging that he had been promised the proceeds of Miss Poundollar's fortune for the rest of his—nine—lives.

INTEGRATIVE AND
TRANSFORMATIVE RELIGIONS
Barbara Hargrove

SETTING A topic of "Problems in the Study of New
Religions" is a little like opening Pandora's box, for
the problems are many and seem to multiply as we work on
them. Since this is the case, I propose to begin at the beginning,
with two tasks which usually come first in the study of any
phenomenon: those of defining the object of study, and of particular subsets or types within it.

So I propose to address three questions: (1) What do we mean
by "new"? (2) What do we mean by "religion"? And finally, (3)
Is it appropriate to deal with the "new religions" as a single
phenomenon, or are there some subcategories which must be
recognized if we are to deal with them in a meaningful way?

I was brought up short on the subject of the first of these
questions last fall, during a series of meetings we had on the
"new cults," when a couple of representatives of the Hare
Krishna group took strong issue to being included in that category. Not only did they object to the perceived negative bias of
the term "cult," but they also said, "You can't call us 'new'
Our roots go back many centuries in the religious tradition of
India."

Moreover, historians tell us that this spate of religious fervor
is nothing new to our society. There have been several "awakenings," including other periods which have featured a turn to the
East, or to cultures other than our own. Certainly there are
parallels somewhere in the past, somewhere in the world, for
each of the groups we study as "new religions."

Nonetheless, there are at least two ways, and probably three,
in which the term "new" can be applied to the present religious
scene, which are meaningful to us as we study it. The first of
these is the common use of the word "new" to mean unusual or

257

exotic. Thus, while Hare Krishna may not be new in India, it is new in America. There is in the movement of "new religions" a good deal of cultural borrowing. Not only is that true, but there is also a strong eclectic element in the present movements, which brings borrowings from a wide variety of traditions into a common system. Also, such borrowings from other cultures are generally adapted to some extent to our own, and in that process become new. Adherents of the Krishna movement here are not really engaged in the same religious worldview or place in the culture as those in India. So even though these are old themes which are taken up, the product is in some measure new.

The second applicable use of the term "new" is to refer to the unexpected, to a change in direction or emphasis, to some kind of reversal of trends. Here we probably have the sense of newness which has most intrigued us as students of religion. The entire phenomenon has been an unexpected reversal of the process of secularization which many scholars still consider to be the overwhelming pattern of our culture, at least in its public manifestations. We really were not prepared for the open, explicit religiosity of the 1970s. Thus, it is a new thing, a problem whose sources and consequences are worth studying.

Yet many of the new movements are also problematic for those who have never accepted the trend toward secularization. They may contain familiar elements—after all, it is difficult to imagine any religion which would be an entirely new creation in human society—but the combination of elements, their type of organization, their total "package," as it were, may indeed be something new, and yet be addressed to the kinds of issues which have been traditionally considered religious. An example here could come from the frequently voiced question, "Is there really anything new in the so-called 'neo-evangelicals' or 'neo-pentecostals'? Or are they just the 'old time religion' warmed over?"

In sum, it would seem appropriate to apply the term "new" to any religions whose ties to the society's recognized organized religion are problematic, in that they (1) are based on religious forms of another culture, (2) present a radical shift or reversal of cultural trends, or (3) offer a unique combination of elements which in themselves may be familiar.

In any case, if religions are considered to be new, then their very classification as religions may raise problems. Ordinary definitions, based on "normative" religion, are not likely to apply in all cases. Luckmann, of course, and others in his wake, have given broader definitions of "religion" than those which have come from the traditional church—perhaps too broad to distinguish between religious and non-religious groups [1,2,3].

It is appropriate, however, to start there, defining "religion" as that which provides the overall blueprint by which persons organize their lives, which gives meaning to one's actions and a sense of identity to the person. Such a blueprint, though, is only maintained in conversation with other people who share it, so it would seem appropriate to require as part of a definition of "religion" some verbalization of the meaning-system, something that stands as its basic myth, and some form of social contact of sufficient regularity to allow that conversation to go on. Usually, to obtain the kind of consensus or consciousness which will make real their definition of "reality," some kind of ritual will be involved, although definitions of "ritual" may need to be loose to encompass the variety of new forms. Thus, for something to be classified as a religion, it should show evidence of some group activity which could be defined as "ritual," and some verbalization of a model or story that could be termed "myth," addressed to general questions of ultimate concern in such a way as to help persons involved find meaning and identity.

One of the problems of such a definition is that it may cast too wide a net. On an individual level, it would seem appropriate to add a measure of saliency or intensity; that is, we would call "religion" only those phenomena which not only meet the description just given, but also have a position of primacy, to say this is *the basic* way in which one organizes the world, *the* community of people which encompasses one's social reality. But sociologically this is impossible. There are clearly members of organized churches whose participation is not on that level, yet organized religion remains something which must be studied if one would understand a society's religious life. So when we run into the question, "Is *est* a religion?" we must deal with the fact that for some of its members it probably is, and if the proportion is at all high, then *est* should be studied as a religious movement. It might, in fact, if we were to act on Charles Glock's (or "Miss Poundollar's") suggestions, be worth our while to try to operationalize some level of saliency and some proportion of the membership, which scholars could agree to recognize as levels at which we would begin to treat a movement or group as religious.

But describing a movement as both "new and "religious" is only to enter into controversy, for what people are saying about these new religions indicates that they could in no way represent a single phenomenon which has arisen out of a single set of needs. On the one hand, we hear that the new religions are too individualistic, too narcissistic, too casual; that they cater to personal emotional experience and have no social conscience. On the other hand, people are alarmed over new religious groups which demand such intense devotion that they cut members off from their families and former friends, make them lose their individuality in some kind of "group-think," are too political, too involved in economic endeavors. Surely all those judgments, if they are based on fact at all, cannot be applied to the same group, nor to the same form of religiosity.

I propose a form of classification for these groups that would address at least some of these problems, on the basis of two polar or ideal types. Primarily the approach is functional, though it is clear that certain structural characteristics flow out of it. It is based on certain social-psychological concepts which have been developed from the foundation provided by Adorno, Frenkel-Brunswik, Levinson, and Sanford in their *Authoritarian Personality* [4] and those who have developed their concepts further, most recently the work of David Loye.

An insight from Loye that seemed particularly helpful in this context had to do with his distinction between two concepts that we often regard as the same, and which we generally give as conditions leading to susceptibility to new religious movements: the concepts of *alienation* and *anomie*. Loye uses these terms in conjunction with a categorization of personality types into "liberal" and "conservative." He goes back to the original usages by which they entered sociological and psychological theory, the definition given by Marx of "alienation," and by Durkheim of "anomie." Thus Loye says of "alienation":

The term was originally used by a definitely leftist social philosopher, Karl Marx, to convey the unhappiness of many with the dominant social systems of his time, to lay the base for protest against these systems, and to serve as a rallying concept for the revolutionary attempt to change these systems—by violence if necessary. Most vitally, in terms of our interest in developing a theoretical framework of wide-ranging usefulness, it was a concept used to express *unhappiness with present norm constraints* and a desire for *violating them to create norms expressive of a better future* [5].

This concept of alienation he contrasts with anomie:

"Anomie," then, was used by Durkheim in his classical analysis of suicide to describe the socially-induced dismay of the conservative side to our nature with any situation that shatters the norms. It was a concept to express the emotional state of feeling adrift in a situation of social ambiguity so characteristic, not only of Durkheim's time, but of the worldwide mood of the 1970s following the protests and aspirations of the 1960s [6].

He goes on, then, to transfer these broad social definitions into concepts of personality types. The liberal personality, he says, is one which finds expression in growth, reaching out, new experience. When such an impulse meets frustration in confining institutional structures which are not elastic enough to allow growth and change, the result is alienation from the structures, an anti-institutionalism that seeks to demolish given forms in the name of freedom. By contrast, the conservative personality is one which finds its expression in supporting given structures, perfecting the ability to play by the rules, learning to understand and use the system in which one is placed. Anomie—normlessness—as Durkheim first described it, is a state of the society in which one can find no pattern, where the rules of the game are unclear, where there seems no firm basis for identity or action; and this is what the conservative personality may perceive in a changing society. Thus, alienation may be seen as the malady of the liberal personality, and anomie as the bane of the conservative.

Ideally, the impulses that we have defined as "liberal" and "conservative" harmoniously co-exist in the individual, who then has both a solid base from which to gain identity and an appreciation of the support that systems can offer, and a willingness to reach out from that base, to grow and change and innovate. Ideally, the institutions of a society, including its religious institution, function to provide a place and an outlet for both functions. Thus, the common story which constitutes myth, and the repetitive actions which constitute ritual, as well as the ethical forms which they support, offer a framework in which the conservative aspects of the human psyche may be nurtured and developed. At the same time, the myth, ritual, and ethics all refer to ideals which are never fully realized at a given time, so that they also nourish the liberal impulse to grow toward that perfection, to create and innovate in the name of an idealized future. When a reasonable balance is maintained between these functions of social institutions, it is unlikely that alienation or anomie will reach levels high enough to call into being many new social movements. Major changes in society, however, tend to upset that balance, and the more rapid the change, the more deep-rooted are the forms of alienation and anomie.

When the imbalance can be recognized to come from sources in the economic or political institutions, and it appears likely that political or economic changes can be affected by direct action, intra-institutional movements tend to arise to correct the imbalance. If, however, recourse through these institutions appears impossible, or the imbalance is perceived to be in the less public areas of family or education, movements may arise from within existing religious structures, which will allow compensation for, or redefinitions of the problem. When the imbalance extends to the religious institution, new religions become the logical outcome—new religions of a type which would bring back the balance by emphasizing whichever of the two functions had been neglected within the normative religion of the society.

An immediate response is to say that the current prevalence of new religions is a clear indication of an imbalance within institutional religion. Thus the task should be to see which function the new groups offer, whether they address themselves to the growth needs and anti-institutionalism of the alienated, or to the identity needs and desire for community of the anomic. If the criticisms cited earlier are accurate, however, it would seem that both types are present in the current scene, thus indicating less an imbalance than a loss of function by institutional religion that is all-encompassing, making it impossible to obtain religious redress for any of the ills mentioned above. I would posit the trends toward secularization and the relegation of religion to the private sphere of life as causes of this failure.

But the primary focus of this discussion is not on the sources of new movements so much as on their nature. Consequently, I would now like to offer a typology, to be tested empirically as we study the new religions. If validated, such a typology might offer significant assistance not only in the study of these groups, but also in gaining insights on the state of the institutional church. It might also offer a basis for analyzing functions of religion in relation to age, social class, and similar variables.

The connotations of such terms as "liberal" and "conservative" tend to get in the way of their use in objective research. I would offer to substitute a typology of religious groups on the basis of placement along a continuum ranging from a pole on one end known as the "integrative" mode, and on the other, the "transformative."[1] Integrative religion would be expected to offer a quite specific form of organization, with boundary maintenance strong enough so that there is no doubt as to who is a member and who is not. Its myths and its rituals would be specific, and be tied to a behavioral code which would make it clear what kind of action was expected of members. Thus, the integrative religious group would be a clearly identifiable community. It is hard to imagine the development and maintenance of such specific codes without a fairly strong organizational focus. One would expect, then, a tendency toward hierarchical organization or strong charismatic leadership—quite possibly both.

Transformative religion, by contrast, would tend to an openness in its ritual and its myth-making, allowing for personal idiosyncracies and interpretations. It would resist set patterns, whether in ritual or in ethics, and would tend toward celebrating individual awareness and growth. "Community" would be defined in terms of interpersonal relations rather than group boundaries. Organizational forms would be fluid, and boundary maintenance so low as to make it difficult to know who is a member and who is not.

Both types would shade off into movements commonly defined as "secular." Insofar as they were expressions of core values around which people organize their lives, I would treat them as "religions," for reasons stated earlier. The secular edge of the integrative groups would probably be a close-knit political cadre; the secular edge of the transformative type would be the open, "consciousness-raising" or "growth" group.

Thus, one might hypothesize that most of the movements which emphasize experience, whether charismatic, meditational, or growth groups, could be classified as transformative, and could be expected to have in their membership a predominant proportion of persons who have opted for alternative religious expression out of a sense of alienation as defined here. By contrast, those groups characterized by firm boundaries, specific dress or behavior codes, and clear organization, whether "Moonies," or Hare Krishna devotees, or Children of God, could be expected to attract a majority of persons who perceive the society as anomic.

Loye, in *The Leadership Passion*, says that leaders of new movements need not only to display liberal or conservative personality types, but also to be active in their style and tend toward extreme rather than moderate commitment to that type. Finally, before a movement can form around them, they need to be able to articulate an ideology which expresses their stance. Ideal types, of course, are by definition extreme, being opposite ultimate ends of a continuum. One may assume, then, that the more nearly any group approaches the ideal-typical designation, the more extreme and intense will be its ideology, and the greater the separation—whether alienated or anomic—from the style and the assumptions of the middle range, in which could be placed most "standard brand" institutional religion.

The relationship to institutional religion of groups extreme enough to be classified as new religions would seem to have some parallels with Troeltsch's three types of church, sect, and mysticism, with the integrative type more sectarian and the transformative more mystical than the more churchly established religions. The experience with sectarian religion in American society has been that, over time, it tends to become more institutional and church-like. Troeltsch is less sanguine about the chances of the mystical type, which he sees as too individualistic to be institutionalized, at least when it exists as a separate form. He says:

Hence at this point there arises the idea of fellowship peculiar to this kind of "spiritual religion": The idea of the Invisible Church, of the purely spiritual fellowship known to God alone, about which man does not need to concern himself at all, but which invisibly rules all believers, without external signs or other human means. The conception of a purely spiritual fellowship, which is carried forward independently by the power of the Spirit, is the background of this sentiment, and in this the individual is there relieved of all obligation to organize and evangelize, and from all connection with ecclesiastical and sectarian organization [8].

This type of religiosity seems more socially viable in Eastern cultures: we find there considerably more institutionalization of such spirituality than appears to be present in many of the transformative movements which could be classified as new religions in America today. Historically, in all cultures, it appears that some balance between these two impulses must be affected, at least on a societal level, for them to have lasting and positive influence.

As extremes, integrative and transformative religion offer different dangers to the society, but dangers nonetheless. The integrative style, were it to become the dominant religious form of the society, presents the danger of authoritarian political structures maintained by religious ideology. It would support the kinds of black-white distinction which lead to intergroup hostility, repression, and war—thus increasing the likelihood of alienation.

The transformative style, were it to become dominant, would offer little basis for social cohesion or any sense of social identity. The transformation toward which it reaches would have to be an internal, private kind, if all structure were eschewed in the name of freedom; and that personal transformation would be difficult, if not impossible, for those who were struggling to meet basic needs of survival or security. Hence anomie could be expected to proliferate.

Thus, for either type to move toward continuing status as a social institution in a reasonably stable society, it would need to incorporate some of the attributes of its polar opposite, so that a balance between integration and transformation could provide a sense of identity and support for growth and expansion. Those groups already less clearly identifiable as one type or the other would seem prime candidates either for institutionalization as a new option within America's pluralist religious system, or for co-optation by some current religious organization, while those nearest the poles might be expected to be less lasting—unless indeed the apocalyptic statements of some of them prove true, and society as we know it is doomed.

In the long run, the significance of these movements lies in the effect they have on the institutional structure. It may not matter greatly whether they become institutionalized as entities, as successful social movements, if some of their ideas and styles are adopted by existing groups even while they fail as movements. If it is true that the simultaneous rise of both integrative and transformative movements represents a loss by the institutional church of power to deal with either alienation or anomie, it would seem clear that neither type of new religion could itself adequately fulfill the religious function of the society. Yet the two extremes seem unlikely to come to terms with one another to present some one new religion which could supplant the church. It seems more likely that institutional religion might absorb the influence of the transformative movements to reverse its definition of itself in such secular terms as are now often used, and of the integrative movements to give it structure and a sense of mission which would counteract its privatizing tendencies.

The rise of the movements seems a clear indication that both trends—secularization and privatization—have gone past the point of functionality. Tracing the development of each type of movement may assist in understanding both the state of the society and that of its religious institution.

NOTE

[1] This use of these terms is somewhat different from that made by Robbins and Anthony [7]. Here the focus is internal: integration or transformation either of the individual personality or of the social-cultural system. In contrast, Robbins and Anthony regarded the integrative mode as one which fits individuals into the system.

REFERENCES

1. Thomas Luckmann. *The Invisible Religion.* MacMillan, 1967.

2. Peter Berger. *The Sacred Canopy.* Doubleday, 1967.

3. Richard Fenn. "Towards a New Sociology of Religion." *Journal for the Scientific Study of Religion* 11 (1972):16–32.

4. T. W. Adorno, E. Frenkel-Brunswik, D. J. Levinson, and R. N. Sanford. *The Authoritarian Personality.* Harper & Row, 1950.

5. David Loye. *The Leadership Passion,* p. 109. Jossey-Bass, San Francisco, 1977. (Italics his.)

6. Ibid., p. 110.

7. Thomas Robbins and Dick Anthony. "Integration, Transformation, or Disintegration: The Social Impact of New Religious Movements." In preparation, 1976.

8. Ernst Troeltsch. *The Social Teachings of the Christian Churches,* II, 745. Translated by Olive Wyon. George Allen and Unwin, London, 1949.

EMERGENT RELIGION IN AMERICA: AN HISTORICAL PERSPECTIVE

Robert S. Ellwood, Jr.

CONCEPTUAL METAPHORS AND PARADIGMS

What basic conceptual paradigms and metaphors do we use in attempting to understand the "new religious movements" of contemporary America? Current methodological discussion in the sciences and social sciences has made this query unavoidable. Since Thomas Kuhn's much-cited classic, *The Structure of Scientific Revolutions* (1962), we have been highly aware that each generation of researchers is likely to have its conscious or unconscious image of what sorts of "reality" are and are not perceivable, or even possible. Karl Popper's discussion of "root metaphors," and Peter Berger and Thomas Luckmann's account of the "social construction of reality," have from the points of view of philosophy and social science presented much the same insight, the insight of the "sociology of knowledge." It is that we, scientists and social scientists as well as everyone else, view the world and its phenomena through the framework of models and metaphoric images and paradigmatic symbol-systems which indicate, fundamentally, what aspects of it are isolated out as significant, even as "real" in the sense of being the parts of the phenomena which give valid clues to the meaning, rather than whose apparent meaning is an illusion to be interpreted by the "real." For every such system both clarifies and obscures; each enables making the distinctions which are necessary to any knowledge at all, and each makes "invisible" that which lacks consonance with its own structure.

In reflecting on metaphors and paradigms used in interpreting "new religious movements," I would like to focus on the matter of synchronic as over against diachronic models. The first emphasizes the short histories of most of the movements in their immediate institutional form, and gives overwhelming hermeneutic importance to their contemporary social context. A diachronic model would be much more historical, emphasizing "behind the scenes" continuities in the "new religions" with similar phenomena in the American past. It might see them as much as the current inhabitants of a pre-existent niche in the American spiritual ecology, as radically new responses to unprecedented situations.

LINKAGES IN SPIRITUAL MOVEMENTS

Consider, for example, American Zen. Many commentators view it as essentially a postwar movement, forever associated with San Francisco "beats" of the 1950s, like Jack Kerouac, Gary Snyder, and Allen Ginsberg, whose "San Francisco Poetry Renaissance" was the bright dawn of the explosive spiritual sunrise of the sixties. The movement toward Zen as a symbol for expressing the alienation these people felt from the Eisenhower era's apotheosis of suburbia was wrought by the influence of the postwar books and American lectures of D. T. Suzuki, and those of Alan Watts, who mostly learned Zen from him. Subsequently, as a result of the zeal for Zen sparked by Suzuki, Watts, and the "Dharma Bums," a number of Zen centers devoted to the formal practice of the Asian faith appeared.

The First Zen Institute of America in New York, associated with the pioneer American Zen *roshi* Shigemitzu Sasaki, and his widow (and Alan Watts's first mother-in-law) Ruth Fuller Sasaki, was founded in 1930. There were a few other Western Zen works before the war; indeed, the first presentation of Zen to America was made by the redoubtable monk Soyen Shaku at the watershed World's Parliament of Religions in Chicago in 1893, and D. T. Suzuki lived and wrote near Chicago for twelve years around the turn of the century.

This is the sort of background which, with a little historical digging, one can find for anything, however, and one could argue it would be only a curiosity were it not for the escalating enthusiasm which made Zen in the fifties and after a significant cultural force. Of much more real importance, it seems to me, is a different sort of historical background: links suggesting continuity between the Zen of the fifties and a broader Anglo-American tradition of alternative religion. I have recently been interested in tracing lines of connection from American Zen to Theosophy, from Theosophy to Spiritualism, and from Spiritualism to Swedenborgianism.[1]

Alan Watts was first introduced to Zen Buddhism, and to D. T. Suzuki, in England in the thirties by the prominent Theosophist and scholar Christmas Humphreys [2]. Suzuki himself, who as Gary Snyder once stated, has undoubtedly influenced world culture more than any other single modern Japanese, was married to an American, Beatrice Lane Suzuki, who was a Buddhist scholar in her own right and a Theosophist.[2] To trace the lineage back further, it is curious to note that there is a 1914 translation of Swedenborg's *New Jerusalem* into Japanese by D. T. Suzuki. That American Spiritualism was, as one can see in the works of its founders such as Andrew Jackson Davis, a quite direct cultic application of the teachings about spirit worlds of the great Swedish sage, Emmanuel Swedenborg, is well known. So is the fact that Theosophy emerged in the 1870s from out of the Spiritualistic milieu; Madame Blavatsky was first drawn to America because it was the homeland of the Spiritualism in which she was deeply interested, and she and her associate Colonel Olcott first met at a scene of spirit manifestation in Chittenden, Vermont. Returning to the Zen of the fifties, one can look for other kinds of lineages with the American past by noting, for example, that Jack Kerouac first seriously plunged into Buddhist study shortly after re-reading Henry David Thoreau's *Walden,* and the immediate occasion was an ongoing debate with his friend Neal Cassady about the teachings of the American psychic Edgar Cayce (who died in 1945), which led Kerouac to search into Buddhist teachings about reincarnation. (Cayce's teachings on such matters were probably heavily influenced by Theosophical literature [1].)

SYNCHRONIC PERSPECTIVES

What is the significance of links like these from the Zen of the 1950s to the Theosophy of the last decades of the nineteenth century and after, when the latter had a social role and literary influence not entirely incomparable to the American Zen of our day—as did Spiritualism in the 1850s and Swedenborgianism even earlier? Are they merely incidental, or are they vital clues to understanding what really underlies each of these spiritual phenomena? Do we, in other words, regard Spiritualism, Theosophy, and Zen each as distinct movements best understood only in their own synchronic cultural context, to which the links of the previous movement are regarded only as "background" or "preparation"; or do we regard each chiefly as an episode in a diachronic tradition of alternative spirituality in America, in which such symbols as trance, the East, charisma, wandering, and the like have always been staples, if each time in different packaging?

Questions like these are commonly resolved before they are really even perceived on the basis of what is showcased and what is left outside the frame by one's operative paradigms and conceptual metaphors. In most twentieth-century study of new religious movements, the paradigmatic weight has beyond a doubt fallen on the side of the synchronic approach, which stresses the distinctness, the separate founding, development, and context, of each movement in its own generation. Nowhere has this been more the case, one might add, than in contemporary studies of the postwar generation of movements. Many have shown great contextual hermeneutic and sociological sophistication, but lack even a rudimentary historical sense.

This bias can be traced to two main sources. In sociology, it is certainly to the tradition inaugurated by the work of Ernst Troeltsch and Max Weber, with its church-sect distinction and the Weberian concept of the charismatic prophet. The paradoxical relation of the sect to mysticism in the Troeltschean picture, which suggests a broad diachronic reservoir out of which sectarianism draws to create its "holy communities" and its anomic, individualistic, parallelism-of-spontaneities mystical groups, offers some food for thought from the other perspective. But classical Troeltschean sociology has emphasized the polar opposition of mighty established church to sect and cult; until in Milton Yinger's schematic work, for example, we find the "cult," the equivalent to the sort of group we are discussing, is characterized as being of small size and short life, centered around a charismatic leader, having beliefs at great variance with those of the community, basically concerned with mystical experience and personal problems [4].

The paradigm is only reinforced by the monumental work of Max Weber, in which the prototypical founder of a new religious movement is the charismatic prophet. He is an *individual* who makes a break with established social patterns and through his charismatic authority legitimates a new pattern, and so makes religion a force for social change; the charisma, and the change, are then "rationalized" by his disciples into a new institution. With this powerful paradigmatic model in mind, small wonder that a generation or two of students tended to emphasize the originality of each founder and to see each movement as without proper father or mother, but as either spontaneously generated or begotten by a social crisis imposed from outside [5].

In anthropology, the great work of Franz Boas, with its field-work orientation and "historical particularism," led to a similar bias against diachronic perceptions. Rightly reacting against certain very premature nineteenth-century schemes of cultural evolution, and influenced by the Neo-Kantianism of Wilhelm Dilthey and the scientific positivism of Ernst Mach, Boas desired above all that anthropology be empirical and specific to the culture about which one is qualified to speak on the basis of empirical research. Each culture should be seen as an entity in itself, he felt. Grand generalizations unsupported all the way through by hard evidence, or based on abstract or metaphysical conceits, Boas much eschewed. While, of course, "deep background" historical research can be empirical, it tends to fall outside the range of primary concerns of one whose training and commitment is toward field-work, and whose orientation is toward seeing each religious experience as its own "historically particular" world of experience in interaction with its particular context [6].

For all that, social scientists will not be without theories, not least in regard to religious movements. But these theories have most been the sort which are comfortable in the Troeltsch-Weber-Boas frame, viewing new religions as activities which rise and fall within a quite particularized time and place, which contrast with more stable religious institutions, and which are contextually engendered in response to a particular crisis or stimulus. Let us look at some of these theories. Most are derived from cross-cultural data, but they will be of no less interest in understanding contemporary American movements for that; we will see how they would fit the case of American Zen.

CONTACT SYNCHRONIC THEORIES

We may begin with two "contact" theories. Alexander F. Chamberlain, as far back as 1913, wrote of "new religions" which spring up as the result of contact with "higher" races and the use of incompletely assimilated ideas brought by their envoys, missionaries, and colonials [7]. (Whether or not Americans would be willing to speak of Orientals as a "higher" folk, it is certainly true that Zen and other specific movements owe much to East-to-West missionary work and imagination, and that indigenous American movements have appeared using imported ideas and practices in new ways.)

In 1943, Ralph Linton wrote of "nativist movements." In contrast to the attempted assimilation of Chamberlain's "new religions," these are "any conscious, organized attempt on the part of a society's members to revive or perpetuate selected aspects of its culture" [8]. The perpetuation of "selected aspects" of a culture, presumably in a process of rapid transition owing to outside contact, means that those elements are given a highly symbolic value, like the rites of the Amerindian Ghost Dance. The more distinctive they are from other cultures, the better. Linton speaks of "magical nativism," centered on the prophet, millennialism, and messianism, in which—as in the Ghost Dance—the native revival is essentially expected to be a magical formula that will reverse the present situation; and of "rational nativism," which makes the selection of elements to perpetuate "realistically" though out of frustration.

It is not difficult to perceive strands of "nativism" in Linton's sense in American religion, particularly those conservative Judeo-Christian movements which counter the pluralism of the "global village." We might note, too, however, that ostensibly exotic or novel religions can also contain nativist strands, perhaps of a nature difficult for conservatism to carry. American

Zen, particularly the "beat" variety, is as much a perpetuation under a new label of the very American transcendentalist outlook and the Thoreau-Whitman lifestyle, as it is East Asian Zen transplanted; in the novels of Jack Kerouac and Robert Pirsig this is very evident.

DISEQUILIBRIUM SYNCHRONIC THEORIES

We shall now turn to two theories of new religious movements centering in a concept of disequilibrium. Anthony F. C. Wallace described what he called a "revitalization movement" as "a deliberate, organized, conscious effort by members of a society to construct a more satisfying culture" [9]. He felt that all religion probably originated in such movements, which can best be understood in terms of five stages:

1. Steady State, the original cultural equilibrium.
2. Individual stress, perhaps caused by rapid transition.
3. Cultural disorientation.
4. Revitalization: the process itself, which in turn has five steps:
   a. "Mazeway reformulation," probably on the basis of a vision or revelation by a prophet.
   b. Communication: the individual becomes a prophet, in the Weberian charismatic sense.
   c. Adaptation: the message finds a viable form within the culture.
   d. Cultural transformation: it is accepted by at least a portion of the population.
   e. Routinization: it becomes stable and "rational" as a new institution.
5. A New Steady State, incorporating the revelation is established.

Wallace indicates that certain areas of choice are left the movement: whether the major symbol is nativist or imported, secular or religious. He has no theory comparable in elaborateness to the five stages to explain on what basis these decisions would be made, which speaks for itself in placing Wallace's model in the synchronic and "historical particularism" camp, rather than the diachronic. Diachronicists might question how much one can ever assume a social or cultural "steady state" as a baseline. Setting that matter aside, however, there is much that is instructive in the pattern. Its general contours have clearly been followed in a number of contemporary American religions, especially those like Transcendental Meditation, Scientology, and the Unification Church, which have had strong charismatic leadership; TM, at least, seems already to have moved well into the last stages of 4. In the case of Zen, matters are a bit more ambiguous, for D. T. Suzuki was not quite the same kind of prophet, and the translation of an already-formed faith is never as clear-cut as the inception of a new one—if that is in fact what we see.

Further insights along the same lines can be found in Neil J. Smelser's notion of the "value-oriented movements," the term in his sociological system which generally covers religious movements, in contrast to the "norm-oriented movement," which espouses political action or social reform. The value-oriented movement is "a collective attempt to restore, protect, modify, or create values in the name of a generalized belief" [10]. "Value-oriented belief," in turn, envisions a modification of nature, the human role in it, or the relations of persons to persons on the basis of setting the desirable against the nondesirable [11].

When do value-oriented movements arise? According to Smelser, in times of ferment and stress, and when alternative means for reconstituting the social situation are perceived as unavailable. And also, we are told, when the worldview is religious, for then protests against the world will become defined in religious terms; when it is not, they will be defined in political terms [12].

The two criteria in the preceding paragraph may involve a certain tautology, for if the worldview of a society is religious, then it would obviously follow that religious means would be perceived as the ultimate and best, if not the only, way of reconstituting the society in a time of ferment and stress. But the very redundancy of the definition helps reinforce in our minds its importance and its applicability to the American situation. The greater popularity and persistence of religious, compared to political *belief-movements* (in contrast, of course, to the pragmatic stasis of American party politics), indicates a society in which a religious worldview is basic. This is most evident in times of crisis, which in the end in America produce more religious revivalism than radical politics. The celebrated counter-culture of the sixties had both religious and political goals, but its political wing has faded even as its religious wing has endured and become routinized, not without converting in the process some prominent erstwhile political activists. The popularity of meditation movements, including Zen, can be seen as a perpetuation into a new venue of the old Puritan and evangelical belief that inner states of consciousness are more important for reconstituting society, as well as saving oneself, than political organization. One must change hearts first, they imply, and only holy people can make the holy community. This is fundamentally a religious perspective, and one whose grip on the American soul is still very strong, however secularized our institutions.

DEPRIVATION AND MONEY

Other refinements of theory about new religions have appeared. Some have argued that they arise in response to situations of relative deprivation. They are the cry of people who do not have what they perceive others of no greater merit to have, but where political means of redress are not available. Norman Cohn, in his classic study of European medieval and early modern millennialist movements, has shown that they had a terrestrial goal—wanting to establish the kingdom of God on this earth—but envisioned a religious, that is miraculous, means to attain it in which the collective faith of the believers was an important aspect [13]. Moreover, he argues, they had their appeal neither among stable peasants nor town artisans well-integrated into guilds, but among marginal, unorganized, atomized populations both rural and urban. They arose especially in times of crisis, like the Black Death, or of war [14].

Kenelm Burridge, in a stimulating study of millennialist movements, has made some strikingly original observations about the great symbolic importance of money—its transfer and spending—in such groups. As though emblematic of the radical reversals imminent in the new age, they tend to demand and receive very substantial donations, and to spend lavishly on conspicuous buildings and other displays. These offer symbols of withdrawal from the ordinary world and foretastes of the paradisal glories to come [15]. One can think of a number of contemporary American examples, from the World Wide Church of God's Ambassador College to the Nichiren Shoshu conventions. This point frequently leads to charges of charlatanism and opportunism, but it is evident in new movements of millennialist bent from Melanesian cargo cults to American adventists, and should be understood in the context of its religious symbolic meaning.

CRISIS AND RESPONSE

What all of these models have in common is a crisis/response pattern compatible with historical particularism. They all obviously contain much truth which has been historically verified, and are of considerable theoretical value. Yet criticism is beginning to emerge of the crisis/response model as a *total* explanation of new religious movements. It does not, for example, usually do very much to tell us *why* certain symbols were adopted by a movement and not others. It does not tell us why some crises seem particularly prolific of new religious movements, and others do not. For that matter, it does not tell us why some movements seem to originate amid no perceptible crisis, *except that created by the movement itself*. W. E. H. Stanner has pointed out that cargo cults (like millennial movements in general) really create their own crises by provoking civil disobedience and economic disruption, and raising eschatological expection to a high pitch, at which prophecy must imminently be fulfilled or it will be disconfirmed [17].

Of course, cargo cults have a general background of intercultural contact and societal transition. But it should be borne in mind that contact, conquest, and transition are really more constants than exceptions in human experience. Every time is a time of change, every age an age of transition, even in the primitive world, however much we try symbolically to negate the realities. But at some points new religious movements occur and at others much less so. Objectively, in America, the 1960s should not necessarily have been more of a time of religious crisis than the 1950s. Vietnam did not have to be more traumatic than Korea; there was no political malaise quite as desperate as McCarthyism; economic and social conditions were actually better and improving. But it was in the sixties that a new burgeoning youth population created its own social and spiritual crisis by project- ing, like the millennial movement, its paradisal vision of a new heaven and earth against realities which, in that light, were dis- mal. This crisis, essentially self-created, spawned scores of new religious movements, and revolutionary politics as well. To find the reason one would not look to the superficial conditions of American society, but to the demographics of a suddenly ex- panded youth population owing to the postwar "baby boom," and even more to the history and dynamics of the traditions out of which the new symbols came. Another important point which Stanner made, and to which we shall return, is that the particular crisis which creates a new religious movement is a "crisis neces- sarily having a religious form"—or, more precisely, the crisis may be secular, but its phenomena are invested with religious meaning. Being religious, the important things about it and the clues to true understanding of it, are its symbolic structures and dialectics.

Before dealing with this very important point, let us turn for a moment to another major critique of the crisis/response model, that of Bryan Wilson in his monumental *Magic and the Millennium*. Wilson rightly points out that the church-sect distinction of the Troeltschean tradition is limited to the Western situation, where sects rebel against a dominant established church; in many less- developed places, the background is not a church, but an amorphous thaumaturgic web of traditional beliefs. He criticizes the "nativism" of Linton and the "revitalization" of Wallace for appearing over-specific, when actually they relate only very broad truths. All new religious movements contain nativist ele- ments, but that is not always their main intention or principal feature. As for the revitalization movement's intention of creat- ing a more satisfying culture, that is not frequently the group's own understanding of its purpose, which will be salvation or religious experience, with creating a better culture in the society at best a latent or secondary goal [18]. Wilson corrects—some would probably say over-corrects—the imprecision of these cat- egories by presenting an elaborate system of new categories.

Two important positive results of Wilson's massive work are of particular benefit at this stage in our argument. First, in reject- ing categories like nativism and revitalization, he takes seriously the religionists' own self-understanding of their goals. That is much the same as saying he takes seriously the symbolic character of religious action, and seeks to find what the conceptual and ritual symbols of the movement are saying, as well as its historical and sociological structures. That is implied in the second point, his use of categories for new religious movements which endeavor to define the movement's total "response to the world" [19]. The movement, in other words, is not a Troeltschean response to a dominant church, nor just a "crisis" response to a particular historical situation, but, whatever its particular trigger, becomes a response by which people articulate their attitude to the entire world and cosmos, and do so in many ways melded together: doctrine, worship, organization, lifestyle. What all movements have in common is a rejection of the goals of the general culture, and a desire to transform themselves religiously into something different from its ideal.

The Importance of Symbols

This kind of separation and transformation in religious terms requires focussing centrally on its symbols, especially the broad focal symbols which seem to sum up the flavor of a wide spectrum of its experience, like *zazen* meditation in Zen and the use of scientific language in Scientology. Symbols are the core of religion; their ability to carry at once meanings on many levels and even meanings in paradoxical relation to each other is one with religion's sense of mystery and transcendence, and its simultaneous expression in several media. H. Byron Earhart has perceptively observed that the basic problem with theories about new religions of the crisis/response sort is simply that they fail to take adequately into account that these are specifically religious movements, and that a religion has certain internal needs and dynamics of its own as a transcendent symbol-system.[3] Renewal, for example, is a fundamental religious symbol which takes many forms of specific expression, from baptism to conversion to orgy. From time to time, the renewal motif appears in a new religion's offering of a new revelation and a new spiritual era. The movement may or may not correlate with social crisis and change. It may, and then again it may not, arise out of the hidden dynamics of a prevailing religion to create its own crisis and allow the renewal motif to emerge in full glory. Or there may be a complex interaction between the two. The movement may appear for its own reasons, but will acquire symbols and organizational and sociological structures conditioned by outer history. But this is something other than saying that the entire movement is to be interpreted in terms of crisis and response, without regard to the inner and enduring processes of religion.

If we begin talking seriously about symbols in religion new or old, we must take into account the diachronic perspective. One inalienable characteristic of sacred symbols is that they always have a past, and come to one as something out of the past. As Mircea Eliade would say, symbols must be discovered; they cannot be invented. The texture a symbol must have to carry polyvalence and paradox—what makes it sacred—cannot be acquired in the one dimension of the present; it can only be acquired through a past, including the discoverer's own past, which gives it meaning in several contexts. Symbols can change meaning markedly, can play innumerable roles, in their migrations down the centuries, but they are only slowly born and rarely die.

To talk about new religious movements seriously as religion, then, requires talking about them as symbol-systems, and to talk about them as symbol-systems requires talking about them so as to include the historical, diachronic dimension, even when they *appear* newborn. For they will nonetheless have symbols, and a moment's reflection will reveal that those symbols are not themselves newborn, though their packaging may be, but have a history which may well do much to explain the genesis of the religion and its meaning.

In the American situation, this is the significance of the passing-of-the-torch of alternative religion from Swedenborgianism to Spiritualism, Spiritualism to Theosophy, and Theosophy to Zen. There are many, many other such passings. What joins them is not an institutional continuity. A significant, but probably not decisive, movement does obtain of individuals between groups like these. But most important, a shared heritage of symbols articulates a certain kind of "response to the world," to use Wilson's phrase. Here are some symbols widely (though not necessarily universally) shared by alternative American religious movements: (1) the central importance of trance or meditation; (2) wandering or itinerancy; (3) the East as a sacred center; (4) charismatic leaders in mystic rapport with an imminent divine reality, and perhaps with intermediate ranks of spirits or masters; (5) connection with radical social movements; (6) a non-dualist cosmology; (7) suffering perceived as impersonal and as the result of the violation of cosmic rules (karma).

EMERGENT RELIGION

What would be an appropriate basic metaphor or paradigm to encapsulate a diachronic perspective? I would like to explore the use of the term "emergent religion." The dictionary meanings of the word "emergent" are several, all of which suggest characteristics of a contrasting manifestation of religion to the established: emerging out of a fluid that covers or conceals; arising suddenly and unexpectedly; arising as a natural or logical consequence of a prior event; appearing as or involving the appearance of something novel or in a process of evolution; and, as a noun, a plant that arises visibly above others, as a tree much higher than the level of the forest, so that it stands out. These definitions of "emergence," we may note, imply that the absolute novelty of the emergent feature is deceptive; it is something that was there all the time or is fully understandable in terms of known logic or processes. But it was rendered imperceptible until the emergence; it cannot enter the range of visibility until changes in the total landscape occur, or a new angle of vision is attained. When this happens, it is likely to seem a novelty, something different and amazing.

An emergent religion, then, is one which appears suddenly and unexpectedly, in a light which makes it stand out from the sea of established religion, like a new volcanic island or a rock revealed by an unusually low tide, and which, though it may be a result of an understandable process and even something which in a sense was there all along, gives an appearance of novelty and contrasts strikingly with the surrounding spiritual milieu. Our hypothesis is that the bulk of apparently "new" and "non-normative" religion in America outside the Judeo-Christian mainstream is really of this character; each emergence of it represents a fresh outcropping of a spiritual perspective always latent in American life, each outcropping being associated with the perspective by certain common symbols and deep structures, and often by definite historical and personal linkages to other outcroppings.

The root metaphors would be ones of emergence: the sea and the submerged rock that always exists, but is only occasionally revealed; the forest in which, from certain perspectives, a tree always stands out as though set apart against the skyline. They are dualist rather than change metaphors. The categories of emergent and established religion represent two modes of religious experience and behavior equally conforming to aspects of human subjectivity, equally long-lasting, and also equally susceptible to polymorphism. A major difference is that the established sort, by nature, takes expression in institutional symbols of visibility and continuity; the emergent fulfills an attribute of its own intrinsic nature by rising and falling, coming and going. As a true opposite, it is the obverse of those values by which established religion is comprehended. It *is* true that, from the perspective of institutionalism, emergent religion is ephemeral and almost microscopic. But the point is, as Troeltsch recognized, that the institutional perspective is simply an expression of a different kind of religious orientation toward charisma, subjectivity, and wandering; the point is not that the emergent tradition itself is comparatively fragile, but that it has to be understood by different means. Compared to the mighty "church" of Troeltschean sociology, its forms are like the amoeba to the whale—tiny, short-lived, continuously dividing, yet in one sense far more immortal.

VALUES OF THE EMERGENCE METAPHOR

This "two sides" metaphor, while of course a metaphor and no more absolutely "true" than any other, brings out some important points about the elusive emergent tradition. First, it gives conceptual priority to the tradition itself, rather than to the rise and fall of individual movements within it. Second, it reminds us that the tradition has a history of its own, and does not begin anew with every new outcropping of it. Third, it shows the two sides are in continual interface and interaction, not least within the psyches of individuals. Fourth, it keeps in mind that the emergent tradition *is* an opposite, and that much of what is true about its structure, meaning, and work can only rightly be understood by turning on their heads the criteria by which we ascertain the same for established religion.

Cautions, of course, are in order. Any paradigm which sets up two "ideal types" can very easily lead to serious misconceptions. The paradigm's significance is not chiefly in the realm of the objective institutional expression of religion. If one were to label all churches and groups in America as "emergent" or "established," the resulting statistics would be very misleading, because some groups have characteristics of both and, more importantly, because people have different sorts of relationships to both. In the case of emergent religion, its institutional expression is only the proverbial tip of the iceberg; the real contours of its influence could only be drawn by taking also into account the great number of people, often people with strong attachments of a different sort to established religion, who privately read its literature and practice its techniques, or even occasionally attend its seances, lectures, meditation meetings, or yoga classes. (This phenomena of itself indicates the very different rules by which emergent and established religion play, for the majority of attenders at all of the foregoing are very likely to be non-members—but how many non-Roman Catholics say the rosary daily or non-Jews attend orthodox synagogues?) In fact, the real divide is not in history or sociology, but within the individual and social psyches of Americans—and here, not in outward sociology, the dualism of the model has some ineluctable significance, since it is related to the basic binary patterns of human thought.

In conclusion, then, our model emphasizes and gives a conceptual framework for such continuities as Swedenborgianism, Spiritualism, Theosophy, Western Zen, and their ambiences. It underscores that each individual movement or personal experience within this stream can be seen as an epiphenomenon of a vaster presence which is, in its way, as puissant and lasting as established religion. But it is different, and works by different laws. Its strengths and weaknesses are, in fact, an opposing complement: it has protean flexibility, where the latter has visible continuing institutional structure; it has appeal to one's sense of being different and special, in place of the establishment's call to one's sense of family and community and place. It continually changes, divides, regroups (though it does also have some small but continuing institutions); it is to church like the sea alive with fragile and mutating amoeba to a whale.

It is also worth mentioning that the emergent religion model far better fits the self-conception of alternative groups than does the historical-particular. For if anything is common to the subjective experience of almost all of them, it is conviction that *what* they are participating in is not rightly understood by emphasizing the smallness, recentness, marginality, and temporal particularity of the group. They may have explanations both metaphysical and sociological for that, and individuals may have some self-understanding of the relation between their own sense of being different and the appeal of a minority group. But they will also insist that, from another perspective, what they are in is old and deep, perhaps more so than less obscure faiths. Spiritualism, not unaware of its parallels with paleolithic shamanism, with some justice calls itself "the oldest religion in the world." Theosophy speaks of its lore as "the ancient wisdom." Zen claims to be the essential but unspoken sermon of the Buddha, if not a wordless message even older. Most claim, too, that some kind of hidden lineage binds them to the primordial source, however frail the current vessels of almost forgotten truth. However one chooses personally to evaluate these claims, a hermeneutical method which does not unduly obstruct phenomenological empathy with the self-understanding of the religion under study ought to be desirable. More than historical particularism, this claim may in fact offer a crucial clue to comprehending not only their inner life, but their place in American society.

NOTES

[1] This lineage, and the development of the concept of "emergent religion," are major topics in my forthcoming book, *Alternative Altars* [1].

[2] She organized the Mahayana Lodge in Kyoto in 1924, and made Kyoto a "nucleus for the spread of Theosophical ideals" [3].

[3] I have found both his idea and his bibliographical references of great value [20]. Burridge [16] makes similar observations regarding millennialian movements and cargo cults. The important question, he says, is to ask what cargo means to the participants, and he comments, "The fact that free access to cargo represents a precisely opposite condition to that presently being experienced should warn us that we are dealing with the symbolic." The state suggests the highly binary nature of symbolic religious thinking, which will appear in the distinction in this paper between established and emergent religion.

REFERENCES

1. Robert Ellwood. *Alternative Altars: Unconventional and Eastern Spirituality in America.* University of Chicago Press, 1979.
2. Alan Watts. *In My Own Way: An Autobiography, 1915–1965.* Vintage Books, 1973.
3. *The International Theosophical Year Book*, 1937, pp. 151, 239. Theosophical Publishing House, Adyar, Madras, India.
4. J. Milton Yinger. *Religion, Society, and the Individual*, pp. 142–155. Macmillan, 1957.
5. Max Weber. *The Sociology of Religion*, pp. 46ff. Translated by Ephraim Fischoff. Beacon, 1963.
6. Marvin Harris. *The Rise of Anthropological Theory*, pp. 250–289. Crowell, 1968.
7. Alexander F. Chamberlain. " 'New Religions' among the North American Indians." *Journal of Religious Psychology* 6(1913):1–49.
8. Ralph Linton. "Nativist Movements." *American Anthropologist* 40 (1943):230–250.
9. Anthony F. C. Wallace. "Revitalization Movements." *American Anthropologist* 58 (1956):264–281.
10. Neil J. Smelser. *Theory of Collective Behavior*, p. 313. Free Press, 1962.
11. Ibid., p. 120.
12. Ibid., pp. 321–325.
13. Norman Cohn. *The Pursuit of the Millennium*, p. 13. Oxford University Press, 1970.
14. Ibid., p. 282.
15. Kenelm Burridge. *New Heaven, New Earth: A Study of Millennarian Activities*, pp. 145–149. Schocken Books, 1969.
16. Ibid., p. 49.
17. W. E. H. Stanner. "On the Interpretation of Cargo Cults." *Oceania* 29 (1958):1–25.
18. Bryan Wilson. *Magic and the Millennium*, pp. 10–13, 485–489. Harper & Row, 1973.
19. Ibid., pp. 18–26.
20. H. Byron Earhart. "The Interpretation of the 'New Religions' of Japan as New Religious Movements." In *Religious Ferment in Asia*, pp. 170–188. Edited by Robert J. Miller. The University Press of Kansas, 1974.

LANGUAGE AND MIND IN THE STUDY OF NEW RELIGIOUS MOVEMENTS

George Baker

SCHOLARS ARE being called to pay closer attention to the language used in presenting the findings of their research to an audience composed, not only of other scholars, but of judges, journalists, mental-health professionals, parents, clergy, as well as followers of both new and established religions. I wish to explore the philosophical and anthropological connotations of several terms that are currently being used in the study of new religions.

Consider the term "new religious movement" as one that refers to an intuitively understood—or at least registered—spiritual or psychological event, a "movement" within oneself. Am I right to assume that, in this sense, everyone reading this definition has experienced a new religious movement? Since we can agree that such movements do indeed take place, and since we may be able to offer our own experience as evidence, our area of disagreement is likely to be confined to the interpretation of the new religious movements of other persons taken singly or collectively. In surveying the terrain of probable disagreement, several landmarks are visible, and they include definitions, spiritual outlooks, and research strategies. My purpose here is not that of offering definitions, although, in the case of "religious," I shall offer one; my purpose, rather, is to examine the philosophical stakes of our definitional options. Afterward, I wish to look at the topic of studying new religious movements from within the perspective of one of those movements. Finally, I shall suggest one way in which scholars, educators—and parents—might respond to the "turning," as Harvey Cox has called it, of young Americans to Eastern religions.

285

I

"New." There may be a religious aspect of our interest in newness. In the Judeo-Christian tradition, God intervenes in history, causes divine disturbances, and thus creates news. The gospel of the arisen Christ was the "Good News." Our interest in hearing the six o'clock news may arise from a spiritual longing to receive word that God is alive in history. Our repeated disappointment with news programs comes from our impulse to ask, Is that *all*? Is there no sign whatsoever that God moves among us? We resign ourselves to being interested in history—to include the history of new religious movements—as a substitute for, or displacement of, our interest in God.

Having resigned ourselves to not getting news about God, we go after news about man. And we do so with a vengeance. In the Garden of Eden man may have been a creature of god, a "theomorphic" being, but now, in the Industrial Park, man is the creature of history, a "chronomorphic" being. Our curiosity about the new religious movements in America is an expression of our chronomorphic persuasion as investigators. Were our persuasion of a theomorphic order, we would be less interested in the newness of religious phenomena than in the underlying divine inspiration. We are chronomorphic sociologists without being aware of it. At bottom, our view of society as a by-product of history is at variance with Christian theomorphic historiography, according to which at one moment in time, that of the Resurrection, the structure of world history was changed by divine intervention. Is it possible that the structure of American history is being changed at the present time by a similar divine intervention, through the agency of the new religious movements? Or, is it imperative that we regard the participation of young, upper-middle class, largely white Americans in the new religious movements as a product of the breakdown of human institutions?

"Movements." The scholar that seeks to observe the movements of new religious groups should ask, In which space do the new movements move? From one point of view, the new movements move in the conceptual space of the scholar's own mind, in which, necessarily, a fixed point of reference exists. So, in thinking about new religious movements, and in trying to devise

ways to measure their movements, the scholar has to ask, What is it from which I am not moving in proposing to study the new religious movements? Where, in other words, is the point of reference which is to be regarded as stationary at the moment of measuring the movements of new religious ideas or groups?

Ethan Allen Hitchcock (1798–1870) would have answered this question by saying that it is our belief in the immutability of nature that makes all scientific beliefs possible, and that our belief in an immutable natural order is tantamount to belief in God. The existence of God, in turn, is the existence of Truth, the Spirit of which was personified in the miracles, or "acting-parables," as he called them, of the Bible [1]. Had he witnessed the events that took place a century after his death, he might have said that the new forms of religious behavior are to be classified as a new species of acting-parables, the principles for the interpretation of which are to be found in the investigator's capacity to be moved by the Spirit of Truth.

Western man seems to have taken his capacity for historical knowledge as the primary evidence of his capacity to be moved by the Spirit of Truth. For this reason, the Jewish, Christian, and Islamic traditions have been historically-oriented and theistic in their outlooks. Western man's knowledge of history is the litmus paper that shows his contact with Cosmic Intelligence. Concomitantly, Western science has required a dualistic frame of reference or epistemology, one in which a sharp division was to be made between the subject and the object of knowledge, between the Self that knows and the Not-Self that is known. In contrast, Eastern man has taken his capacity for personal Enlightenment as the primary evidence of his capacity to be moved by the same Spirit of Truth. For this reason, the great traditions of Asia have tended to be socio-psychologically oriented and pantheistic in their spiritual outlooks. Eastern science has required only a monistic epistemology, for the principles that govern the object of empirical investigation are to be discovered in the consciousness of the researcher. Maharaj Ji, the youthful Perfect Master, expressed this primordial Eastern point of view in a poster that read, "The force that moves the atom moves you."

"In America." In not having our title "Program for the Study of New American Religious Movements," we opened the door

for studying new movements that are "in America" but not "of America." In delimiting our subject in this way, we seem to have excluded the new American religious groups overseas. American monks are practicing Buddhism in Korea no less than Korean pastors are practicing Christianity in America. It may be useful here to distinguish, as an example of a general phenomenon, between Korean-American movements and American-Korean movements. It may well be that two movements co-exist under the same denominational umbrella. The activities in America of a Korean religious elite and its Korean followers may form one movement, a Korean-American one; while the activities of an affiliated American religious elite and its American followers may form a second movement, an American-Korean one. The leaders of the two movements will naturally draw their ideas and practices from their respective spiritual traditions, Confucian or Buddhist in the one case and Christian or Jewish in the other. The problems of intercultural and interspiritual communication that may be experienced by the members of the two elites may at times be severe.

"Religious." One of the senses of this discussion is that when we say "new religious movements" we have two options with regard to the definition of "religious." Each option offers advantages and disadvantages, and each brings with it problems of language and philosophy.

The first option is to leave the term "religious" undefined or primitive. We would then use "religious" as the starting-point, or irreducible terminological unit, of our investigation. Taking this option, we have, as our first axiom, the proposition, "Man is a religious being." Having said this much, you interrupt to ask, "What do you mean?" I have to reply by repeating or paraphrasing my statement: "Man is a religious being, or said differently, man's being or nature by any other name is still religious." You may become annoyed by my stubbornness.

The second option is to take the term "religious" and reduce it to something else, or, if not "reduce" it, to translate it into other terms. We might say, for example, that by "religious," we mean the process of ascribing ultimate meaning, or the handling of uncertainties of a cosmic order, or the symbolic repairing of the traumas of childhood and the failures of adolescence. The problems of this option are varied and complex. I may say, for example, that by "religion," I refer to the design according to which a person organizes his or her life in a meaningful way, and out of which he or she derives a sense of ultimate identity. You may want to reject this definition by an argument like this one:

The ability to organize one's life around ultimate concerns is the outcome, not the starting-point, of religion. The person that 'converts' to a religion need not, at first, be regarded as capable of following that religion. His state-of-being during the period that he matures on what has been called the 'path before the Path' is that of a sinner. (And I take it that 'sinner', by definition, is a person that lacks the discipline required of a true follower of any religion.) *My* first axiom is this: as he is, man is not a religious being, he is a sinful being, a sinner.

In this argument, you have chosen "sinful" and "sinner" as your primitive terms, and I may be left wondering how your sinner is ever going to become religious.

From another quarter of this discussion, little concern has been expressed about the need to make air-tight definitions of such terms. Theodore Roszak has suggested that terms like "consciousness circuit" and "All that!" might serve to point to the spiritual interests of this, the Aquarian Age. This lack of concern about our use of terms like "religious" and "secular" may arise, not out of neglect, but out of a new vision, which, in technical theological language, might be called "neo-pantheistic" or "neo-panentheistic." If it is true that a seed of the Divine Principle is to be found in every human activity, then there is little point in trying to devise definitions that make antonyms out of the terms "religious" and "secular."

What does not emerge clearly from this way of considering the problem of terminology is an idea about the relative place of that which is to be called "All that!" or the "religious quality" in the life of human beings. Often this religious quality is spoken of as if it were a quantity; but in speaking of some persons as being, or as having been, "more religious" than others, in effect we are treating religion as if it were a special brand of human motor-fuel. Christians speak of a person's being "filled" by the Holy Spirit. In speaking this way about the religious quality, we inadvertently "exteriorize" religion; that is, we treat religious quality, however we may care to define it, as if it were an accessory after the fact of human life.

In thinking of men and women as socio-biological instruments that are engineered for survival on the planet Earth, we tend to regard their activities associated with food, clothing, shelter, and reproduction as their primary functions. In such a scheme, the religious quality is left out. In consequence, we find ourselves having to talk about religious behavior as if it were an activity that, when compared to sex or food-gathering, must be regarded as secondary. For this reason, it may be that in deciding upon a terminological strategy for studying new religious movements we will have to face the difficult question: Where is religion in human life?

Perhaps the sharpest contrast between modern and pre-scientific theories of religion is to be found in answer to this question. Religious teachers and teachers of diverse epochs and cultures in one way or another have said that religion is built into the system in which mankind, organic life, and the cosmos co-exist. Religion, in this view, is not to be regarded as a social institution, a belief-system, or an accident of culture, but as an aspect or component of the design of the world-system. Man, as the micro-system, has a homologous relationship to the universe, the macro-system, and the aim of religious instruction is the proper understanding of that relationship. Traditional religious education is an institutionalized exegesis of "so" in the aphorism, "As Above, so Below." In contrast, modern, anthropologically-oriented scientists have said, in effect, that man's relationship to the universe is a homomorphic one, and that beliefs to the contrary are products of fantasy.

If we answer the question, Where is religion in human life? in one way, we will have to agree with the Buddha that one's "Original Face" is the linkage between mankind and the cosmos, and that enlightenment will consist in an understanding of the unity of human and cosmic realms. If we answer the question in another way, we will have to agree with Western social scientists that have said that human patterns may be studied and understood without reference to cosmic designs. Ultimately, either answer is going to be a religious answer, in that it addresses the religious question of man's ultimate place in the cosmos.

Are we to say that all answers to such questions are "religious" in the same sense? What, for example, is to be called "religious" in a Buddhist sense? I asked this question of an

American lecturer at the Nyingma Institute in Berkeley. He replied that it was a *re-ligio,* a "tying-again," to the Godhead. In Buddhist terms, this process meant a return to the reality of the Buddha, Dharma, and Sangha. The quality of that experience, he implied, could be called "religious." Another Buddhist teacher, Suh Woon, a Korean monk who resides at Sambosa Temple in Carmel Valley, compared the essential experience of Buddhism to the moment in which a woman discovers that her purse is missing. At that instant she asks, purely and simply, Where is it? At that moment she receives a foretaste of what Zen Buddhists have called the "mind-of-great-doubt," and what the monk called the "pure-question-mind."

Are we to say that the Buddhist's experience of great doubt is to be regarded as the same as, or the equivalent to, the Christian's experience of repentance or surrender to God? If so, then the term "religious" may be used in discussing both the Buddhist and Christian systems. We might then say that where a Buddhist speaks of "no-self" and denies the existence of an independent, permanent ego, the Christian speaks of "self-less" devotion to God and affirms the union of his will to that of God.

Let us set aside the comparative study of spiritual traditions, and now try to classify religious qualities on the basis of our own observations and experiences of the universal, human life-cycle: birth, childhood, adolescence, adulthood, and death. Clearly, the religious qualities of children, adolescents, and adults are profoundly different. The religion of childhood, in America the religion of Christmas presents and Easter eggs, is of a different quality than the religion of adolescence, which, in turn, is a religion of great accomplishment and heroic vision. The business of childhood-religion is wonder, and the child's quality of understanding might be termed "pre-religious." The business of adolescent-religion is action, and the adolescent's quality of understanding might be termed "proto-religious." The word that I would use to describe the business of adult-religion is "impartiality," by which I mean a state of natural, holistic truthfulness. In such a state, an adult's behavior and quality of understanding may be termed "religious."

To define "religious" along these lines would be to suggest that few of the new movements are religious, but that most are "proto-religious," and that some are "pre-religious." Such a description would square with the well-known fact that the population of the new movements is largely made up of adolescents and post-adolescents. Only a few of the new groups are made up largely of persons "over thirty." Some of these older persons may have come to accept their "conditioning"—their karma—as a permanent feature of their spiritual landscape, but may have taken, nonetheless, impartiality as their aim. For such persons "impartial" may be synonymous with "religious," "moral," "mature," and, possibly, "normal."

II

From the *Heart Sutra*, we learn that "Form is Emptiness, Emptiness is Form," a proposition that has been explained in America by Zen teachers as the foundation of a theory of no-mind. In this theory, the mind-of-discrimination is regarded as the mind-of-attachment, which is the source of suffering. Non-discrimination is, therefore, said to be the highest form of discrimination, and non-action the most effective form of action. The practice of non-discrimination in everyday life, which includes the practice of "just sitting," has been called by a Korean master "keeping a 'don't-know' mind." Recently, I wrote to one of his American disciples, Bhikshu Mu Bul, whom I had met in Korea, and asked him, How does one study the new religious movements with a don't-know mind? The instructions from his teacher, Seung Sahn Soen Sa, who resides in the Providence Zen Center, and whom I later met at his new Zen Center in Berkeley, were these: Read his Zen stories and Dharma lectures [2], and after reading them were I still to have a question, to read them again, and if I still were to have any doubt, to read them a third time. If, after the third reading, I still had doubts, then at that point I should ask his teacher who would give me an answer [3].

Implicit in his teacher's advice and, as I found out, in his writings, was what I took to be a Buddhist assumption about the spiritual character of biographical research: by studying the lives of persons to whom an understanding of a teaching has been passed, one may learn how those persons manifest the original insight of the founder of the teaching, in this case, the Buddha. His advice, in short, seemed to be this: Study me.

At this point, I realized that my intellectual identity was being brought into question, for two quite different sorts of study of new Buddhist groups were imaginable. The research of a Buddhist student will be directed toward the discovery, in the words and actions of his Asian teacher and his teacher's typically Anglo-American representatives, of a living expression of the Way of Non-Attachment. For him, the learning-value of studying the lives and teachings of American monks is potentially the same as that of studying the lives and teachings of ancient Chinese, Tibetan, Thai, Korean, or Japanese masters. In contrast, the research of a non-Buddhist student will be directed toward discovering in the behavior of American followers evidence bearing on the nature of their attachment to an imported, Eastern tradition or on the nature of American society.[1]

I returned to my question: How to study the new religious movements with a don't-know mind? I speculated that a Buddhist answer might take a form like this: The teachings of Buddhism lead to a knowledge of transience, not of forms, as in the West. Such knowledge is to be found in the space between categories of analysis. To be aware that such space exists is to be aware of the limited, transient character of one's present understanding. To study with an awareness of that transience is to study with a don't-know mind.[2]

The doctrine of no-mind has been presented in other Buddhist quarters as a doctrine of no-self. Restated, my question would be, How is it that research on the new religious movements may be carried out if there is no researcher? In other words, If there is no being that possesses a Self that is capable of doing research, how is research to be carried out? I received an unexpected reply to that question from Bhikshu Hei Myong, an American disciple of another Korean master, Ku San, whose Dharma lectures have been translated and published by his Western disciples [5]. I wish to paraphrase the relevant sections of his letter in order that, by appreciating the aesthetic lines of a Buddhist philosophy of science, we may gain a sensitivity to the aesthetics of Western research. In the following analysis of the task of studying the new religious movements, written from a monastery in Korea by a Buddhist monk who had been raised in California and ordained in Thailand, no attention is given to matters of terminology, soci-

ology, or history. The emphasis, rather, is on a proper understanding of mind and process.

Your statement [he writes] that research on the new religious movements cannot be done if there is no "doer" raises some intriguing
questions that enter into some of the most profound areas of Buddhist
epistemology. What is reiterated throughout the Mahayana texts, and
particularly in the works of Bojo, which we are translating, and in the
works of other Korean masters, is that it is essential for us to recognize
the fundamental identity of the mind: The knower, or, more precisely,
the "subject" of empirical knowledge, and the "objects" of that
knowledge, be they mental or physical, are of one nature.

In the Chinese Mahayana conception, the term 'mind' actually embraces both subject and object. 'Mind' is therefore a general term that
refers to two specific aspects of consciousness: essence and function.
'Essence' refers to the immutable quality of the mind, that is, the mind
in its passive aspect as a 'suchness' that integrates all phenomena into
one unity. 'Function' refers to the ability of the mind to adapt to any
conceivable situation in any conceivable manner; that is, this adapting
is the active aspect of mind that is able to manifest the phenomena of
the universe in all their diversity, and which makes possible the wide
range of responses of which beings are capable.

Improper understanding of the essential identity of these two elements bifurcates the perceptual process and thereby destroys the ability to know intuitively without the need of a subject-object division.
These dual modes of thought are one of the most virulent features of the
human psyche, and are ultimately what sustain our continued existence
in Samsara, the Sea of Suffering, for they hinder that transcendent,
all-embracing vision which characterizes liberation. It is indeed this
habitual discriminative thinking which 'Mu,' 'What is it?' and other
hua-t'ous, or koans, are designed to eliminate.

Now, for you to say that there is no doer and hence no research
which can be done, shows a proper understanding of the meaning of the
essence of the mind as an integrative suchness; but, this view tends to
ignore the functioning of the mind which can produce anything, provided the necessary conditions are present. Actually, it is precisely
because the mind is not a 'doer' and just a 'suchness' that it can give
rise to such a wide variety of responses. If the mind were something
tangible which could be categorized into some kind of convenient conceptual compartment like 'doer,' or 'mind,' or 'soul,' or whatever, it
would be subject to a limitation. Its operation, that aspect of functioning, would accordingly also be limited. Thus this 'suchness' cannot be
categorized into one tight compartment, and its ability to embrace all
pluralities enables the mind to adapt limitlessly and deal with any possible problem.

So, you see, to do research without any doer really presents no
problem at all; for, by simply abiding in 'suchness,' you gain an all-

inclusive perspective which enables you to penetrate to the heart of any problem and arrive at the most accurate of conclusions. It is precisely because we are not 'doers' that, with proper training and development of our latent potentialities, we will be able to do anything—and yet remain unaffected throughout.

From a different standpoint, we can perhaps say a bit more simply that there is no 'doer,' but there is 'doing.' For the conditional nature of all formations, be they physical or mental, assures us that if there is a cause, either a material element or a mental intention, there will be an effect resulting from that cause. In this case, because there is an intention to do research on the new religious movements in America (an intention that itself has arisen due to other conditions, such as an invitation to take part in the project, etc.) action takes place. If that action is sustained then an effect, a conclusion, will be produced.

So, from this standpoint, the problem of an innovative perspective towards research on the new religious movements does not even arise. The research will happen because the conditions for it to happen are present. One need only stay detached from the process, permit the necessary conditions to manifest naturally, and the conclusion will take care of itself. And, paradoxically enough, the work will probably come out better for it, because one is not trying to put intentional direction over a complex combination of conditions about which it is impossible for one to know fully, and hence over which it is impossible to have full command. These ideas come together as a simple application of the not-self doctrine about which you probably heard a great deal from the Theravadins in Thailand [6].

In this straightforward, Buddhist analysis, the research problems associated with the study of new religious movements are no different from the ordinary problems of life. One does notice a difference of terminology: the Western scholar has no term like "integrative suchness" and the Buddhist scholar apparently has no need for a term like "religious quality." This difference of terminology arises from a difference of philosophical and anthropological accent. How far does this difference extend? Does it continue to exist at the level that is not that of belief about oneself, the world, and the process of cognition? Or is it that at that level, which is beyond philosophical speculation, the great religious and phenomenological teachings converge?

The letters from these two American Buddhist monks point to the possibility of an enriching interpenetration of ideas between scholars and members of the new religious movements. Since all minds are of a common human nature, nothing is gained by trying to oppose "our thinking" against "their thinking." We may discover that the Lord has provided Americans with new epistemological wineskins in the teachings of new religious groups.

III

Meanwhile, the turning of young Americans to Eastern religions may be explained from one anthropological point of view as a matter of cultural blindness. These young Americans no longer "see" the Western religions around them. What appears to many Euro-Americans, and to some Afro-Americans, as Catholicism, Judaism, and Protestantism—and what appears to many second- and third-generation Asian-Americans as Buddhism—is not religion, but empty ritual. When we ask, in turn, Why is such not-seeing so widespread at this time? we may answer by saying that young Americans have not been taught to see the religious dimension and significance of the "empty" practices of their parents. This not-teaching, in turn, comes from another practice, that of non-education about religious questions and values. Having separated church and state in the minds of young Americans, we should not later be surprised to learn that our fellow citizens have no need of church.

We do see, however, that our children, students, and neighbors do have a continuing need for religion. Our question seems to be, Why not a need for the established religions? We will, of course, gain nothing by citing Christian and Jewish scriptures as evidence of the heterodoxy of the new "para-Christian" and "pagan" religions to which they belong. (Someone may ask us, How do you know the Bible is orthodox?) A different kind of response is needed, one based on a re-examination of the assumptions that underlie our own spiritual outlook; for these assumptions at another level of analysis are conclusions about human life, the validity of which we seldom question.

In this process of re-thinking, while keeping a "pure-question" mind, we may discover that it is precisely our deep-structure conclusions which are under study in some of the new religious movements. We may discover at that point that members of the "old" religious movements may participate in that study, as the following dialogue between a Methodist mother and her Zen daughter suggests:

Mother, I would gladly be a Christian if you could explain to me what being a Christian means. You used to say, "A Christian believes that Jesus died for our sins," but your statement explained nothing to me. Meanwhile, I prefer to go to the Berkeley Zendo and sit, and, as you once said, "do nothing," than to go to church and kneel and do nothing.

Her mother, having gone to the trouble of reading what American scholars have written about new religious movements, and having thought comparatively about her own religious experience, offers this advice:

You don't have to take what I say literally. The story of the life of Christ, and, for that matter, the story of the life of the Buddha, may be taken allegorically. Taken that way, the truth of Christianity is embedded in the allegorical structure of your own mind, but you should understand that that truth cannot be received in one sitting.

You should also understand the danger of symbolic interpretations: If you go around making allegories out of everybody's history, what do you do when you come to yourself, to your own experience? Is that experience real, or is it just a symbol of a potential experience?

You will agree that what counts is the possibility that someone— myself, in particular—actually might live a unified, enlightened life on the basis of a teaching. The story of Christ, taken either as history or as allegory, could lead both of us to that possibility. So it's neither that Christ actually lived and died for our sins, nor that he did not actually live and die for our sins.

NOTES

[1] In ethnographic language, research may be "emic" or "etic," that of an insider or that of an outsider. Both sorts of research seek the truth, but emic Buddhist research seeks the truth about man as an underdeveloped, spiritual being, while etic Buddhist research seeks the truth about man as a highly-developed, historical being.

What counts as research also depends upon cultural factors, the influence of which is profound, but difficult to discern. What Koreans might undertake as social science research, Americans might regard as policy articulation; and what Americans might undertake as a "redeployment of forces," as in the case of the proposed military withdrawal from Korea, Koreans might regard as a restructuring of national priorities and values [4].

[2] Bhikshu Mu Bul corrected me by letter, and later in person, by saying that the aim of Zen is not philosophy, not a new theory to explain things: Ten thousand questions all come back to the one question—don't-know mind. So long as the questioner is separated from his question, he thinks of theories of knowledge and research. Symbols only lead to a knowledge of symbols, but Zen meditation, which is before thinking, leads to knowledge of one's original nature.

REFERENCES

1. George Baker. "The Gnostic Hermeneutic of E. A. Hitchcock, U.S. Army." In preparation, 1978.

2. Stephen Mitchell, editor. *Dropping Ashes on the Buddha: The Teaching of Zen Master Seung Sahn.* Grove, 1976.

3. Bhikshu Mu Bul, Providence Zen Center, 48 Hope St., Providence, Rhode Island 02903. Personal communication, August 2, 1977.

4. George Baker and Michitaka Nakahara. "Silence in Japanese Policy toward Korea." *Journal of East and West Studies* (Seoul), 7 (1978):39–62.

5. Ku San. *Nine Mountains: Dharma-Lectures of the Korean Meditation Master Ku San.* 3rd rev. ed. International Meditation Center, Song Kwang Sa, Seung Ja Gun, Cholla Namdo 543-43, Republic of Korea, 1978.

6. Hei Myong, International Meditation Center [5]. Personal communication, July 20, 1977.

CONTRIBUTORS

SYDNEY AHLSTROM is Professor of American and Church History, Yale University, and has written several volumes on American religious history. His most recent works include *Religion and the Dilemmas of Nationhood* (1976) and *A Religious History of the American People* (1972).

DICK ANTHONY is a Research Associate with the Program for the Study of New Religious Movements in America. With Thomas Robbins he has published many articles on the new religious phenomena, including "Getting Straight with Meher Baba." With Robbins and Robert Bellah he is also co-authoring *On Religion and Social Science: Toward the Non-Reductionistic Study of Religion*

GEORGE BAKER, formerly a Fulbright scholar in Mexico and a lecturer with the University of Maryland in Japan, Korea, and Thailand, is currently Associate Director of the Program for the Study of New Religious Movements in America.

ROBERT N. BELLAH is Ford Professor of Sociology and Comparative Studies, University of California, Berkeley, and is well-known for his books and articles on the sociology of religion. He co-edited *The New Religious Consciousness* (1976) and has published *The Broken Covenant* (1975) and *Beyond Belief* (1973).

FREDERICK BIRD is Professor of Religion and Sociology, Concordia University, Montreal, Quebec, where he directs a study on new religions and parareligious movements with support from the Quebec Ministry of Education. He is currently preparing a volume on religious responses to poverty in the United States.

WALTER CAPPS is Professor of Religious Studies and Director of the Institute of Religious Studies, University of California, Santa Barbara. He has published *Seeing with a Native Eye* (1976), a volume on native American religion, and *Hope Against Hope* (1976).

JOSEPH P. CHINNICI is Associate Professor in Church History, Franciscan School of Theology, Berkeley, a member of the Graduate Theological Union.

HARVEY COX is Victor S. Thomas Professor of Divinity, Harvard Divinity School. *Turning East: The Promise and Peril of the New Orientalism* (1977) and *Seduction of the Spirit* (1973) are two of his most recent works.

EMILY CULPEPPER is a graduate student at the Harvard Divinity School and has written on women and religion, including an article in *Second Wave* entitled "Female History/Myth Making." She has also produced a film, *Period Piece,* distributed by Insight Exchange.

JOHN DILLENBERGER, formerly Professor of Historical Theology at the Graduate Theological Union, is the President of the Hartford Seminary Foundation in Connecticut and is known for his anthologies of the writings of Martin Luther and John Calvin. He has recently published *Benjamin West* (1977), a study of religious art in America.

ROBERT S. ELLWOOD is Bishop James W. Bashford Professor of Oriental Studies at the School of Religion at the University of Southern California in Los Angeles. He has written *Many Peoples, Many Faiths* (1976), *The Eagle and the Rising Sun: Americans and the New Religions of Japan* (1974), and *Religious and Spiritual Groups in Modern America* (1973).

ELDON G. ERNST is Professor of American Religious History and the History of Christianity, American Baptist Seminary of the West, a member of the Graduate Theological Union in Berkeley. His most recent work is *Without Help or Hindrance: Religious Identity in American Culture* (1977).

LANGDON GILKEY is Shailer Mathews Professor of Theology, The Divinity School, University of Chicago. He is known for his books on contemporary theology, including *Reaping the Whirlwind: A Christian Interpretation of History* (1976), *Catholicism Confronts Modernity: A Protestant View* (1975), and *Naming the Whirlwind: The Renewal of God-Language* (1969).

CHARLES Y. GLOCK is Professor of Sociology at the University of California, Berkeley, and has published several major studies on religion in the United States. He co-edited *The New Religious Consciousness* (1976), *Religion in Sociological Perspective* (1973), and *Beyond the Classics?* (1973).

DANIEL GOLEMAN is Associate Editor of *Psychology Today* and has written *Varieties of the Meditative Experience* (1977).

BARBARA HARGROVE is Associate Professor of the Sociology of Religion at Yale University Divinity School, and is President of the Religious Research Association. She has published *Reformation of the Holy* (1971) and is currently working on a successor, to be called *The Sociology of Religion: Classical and Contemporary Approaches.*

J. STILLSON JUDAH is Librarian Emeritus and Professor Emeritus of the History of Religions, Graduate Theological Union, and Adjunct Professor, Pacific School of Religion. His most recent volume is *Hare Krishna and the Counterculture* (1974).

MARK JUERGENSMEYER is Associate Professor of Ethics and the Phenomenology of Religion, Graduate Theological Union, and Visiting Associate Professor of Religious Studies, University of California, Berkeley.

JACOB NEEDLEMAN is Director of the Program for the Study of New Religious Movements in America and Visiting Professor of Comparative Religious Studies, Graduate Theological Union. He is also Professor of Philosophy, San Francisco State University. In addition to *The New Religions* (1970), he has recently published *A Sense of the Cosmos* (1975) and *On the Way to Self Knowledge* (1975).

CHARLES PREBISH is Associate Professor of Religious Studies, Pennsylvania State University. Most recently he has published *Buddhism: A Modern Perspective* (1975), *Buddhist Monastic Discipline* (1975), and has a study of American Buddhism in press.

THOMAS ROBBINS is Assistant Professor of Sociology, Queens College, City University of New York.

JAMES T. RICHARDSON is Professor of Sociology, University of Nevada, Reno. With Mary W. Stewart and Robert B. Simmonds, he has co-authored *Organized Miracles* (1978) and numerous essays in the field of new religions. In addition, he was the editor of an issue of *American Behavioral Scientist,* XX (4), which dealt with the study of "conversion" and "commitment" in contemporary religion (1977).

THEODORE ROSZAK is Professor of History and Chairman of the Religious Studies Program, California State University, Hayward. His works on American culture include *Unfinished Animal* (1975), *Where the Wasteland Ends* (1972), and *The Making of a Counter Culture* (1969). His latest book is *Person/Planet* (1978).

ROBERT B. SIMMONDS is Associate Professor of Sociology, State University of New York, Cortland.

ARCHIE SMITH, JR., is Associate Professor of Religion and Society, Pacific School of Religion, a member of the Graduate Theological Union in Berkeley.

MARY W. STEWART is Associate Professor of Sociology, University of Missouri, Kansas City.

DONALD STONE is a graduate student in sociology at the University of California, Berkeley, and Research Associate with the Program for the Study of New Religious Movements, Graduate Theological Union.

CLAUDE WELCH is Dean and President of the Graduate Theological Union in Berkeley and has published *Protestant Thought in the Nineteenth Century* (1972) and *Graduate Education in Religion: A Critical Appraisal* (1971).

ROBERT WUTHNOW is Assistant Professor of Sociology, Princeton University. His work in the sociology of religion includes *The Consciousness Reformation* (1976) and Experimentation in American Religion (1978).

INDEX

NOTE: The index contains several collective categories: The names of specific new religious movements appear under New Religious Movements. Terms with special significance in the study of new religions are listed under Definitions. Public and scientific issues related to the contemporary new religions appear under Issues and Research. Other collective entries are American Religious History, Buddhism, Christianity, Feminism, and Roman Catholic Church. Items entered in collective designations generally do not also appear in the body of the index.

New religious movements *(continued)*
fundamentalist groups: 16; *See also:* Fundamentalism; Ghost Dance: 272; Holiness secession: 16, 214; Jehovah's Witnesses: 6, 16, 36, 214; Landmark movement: 15; New Thought: 18, 36, 186; Oneida: 14; Oxford Movement: 73; Perfectionism: 14; Religion of Humanity: 36; Russelite movement: 16; Seventh Day Adventists: 35, 214; spiritualist groups: 14, 17–18, 270; *See also:* Spiritualism; Theosophy: 18, 36, 174, 191–96, 269–70, 279–83; Transcendentalism: 6, 13, 18, 273; Two-Seed-in-the-Spirit Predestinarian Secession: 15; Vedanta: 36, 199

20th century: Arica: 180, 185, 187n.1; Baba Lovers: 220; *See also:* Meher Baba; Black Muslims: 15, 36, 214; Buddhism, *See:* Buddhism; Children of God: 76, 264; Christian World Liberation Front (C.W.L.F.): 236, 245, 250n.11; Divine Light Mission: 77, 180, 182, 183, 187n.1, 190; Eckankar: 190; *est:* 145, 147, 148, 150n.4, n.7, 259; Feminism, *See:* Feminism; Gurdjieff, *See:* Gurdjieff, G. I.; Hare Krishna, *See:* International Society for Krishna Consciousness; Healthy, Happy, Holy Organization (3HO): 53; Hinduism, *See:* Hinduism; Institut de Yoga Sivananda: 178, 180; Integral Yoga Institute: 178, 180, 182, 184, 187n.1; Islam, *See:* Islam; Jesus Movement: 80, 177, 182, 235, 236, 242, 245, 247; Moorish Temple: 15; Orthodox Roman Catholic Movement, Inc.: 34; Pentecostalism: 6, 16, 63, 214, 258; Process: 76; Radhasoami: 190–99; Rastafari: 214; Scientology: 76, 145, 180, 182, 185, 187n.1, 196, 274, 278; Self-Realization Fellowship: 174,

178, 187n.1; Silva Mind Control: 178, 180, 185, 187n.1; Sri Chinmoy: 180, 183, 187n.1; Subud: 178, 180, 185, 187n.1, 221; Sufis: *xiv,* 13; Tai Chi Chu'an: 178, 180, 181, 187n.1; TM, *See:* Transcendental Meditation; Unification Church, *See:* Unification Church; World Wide Church of God's Ambassador College: 276; Young Life: 204

New Rome, America as: 98n.4
Nichiren Shoshu, *See:* Buddhism, movements
Nietzsche, Friedrich: 18, 111
Nixon, Pres. Richard M.: 77
and Unification Church: 91–92, 98n.6

Objectivity, *See:* Issues
Olcott, Colonel: 269
Oriental religions, *See:* Eastern Religions
Ornstein, Robert: 147
Ouspensky, P. D.: 19

Paine, Thomas: 53
Paradigm: 267, 270, 280, 282
changes in: 114
Park, Pres. Chung Hee: 92
Pavlov, Ivan P.: 55
Pentecostalism, *See:* New Religious Movements, 20th century
Pennsylvania: 4, 19
Perls, Fritz: 164
Philosophy of science: 142
Pilgrims: 84
Pluralism, cultural: 43, 211, 216; legal: 31; religious: *vii,* 27, 35 78, 110, 163, 166, 272
in America: 4, 5, 12, 19, 24, 29 36–42
and Unification Church: 90–91
Poland: 72
Polanyi, Karl, cited: 67
Polanyi, Michael, cited: 150n.2
Polarity therapy: 192, 197
Polemic themes, in religious history: 126–29, 136, 202–05
Polytheism: 8